Thok Nath ~ English Dictionary

Eastern Jikany Nuer Dialect

Lual Chany Chol

ISBN 978 0 6486541 0 0

South Sudan Workshop Programme, Juba

Published by Africa World Books Pty. Ltd.
(www.africaworldbooks.com)

Design and typesetting: Africa World Books

Preface

There are two main reasons for a dictionary in terms of which its degree of excellence and achievement must be measured:

- coverage
- definition

In regards to coverage, readers have to be assured that the words they need to understand and use are included, up-to-date in all aspects, and disciplines.

In regards to definition lies semantic analysis with lexicographers ensuring that every sense of a word is given as it occurs in current usage.

A preface is not, of course, the place to specify the whole range of features that mark a book, and I must reluctantly pass over many another of the learner's needs.

Lual Chany Chol
Thok Nath linguist, Jikany dialect

Contents

Introduction

Welcome to the first Thok Nath English Dictionary of Eastern Jikany Nuer Dialect. In this dictionary, I have tried to provide the learner with the best definitions in the English language so that he or she can pick up the meaningful expressions in this language.·

Fast Access

Learners should not waste their time with irrelevant meanings. All definitions are in frequency order with the most common ones first. The common words act as visual indexes to help the learner's access the meanings of long entries.

Spoken Thok Nath

To study the spoken language you will face several dialects, Jikany Doar, Jikany Cieng, Gaatjaak and many minor dialects.

Frequency

Learners are interested to know which words are common and which ones are unusual. Many Thok Nath words are of three to four generations and are not any longer commonly used. Here I will list the common words of Thok Nath according to their zonal usage.

Phrases

Thok Nath is expressed through some basic combinations of words in that Location. Throughout this dictionary full treatment is given to each phrase or Word.I am greatly concerned to help those who would like to learn this language for any purposeful goal, both the native speakers and those learning the language. It is my sincere hope that each finds it useful and informative, and I will welcome any comments.

Lual Chany Chol

How to Find What You Want

The alphabets

Thok Nath, like most other languages, has alphabets. The first linguists who designed this language's alphabets used the Latin alphabets as basis and added some other letters.

The followings are the capital letters of the alphabets:

A A̱ B C D Dh E E̱ Ɛ Ɛ̱ G
H I I̱ J K L M N Nh Ny Ñ
O O̱ Ɔ Ɔ̱ P R T Th U W
Ä Ë Ɛ̈ Ö

The followings are the small letters of the alphabets:

a a̱ B c d dh e e̱ ɛ ɛ̱ g
h I i̱ j k l m n nh ny Ñ
o o̱ ɔ ɔ̱ p r t th U w
ä ë ɛ̈ Ö ¨

¨ is used above or below vowels to mark short stressed vowels, e.g.
ä a̤ Ÿ e̤ ɛ̈ ɔ̤ i i̤

Pronunciation

The phoneticians who studied this language decided on various signs to identify the different phonemes of the language.

To help the learner to identify the sounds, I give a pronunciation guides:

A	sounds as	U in	Cut	e.g. Gat
a̲	sounds as	A in	Far	e.g. Ha̲n
B	sounds as	B in	Bar	e.g. Bar
C	sounds as	Ch in	Chair	e.g. Cak
D	sounds as	D in	Dark	e.g. Dap
dh	sounds as	Th in	Although	e.g. Dhol
E	sounds as	Ee in	Feel	e.g. Duel
ɛ	sounds as	E in	Get	e.g. Rɛk
ɛ̈	sounds as	E in	Petty	e.g. Pɛ̈t
G	sounds as	G in	Gas	e.g. Gat
H	sounds as	A in	An	e.g. ha̲n
I	sounds as	I in	This	e.g. Thin
i̲	sounds as	I in	Will	e.g. Kit
J	sounds as	J in	Jam	e.g. Jiop
K	sounds as	K in	Ask	e.g. Kak
L	sounds as	L in	Lamb	e.g. Lat
M	sounds as	M in	Mat	e.g. Mat
N	sounds as	N in	Noun	e.g. Nath
Nh	sounds as	N in	Knock	e.g. Nhok
Ny	sounds as	Nge in	Strange	e.g. Piny
Ŋ	sounds as	Ng in	Wing	e.g. Ŋol
O	sounds as	O in	Boy	e.g. Thok
O̲	sounds as	O in	Old	e.g. Lo̲c
ɔ	sounds as	O in	Got	e.g. Lɔc
ɔ̲	sounds as	O in	Lot	e.g. Lɔ̲t
P	sounds as	P in	Part	e.g. Pat
R	sounds as	R in	Ram	e.g. Ruac
T	sounds as	T in	Tale	e.g. Tuac
Th	sounds as	T in	Theme	e.g. Thur

U	sounds as	U in	Flu	e.g. Bul
W	sounds as	W in	Wine	e.g. Wan
Y	sounds as	Y in	Yawn	e.g. Yaŋ

Compound words

E e
E e Sixth letter of Thok Nath I i
I i Eleventh letter of Thok Nath Ö ö
Ö ö The thirty first letter of Thok Nath U u
U u The twenty fifth letter of Thok Nath

A

A The first letter of Thok Nath alphabets

A An article for singular nouns, e.g. a gat, a wut

Aah An angry word usually said with pushing a finger or stick at

a person when angry

Aha A word which is usually said when listening carefully.

Aal A word which is said when one is not ready to interfere in someone's problems or troubles.

Ala A surprise word which is usually heard or said when something has gone wrong or spoiled.

Aie A word which means no or not.

Ay No or not

Aay A sound of series laughing.

Ayoow A sound or cry of mourning, weeping or lamenting.

Aöö A regrettable word which is always said when a thing or things got spoiled or misused.

A̲

B

Ba 1. The eighth letter of Thok Nath. 2. A future reference expression as prefix.eg Ruac æmœ ba lat iruun: *This talk will be discussed tomorrow.*

Bab To push something out unknowingly when doing something nearby.

Babbraar To push outside something usually: fish when fishing; charcoal when cooking or someone in a dance

Babraari Plural of *Babraar* being the action of pushing a thing out, as explained above.

Bao A kind of wild tree which has yellowish fruits when ripened.

Baow Plural of Bao being a kind of tree that has fruits which look yellowish when ripened as explained above

Bac 1. A person who usually does anything badly. 2. To hand something on the wrong side.

Baac State of doing things badly.

Bay 1. Failure to recognize or identify someone or something. 2. A condition of water surface when disturbed by a moving body or object.

Bal A large cut on someone or animal.

Baal A hard neck muscle meat which is not always chewable.

Baali Plural of Baal neck hard meat as explained above.

Balbal 1. State of being quite sharp or that cuts quickly or faster. 2. A slang for a person that joins or jumps into any talk.

Balbaal 1. Plural of Balbal being how fast a sharp tool cut as explained above. 2. The behavior where one jumps into any talk.

Bam 1. A type of small or tiny bluish beads for decoration. 2. Part of human body below the belly or above female genital organ. see Juäk (Male organ).

Ban 1. A bed bug 2. To run a race or competition. 3. Rectangular shape with four corners.

Banban Having four or so many corners.

Banjiar To act in away of cheating when dividing something where you take a big or greater part of it.

Baaŋ State of being useless or helpless person.

Baŋ 1. Nothing, useless or helpless. 2. River bank or shore.

Baŋbaŋ A type of wild plant.

Bak 1. Fish movements out from the river in a rainy day. 2. To cut a wood or whatever object into many pieces. 3. Headache. 4. A piece of a wood or whatever that is cut to so many pieces. 5. To pass or go to someone who would like to share a trip or a journey with. 6. A crack on hard surface or soil. 7. To open gourd, pumpkin etc.

Bakbak A cracked piece of wood or bone.

Bakbakni Plural of *Bakbak* being a cracked piece of wood or bone as explained above.

Bap 1. To take or collect along something or animal on the way. 2. Sound as that is heard when someone has fallen on stomach or belly. 3. Lying on stomach or belly as that of a baby or a soldier.

Bapbap State of being not so high nor raised up.

Bappiny 1. State of moving on stomach or belly. 2. To knock down someone or something when in a hurry or in panicking.

Baar 1. A type of plant that looks like sorghum in early stages of growth. 2. Plural of Bar being whatever is trusted to someone to carry along to other people in a distance.

Bar 1. To run away or to escape any danger that is about to hit or attack you. 2. To take along someone or something when on journey.

Barbar State of feeling weak or shivering due to weakness or fear.

Barkak Hoof of an animal or the hard shell of a fruit.

Barkakni Plural of *Barkak* being the hoof or hard shell as explained above.

Barpiny To knock down someone or something suddenly when in a hurry.

Baroa A kind of plant.

Baroani Plural of *Baroa* being a kind of plant such as okra as explained above.

Bat 1. A piece of dried fish (Liac). It becomes a plural when a stress is put on (a). 2. The fluid that flows out through the mouth when one in deep sleep.

Batbat Slang for he/she who involves others in his/her own troubles or problems.

Batnyaaŋ To involve someone into one own difficulties or troubles.

Baath State of being seriously affected, chock or severe panicking.

Bath 1. Lost or missed the way or the point. 2. Having been overcome by sad news or events.

Baw Statement for terrifying or frightening a child, prisoner, captive or enemy.

Bawbaw State of being quite frightened or in great fear.

Bäy State of having lost the original taste as that of fermented grains.

Bäyba̱y Having that taste of fermented grains.

Bäl 1. To jump over something or someone. 2. Container made by cutting a gourd into large pieces. It is used for cooking preparation of food stuff without touching milk(Nuer tradition).

Bälbäl State of having lost or has no taste due to having been over used or diluted with water.

Bälmän A name of a certain type of bony fish.

Bään A name of a child born during death ritual ceremony.

Bän A ritual which is performed after death.

Bänbän State of such ritual ceremony after death.

Bäŋ Hut entrance which looks like veranda.

Bäñni Plural of Bäñ being a hut entrance that looks like veranda.

Bäk 1. A ritual which is performed by cutting a sacrifice animal into two parts as part of traditional belief. 2. The fish movement outside the river water into rainy cold fresh water.

Bäny 1. To leave something or someone behind. Eg Cu hä bäny piny: *Do not leave me behind.* 2. To own a lot of cattle particularly cows (a Dinka word).

Bänypiny To leave something or someone behind.

Bääp To cause someone to lose patience due to bad news.

Bääpbääp A way of walking when overcome by sorrow or sadness.

Baär 1. Bow and arrow. 2. State of being tall or long eg Mi bäär: *Long*, Ram mi bäär: *Tall person or human being.*

Ba̲r 1. State of being tall or long. 2.Gun shot or arrow shot. 3. Local art where a cow vein is opened to drain some blood. 4. Plural of Bär being an Anyuak man or woman.

Bärbär 1. State of being quite tall or long.2. A slang for an issue that does not concern a person.

Bät Small fish which is swallowed by big one.

Bätni Plural of Bät a small fish as explained above.

Bäthbäth State of being very slight as that of porridge or fast food.

Baŋ State of helpness habit learned by a child due to bad rearing

Ba̲ŋni Plural of Ba̲ŋ being another pronunciation of Bäñ part of a hut as explained above.

Ba̲t 1. To swallow something. 2. A thin piece of dried fish.

Bec To admire someone or something.

Beec 1. A person who admires whatever comes to his/her site. 2. Plural of *Bec* He/she who admires with slight different in pronunciation.

Bel 1. State of blame as when someone has done wrong deeds or actions. 2. Black smith.

Beel 1. State of blacksmith work of forging of tools out of metal or iron. 2.A type of grains (sorghum).

Belɛgak A type of grass.

Belriakä A kind of plants or grass.

Ben Coming, have / has come or have / has arrived.

Benbɛn State of being in a hurry after someone or something

Beŋ Not straight due to bending to one side.

Beŋbeŋ State of walking while expecting something to appear or to attack.

Ber 1. Come,report or show up. 2. To tie grass with rope when thatching hut roof. 3. A bundle of tied up grass for thatching a hut.

Beer Plural of Ber a tied up grass for thatching as explained above.

Berber Come come when calling someone in a distance to come quickly.

Bet Plural of Bet being bad deeds of someone.

Bëëc She/he who admires something or someone.

Bɛ He/,she/ or it will.eg Bæ ben iruun: *He/she/it will come tomorrow.*

Bɛɛ He,/she/it is coming.

Bɛc The pain or whatever that makes a body painful.

Bɛcbɛc State of being painful or difficult to deal with.

Bæcbæac Plural of Bæcbæc being whatever causes pain or suffering.

Bɛl 1. Plural of *Beel* the sorghum or grains as explained above. 2. To blame someone.

Bɛɛl State of blaming someone for wrong or bad done to one.

Bɛɛŋ A pain which starts on human body due to a wound or injury.

Bɛŋbɛŋ 1. Having become full with water to the banks as a case with flooded river. 2. Slang for severe fever with high fever.

Bɛp Having round shape as that with belly or gourd container.

Bɛpbɛp Small with round shape.

Bɛɛr 1. Someone who is good in dancing 2 State of.dancing according to the music or tunes. 3. The flag or anything which indicates or gives signals.

Bɛrbɛr State of being shaky as when dancing, shivering or being shaken by winds.

Bɛt A hasty way of drinking, milk, beer, water, etc.

Bɛtbɛt State of having hasty way of drinking much of water,milk or whatever when thirsty or feverish.

Bɛw Sharp noise of a baby, child, or a goat.

Bɛwbɛw State of such noise either when talking,crying or wailing continuously.

Bëcbëëc Plural of Bɛcbɛc being a state of pain as explained above.

Bëër State of being the best dancer in the group.

Bi 1. You will (singular). Eg Bi ben ithaar?: *Will you come next year?* 2. Second person for coming as in eg Bi ni?: *Where do you*

come from?

Bia You come for more then one person.

Bic State of being not any longer strange, but normal

Bi-hän I will. Eg Bi han ben: *I will come.*

Bi-kɔn We will. Eg Bi kon kie bi ney ben: *We will come.*

Bi-kɛ/kɛn They will. Eg Bi ke kie bi ken ben: *They will come.*

Biir A person who decorates peoples by cutting shapes on their

bodies.

Bil 1. Colour of a cow usually with dominant colour (red, grey, black etc) with some whitish spots on both sides of the belly. 2. The appearance of bright colours in darkness or in cloudy weather. 3. A name of a cattle camp e.g Bil Kec, Bil Nyapan etc 4. To make or to colour one own face, utensils or walls.

Bilbil 1. State of shining or glittering as that of flash light or fire. 2. A name of Alcohol distilled from fermented grains or dates.

Bieeth Plural of Bith a type of metallic tools as explained below.

Biem To filter local beer with cloth bag known as Nyoŋɛ.

Bieem Plural of Biim a person who attacks or waylays as explained below.

Biew 1. Having lost taste or changed taste due to overstaying in water. 2. A kind of stick which is not well decorated.

Bieer A man who makes scars on the face or body skin as decorations.

Bim State of waylaying in order to kill or beat up someone who did bad.

Biim A person who waylays and attacks people to kill or to beat them up.

Bimbim A village north of Yomding near to Nyäŋ swamp.

Binybiny Appearance of disturbed water signs or oil dots on the meat soup.

Biɛɛl Plural of *Bil* the colors as that of cows or whatever as explained above.

Biɛr The appearance of lightening strikes in cloudy weather..

Biöp 1. The shape of lips as when one is very angry or about to weep. 2. The water of fermented grains.

Bip To have very quick admiring habits or manners.

Bipbip State of having such a habit of admiring very fast.

Biy A noise or sound as that is heard when two iron or metallic tools are hit.

Biw 1. Noise or sound as that is made by kids. 2. To jump over something usually bush, waters or fence.

Biiy Cloth or a piece of cloth.

Biiyni Plural of Biiy a piece of cloth as explained above.

Bilɛ A temporary small shelter for keeping calves, lambs or puppies.

Biri To prick and cut on someone skin to make decorations.

Biir Those small scar dots on the skin which is made for decorations.

Birbir State of one direction movement without looking back or turning.

Birbir State of being shaky due to wind as a case with flag or due to cold, fear or being feverish.

Bit 1. State of great silence. 2. One hundred or Kuor.

Bitbit He/she who keeps or always in silence all the time and not troublesome.

Bith 1. A type of spear which has some sharp teeth. 2. One of the rips of animal(cow or human being).

Biwbiw The noise as that of singing or weeping continuously.

Böc To stop doing something due to difficult situation.

Bööc Stoppage due to exhaustion or having ruled that it is not possible to continue.

Bök To throw a stick, stone, etc at someone or something.

Böök State of series throwing of sticks, stones, mud stones, etc.at peoples or animals.

Böl 1. The flame of fire. 2. A type of plants which causes poisoning.

Bööl Stage of glowing fire where it becomes red in colour.

Bölböl Glowing fire or slang for fat meat.

Bölreal A type of plants which grows in old compound.

Böŋ State of having favored one person than the other one (s)

when separating two persons fighting.

Böŋni Plural of Bööŋ a large whitish marine bird as explained below.

Böŋ rɛɛc The behavior of favoring one person when two are fighting.

Bööŋ A large whitish wild duck which lives on fishing

Böm Cow hump, or a deformed person back being a T.B victim.

Bön Plural of Bon being a knitted work which is worn for dancing purposes as explained below.

Böny 1. Plural of *Böny* to dodge a stick or whatever as explained below (stress on ö).

Böny 2. To dodge something harmful or dangerous.

Böy A cow ornament made out of large shell nut pierced together as necklace.

Bööy Plural of *Böy* a type of nut as explained above.

Bör 1. White or whitish. 2. A kind of whitish bead which is worn as row pieces on each ear of a woman. 3. State of feeling much heat or body temperature rises due to sickness. 4. To make or cause a local pipe become hot as part of smoking.

Böör 1. Whitish in colour for both cows and goats. 2. State of pains as when in fever or in general pains. 3. Plural of *Bör* being that kind of beads which is worn on ears.

Böw Goat.eg Ti dæl mi böw: *You have got a goat.*

Böwni Plural of Böw being a goat as explained above.

Böt Barren animal both goats and cows or those do not produce.

Bo̲t Plural of Böt a barren cow as explained above.

Bo Also, so or like that. Eg Ti thin bo? Are you also included?

Boak To rob someone luggage or cattle while on a journey.

Boäk 1. The sun bending to the west Boäk caŋ 2. To bend to one side.

Boar Shame or whatever causes shame or state of shamefulness.

Boath Having much to do with hunger Bœth starvation or famine.

Boäth To bend one back down as when walking in order not to be seen in **a** distance or when passing below a low roof.

Boäw A yellowish fruit of a wild thorny tree of savanna forest.

Boc 1. To touch the area around the kidney of someone to stimulate him/her to laugh. 2. State of being coward or cowardice.

Bohm State of being very strong, powerful, hard or difficult to throw, cut or uplift.

Bok 1. Nuer pronunciation for a book (borrowed from English).2.A kind of snake 3. A colour or kind of certain species of cows with bluish eyes. 4. State of food soaked and stayed in water for quite a long time or a dead body before burial. 5. A type of short grass with almost yellowish and greenish flowers.

Bokni Plural of *Bok* either a book or the colour as explained above.

Bokbok State of shaking or not steady as when the wind blowing over the grass stalks or trees.

Bol 1. A name of a child born after twins. 2. To prepare fire with cow dungs.

Bolbol State of having something looks fat or huge.

Bolreal A type of plants which grows in old compound.

Bolwijuàt A bird with a protruding feather on its head.

Boŋ To throw someone down when wrestling or fighting.

Boŋboŋ A game like play which is practiced by kids, babies or children.

Bon 1. To reject the share because it is too little or small. 2. A long knitted threads or strings which is worn around the waste for dancing. It looks like Yoa but longer.

Boon A person who always rejects his/her share as explained above.

Bony 1. To dive or dip one body into the water usually when swimming or bathing. 2. To dodge something harmful or dangerous tool or device.

Bonybony Slang for a person who does not keep his/her first statement or he/she who denies whatever he/she said early.

Boyboy State of being whitish as a piece of paper, chalk, cloths etc.

Bohr 1. The outer part of placenta. 2. A type of marine grass which is served to calves.

Bor 1. Clay or fireplace for cooking. 2. To fill a pot or whatever by dipping it into the liquids such as water. 3. Plural of Boar being the shame or bad name.

Borbor The noise that is heard when filling a narrow opening container in liquid.

Bot 1. To lick fingers after eating very delicious food. 2. Wound or injury.

Both 1. Sticky substance that looks like rubber or whatever. 2. To pull along with a rope or stick an animal or a human Being. 3. Hunger, starvation,famine or lack of food. 4. To do something with neighbor support such as thelocal beer. 5. To bend down a little as when entering a hut door. 6. Having been decayed as a case with meat,fish or bad grains.

Bothboth 1. Having decayed or decomposed as with grains. 2. State of being quite thick in body. 3. Having been bended or in bending appearance or position. 4. That is elastic as that of sticky substance such as rubber. 5. State of being in bending position as when attacking animal in hunting.

Bowbow 1. Being easy to release blood or fats. 2. State of being frightened and ready to run for life.

Buk 1. To put some ashes on a cow or a goat to earmark it for ancestral gods or kujurs. 2. To put ashes on a sacrifice before slaughtering or spearing it or to smear oneself with ashes as an ornament 3. Water spirit, local god or kujur among Nuer.

Budh 1. Sound of heavy falling object. 2. A heap of cow dung. 3. Add mud on wooden walls.

Buɔk 1. A black and white monkey. 2. Having got decayed or spoiled such as a dead animal or fish. 3. To rob or take someone property by force when he/she on a journey. 4. To play in water after one finished bathing.

Buɔ̱k To bend something or someone.To defeat people or force them **to** retreat or run.

Buook A black and whitish monkey.

Bul 1. One of Nuer sections in western Nuer. 2. A drum or drum dance. 3. Slang for the final settlement of the marriage where dowry is paid. 4. To roast fish, meat or clay utensils. 5. Slang of burning heat due to rise in temperature. 6. A clay made pot or container.

Buli 1. State of having much to do with Bul Nuer. 2. Plural of Bul as a clay made utensil or container.

Bulbul 1. A type of insect which looks as if it is tied on the middle or waist. 2. Having much meat, fat or fleshy. 3. Slang for such insect where it looks as if it doesn't feed.

Buliak A kind of fish which fills itself with air to appear fat or huge to frighten the other big fishes.

Bu̱ɔl 1. Plural of Bul being the drum as explained above. 2. A roasted thing. 3. Dark red colour as that of decayed blood.

Bu̱ɔ̱ɔl 1. Plural of Bu̱ɔl a roasted thing as explained above. 2. Having got roasted.eg Riŋ cæ buåål kua dääk: *The meat is roasted, you divide it.*

Bum 1. To consolidate to endure hardships as in Bum rɔ : Don't lose hope. 2. Plural of Buœm that is deformity as explained above.

Bu̱ɔm State of having signs or organs not like the rest of people.

Bumbum 1. Powerful and energetic person. 2. Strong or solid and hard to break item.

Bun Plural of Buon which is a group of people, things, cattle or wild animals as explained below.

Buny A mouthful of milk, beer or any drinkable liquid.

Bunybuny Being short and thick as that of horns, fingers etc.

Buoa̱ni Plural of Buœn a group or state of being in a group as **explained** below.

Bu̱ɔn A group of anything.

Buöny Plural of Buony being an Ethiopian as explained below..

Buony 1. An Ethiopian. 2. To dive in water when in a river or water pool.

Buonybuony State of being short, thick or fat.

Bup 1. A noise or sound of a falling heavy object. 2. A state of lying on stomach.

Buup Epidemic, unlimited famine, disease, disaster etc.

Bupbup A noise of falling objects on flat surface.

Bur 1. Collection of huts, cattle or a group of anything. 2. The roaring of a bull or lion. 3. State of being short or low as that of trees. 4. State of being covered with flies,ants etc. 5. To prepare a fish to be cooked when it is half dried see Burɛ.

Buur A bundle of grain, maize stalks in one place.

Buuri Plural of Buur being a bundle of grains stalks as explained above. eg The current Buuri suburb of Khartoum City is a Nuer name for grain bundles.

Burbur 1. State of being short and fat. 2. A kind of insect that attacks the cattle in the evening.

Buor 1. A kind of grass that grows in water and is served to calves. 2. To mock or make mockery on someone. 3. A kind of membrane which makes up the placenta. 4. To make such noise as that of cattle when released for grasing or when about to cross rive

Buɔ̱t 1. A colour usually a mixture of orange and white on cow only. 2. Wound or injury. 3. To spend a day.

Buɔ̱ɔ̱t Plural of But that is wound as explained below.

But 1. Wet or moist place usually a room or shadow of a tree. 2. Bush or shrub trees. 3. A wound or injury.

Butbut Bushy trees or place where short bushy trees are found.

Butbutni Plural of Butbut being bushy tree as explained above.

Buuth State of being fat in early stages such as a baby, calf etc.

Buthbuth 1. State of being fat as with the calves or babies etc. 2. State of food spoilage or decaying.

C

Ca A word which is used for past tense, meaning was, were, and did.

Caa Reported speech word, meaning what happened eg. Caa thok Nööŋ: *A mouth (news) was brought*. Caa nañ: *It was taken.*

Cä The sound of the twenty fourth letter of Thok Nath, or first person statement for I have, e.g. Cä bi be̱n : I will not come. Cä be̱n : *I have come.*

Cac To move in group at ago in one line.

Cacac 1. State of having little or shallow water as in a pool. 2. A dancing fashion or walking styles.

Cääc To make precautions or preparations before time.

Cay Burun tribe of Eastern Upper Nile State or whatever is done or brought from this tribe.

Caay A surprise word when one finds someone continuing doing something he/she was actually been warned of.

Cak 1. A kind of insect that sticks on animals, human being in order to suck blood. 2. Milk or plenty of milk. 3. To create or make for the first time.

Caak 1. Plural of Cak the plenty of milk 2. To shelter under a roof or leaves in raining day.

Cakcak Ability to create or make some faults or untrue statements as in a court.

Cäk 1. Plural of Cak being the milk as stated a.bove. 2. The creator, the Almighty God. 3. The deformed person or animal etc. 4. All abnormality in anything created.

Cal 1. The area above each leg and below the belly. 2. To be resembling father, mother or any other relative sees cät.

Caal A small frog which is used for fishing as a snare.

Calcal 1. Being quite thin. 2. A style of walking.

Cäl 1. The biggest fish in river Nile–..Nile Perch

2. A slang for this big Nile fish which can not harm because it has no teeth.(Proverb).

Ca̲l Plural of Cäl being the Nile biggest fish as explained above.

Cam 1. To eat food or whatever eatable. 2. Left-handed person or the left side direction. 3. To hand up something to someone on the wrong side or opposite.

Caam 1. Sharp pain as that troubles the stomach. 2. Consumable goods such as fish,dura (sorghum) etc.

Camcam Whatever is eatable, usually food etc.

Cäm Plural of cam being a left-handed person as explained above.

Cämɛ That food substance which is put on the hook for trapping fish.

Can 1. Poor, helpless person. 2. State of poverty or lack of property or people. 3. To take position as when fighting with sticks. 4. State of having been bended down by heavy winds or large flow of water.

Cancan 1. State of being overwhelmingly covered by water. 2. A wild plant which cures certain diseases or sickness.

Cään Water flood or that water which overflow banks of a river.

Äncän State of causing delay as when people at the point of starting or leaving.

Caŋ To put away something so as it is not seen by passer-by.

Caŋcaŋ State of being not ready to join people in doing something.

Caŋcaaŋ The way a youngman or a thief moves along waiting to meet his girl friend or to steal.

Cäŋ 1. The sun. 2. Today or this date.3. Home eg.Cäñ læp æloñ, æn cäñ æmæ.Tä cäñ : *The sun sent hard rays. This day, I am at home.* 4. A Leather string for tying a piece of skin around the waist by womenfolk. See cäŋ yät.

Cäŋäŋ State of being not well made, built, created or designed.

Cäŋdäär mid day, at day time or during the day time.

Cäŋkuɔth Sunday or the God day or the praying day.

Cany 1. To reject, to push away something because you do not need it, her or him. 2. To refuse fighting someone who is too young or too old.

Canycany 1. Style of eating when one has no interest or appetite for that type of food. 2. Lack of appetite for food or any other thing due to being dirty, not well cooked or too little.

Cääny A feeling when one dislikes, or hates anything given to, usually food, place, water,etc.

Cap Full of water, butter or fat.

Capcap 1. Being well filled with water or butter. 2. A person who talks a lot or join any talk.

Cäpcäp A slang for short and fat person.

Ca̲p A way out, plan or better idea

Ca̲a̲p Plural of Ca̲p better idea or plan as explained above.

Car 1. To put thing in order, in line or in parade. 2. State of not being ready to join people in meal etc because it is too little for many hands.

Carcar Being in one line or the same level of height or has been leveled.

Carcaar A device for cutting either wood or iron pieces such as sawing machine.

Carɔk Any problem, trouble or difficulty caused or brought by a person from distance place.

Carɔkni A plural of Carɔk being trouble as explained above.

Cär Plural of Ca̱r thinking as explained below.

Cäär A black cow or goat.

Cärcär To make unnecessary delaying particularly when people are about to leave.

Ca̱r 1. A black colour or darkness. 2. To think.

Ca̱a̱r Plural of Cäär a black or dark colour as explained above.

Cat 1. Bend down something,to tilt or adjust it to the right position. 2. To lie down as when one is resting.

Catcat To have something in a bending position.

Cät 1. To resemble, to look like, to have the same appearance. 2. To put a container or utensil on the right position.

Cäät Resembling in appearance or in structure.

Ca̱a̱t To slipper due to soft surface.

Ca̱tca̱t State of slippery surface usually after rainfall in muddy soil.

Cath A borrowed word from Dinka for walking usually a child way of learning how to walk.

Ca̱thca̱th A state of being mobile as that with a child who learns how to walk.

Ca̱w 1. To wash something without soap. 2. The noise or sound which is heard when one is inside water bathing or wading.

Ca̱a̱w Noise of birds or fishermen when operating or landing on water surface.

Ca̱a̱wca̱a̱w That noise one hears when crossing,playing or disturbing water.

Cawcaw 1. A song, which is, sang by young ladies in drum dance.
2. That water without mud in the river or water ways.

Ca̱y 1. To pour some water on hard surface to make it soft when digging.
2. To cool down a hot object in order to handle it.

Ca̱yca̱a̱y Very little quantity of liquid (water, milk, beer, etc) that cool down the needs or thirst.

Ceth Stool, or that waste the body releases or the shit.

Cɛ 1. He/she has come as in Cɛ be̱n.

Cɛ mith, cɛ wä: He/she has eaten and he/she has gone. 2. Not as in: Cɛ bi wak: *He/she will not cry.*

Cɛc 1. To dissuade someone so as to tell him something. 2. To take a different route as when on a journey.

Cɛc-cɛc A person who does not conform to the group plans or who goes astray.

Cɛl To make a piece of wood, iron or bone from the main stem or body.

Cɛl-cɛal Plural of Cælcæl being a small piece of wood, bone, iron etc.as explained above.

Cɛm A noise of a moving object outside the hut.

Cɛm-cɛm Unnecessary movement usually by children as when they are playing.

Cɛn-cɛn A group, troop or good number of youth ready to carry out any task.

Cɛp 1. To cut down some grass with a long knife. 2. A sign or noiœe of someone moving or passing by.

Cɛp-cɛp State of such frequent movements as explained above.

Cɛth Plural of Ceth being the stool or stomach waste as explained above.

Ci 1. Have, done, made eg. Ci kɛ wä: *They have gone*

Ci maath: You have drunk. 2. Ci: Not, negative for 2nd person, eg. Ci bi wä: *You will not go*. Ci bi be̱n: *You will not come*.

Cia For both plural have/ have not second person plural or group, eg.Cia wä: *You have gone*. Cia tɔ̱ɔ̱c: You have lied down. Cia bi wä: *You won't go*. Cia bi tɔ̱ɔ̱c: *You won't lie down*.

Ciac A side route or path.

Ciak State of being quite short and not tall.

Cial A piece cut from the main object usually wood, bone, horn, nail, etc.

Cial-ciaal Plural of Cial being a piece of the main object,wood, bone, horn or nail.

Cian A cursed or has been wished bad luck. See Cien.

Ciaŋ The way or normal ways of living.see Cieŋ.

Ciar The movement of stone or whatever over surface, opened ground or water.

Ciaar To go astray to run for life when in danger.

Cic A failure to move regularly or steadily due to troubles on joints

Cic-cic State of having stiff joints that cannot allow one to walk or move, or bend down.

Ciek Woman of all folks,see Män.

Ciel 1. Elbow or the joint of one hand. 2. To peel the sugar cane as when one wants to chew it

Cien 1. To curse or call bad fortune to affect someone for having done bad. 2. Intestine

Cienɛ A kind of small fish which jumps up when water is disturbed.

Cieŋ 1. Home, where one lives or stays. 2. Clan or big family under one founder, eg.Cieŋ Waloak Cieŋ Yol. 3. To live, see Ciaŋ. 4. A type of smell as that of fish.

Cieŋ-taŋ An unknown place or region Nuer refer to,in order to convince their subjects.

Ciey Iron wire as that is used for tying up things.

Ciey-ciey 1. Troublesome person or child who does not accept advice.

Ciey-ciey 2. The noise of flowing liquids such as water, blood, milk etc.

Ciep A piece of meat or any other object

Cier One of stars that helps in locating directions or assessing seasons.

Ciet 1. To wear or put on the best clothes or whatever. 2. Style of spitting saliva as part of the culture. 3. To have one hair cut to a certain fashion or style.

Ciew 1. State of becoming quite grown up to adult. 2. Having ripened as with sugar canes, or state of being quite matured

Ciɛk 1. State of having grains got ripened, eg. Bɛl bi kɛ ciɛk: The grains will get ripened. 2. To praise some good work done.

Ciɛk-ciɛk State of being quite short in height, or length.

Ciɛm To kiss. To express the love by action.

Ciɛn To curse or call bad fortune to affect someone for having done wrong.

Ciɛw State of being quite thin or slim.

C̱ik 1. Iron or metallic ring usually from Copper, Gold, Silver, etc. 2. A kind of fish that has no scales usually black in colour.

Ci̱ik Plural of Cik being the metallic ring as explained above.

Ci̱ŋ-ci̱ŋ State of having fish smell.

Ci̱l-ci̱l State of being little or small in body size. See Cin-cin

Ciök 1. Plural of Ciöök being the leg 2. The beginning of a topic. 3. The war **songs** for gathering. 4. Poles or stands which support a container up.

Ciöök 1. Leg, war rehearsal or marriage ceremony songs. 2. Wooden stands which support up a container.

Ciöt 1. Name 2. To pluck out, or to force out whatever such as a baby at delivery etc.

Ciööt Plural of Ciöt being the name, as explained above.

Ciöör Plural of Cor being blind. State of being blind or blindness.

Cip Being a small piece as in Cip-cip.

Cip-cip State of being very small piece of anything.

Ci̱r A type of tobacco with long thin leaves.

Cir-cir 1. That cannot be stopped easily, or quickly. 2. A kind of insect or worm that moves on several legs. 3. Being quite small and narrow in size as with tobacco leaves.

Ci̱t To pass watery stool as when with diarrhea or dysentery.

Ci̱th State of passing watery stool as when suffering of diarrhea.

Ciw A kind of disease which affects the children or babies, see Wɛth.

Ciw-ciw State of being quite thin or slender as that with body or anything.

Co A short form of Cow being the husband, eg Næmæ æ co nyimaar: *This is my sister husband*

Co nyal: The girl husband.

Coa That whatever to do with husband, eg 1. Räw Coa: The husband dance, eg.2. Man Coa: The husband sister.

Coa̱ Bone or piece of bone, see Cɔ̱w.

Coal Person invited to attend a function because he /she is not related to the concerned family.

Coaal Plural of Coal being the invited person as explained above.

Coak 1. Plural of Cok the black ants. 2. kujur man or woman.

Coc A way of sitting in a tight place or a woman way of sitting at delivery stage.

Coc-coc State of being so tighten or squeezed in small space.

Cok 1. Black ant, see Rɛl for white ant. 2. The kujur man or woman. 3. To mix food of differing ingredients in order to have good taste. 4. The cattle way of treading soil in rainy season. 5. State of being alone in the place.

Cok-cok State of doing simple, minute thing or minor issue (s).

Cok-coak Plural of Cok-cok being semi idle or doing meaningless as explained above.

Col 1. To call or to name a person or a dog etc. 2. To compensate by naming a baby born after a dead child. 3. To invite a person. 4. Black or dark.

Col-col Great darkness or state of being completely dark.

Com 1. To clean by making the final touches on wooden or clay container or device. 2. Delicious or tasty food. 3. To instigate a person to fight or do something good or bad.

Com-com State of being quite delicious or tasty.

Cohm The failure to take a decision or suffering of indecision.

Com-coum Plural of Com-com being whatever delicious as explained above

Com thin To tackle something beneficial. To instigate someone to do something good or bad.

Con-con 1. A condition of pulling contest where the contesting parties pull a rope. 2. A mixture of dead grass and marines in water.

Cony To shape the horns or hands into the wanted style or shape.

Cony-cony State of having such shape of horns.

Conyony Series conformation in a fight or combatting.

Coñ To close one hands or whatever that can be closed or put together such as paper, piece of cloth or skin.

Coñcooñä State of being in a closed position. Eg Jiæc rœ æñu tii coñcooñä mœ? *Get up why are you in such a closed state?*

Coñoñ 1. A kind of beans. 2. A state of being in one position for quite a long time.

Coy 1. That noise, one hears when water is poured on fire or hot utensil. 2. Sharpness a thorn pricking.

Cooy The noise of water on glowing fire.

Coy-coy State of such noise when water, fats put or pour on fire.

Couny The bull with one left horn bending as explained above.

Coap A state of what to do with Cop eg Thok Coap as explained below

Cop 1. A long stick which is used for digging soil to sow seeds. 2. To reach or arrive. 3. A hand wrist. 4. State of being well fitted or exact to the intended position.

Coplæær To catch up someone who has gone ahead or whatever is taken **without** your notice.

Copni Plural Cop a hand wrist as explained above.

Cohp Full of water, fat or butter usually food or compound.

Cor 1. Blind man,woman or animal see Ciöör 2. Decomposition of the flesh as a result of decaying or rottening

Cor-cor State of flesh decomposition or decaying.

Cot-cot 1. A cow or bull that has no horns. 2. State of being quite small or tight as a case with a room.

Cot-coat Series confrontation that amount to facing one another in a fight.

Counh To have appeared towards the speaker or passed near or beside him/her.

Coupe A floatable material that is added to snare to indicate that a fish is about to swallow it when fishing in a river.

Cour Vulture, a bird which feeds on dead human beings and animals.

Couw To boil some items so as not to get decayed or spoil, such as meat, fish etc.

Cow 1. Husband or friend (male) or Lom see :Concubine. 2. Plural of Cow as explained above with stress on (O). 3. Plural of Coa being a bone as explained above.

Cow-cow State of being quite difficult to break and that causes much saliva.

Coth 1. To rub away the dirt of the body. 2. To smear the body with oil, fats or butter.

Cooth State of having passed near the speaker.

Cothjɔɔr To rub away the dirts of whatever oil,soil etc.on the body.

Cöc To raise one hand as when about to hit or spear.

Cöc-cöc The stage of being ready to spear or hit.

Cöl A clay made container that can not stand without support.

Cöl-cöl 1. That can not stand a lone. 2. A person whose back is quite stiff, hard to bend.

Cöm Snail

Cööm Plural of Cöm being snail as explained above.

Cör Plural of Cour the vulture bird that feeds on human and animal flesh.

Cöt To press in order to squeeze out some thing such as baby at delivery, or stool.

Cu A prefix which is used in the past tense as well as negative form, eg. Cu kɛ be̱n: *They came*. Cu kɛ wä thin: *They went in*. Cu wee thin *Do not go in.*

Cua I was, as for eg. Cua wä: *I went*, Cua kɛ bök: *They were thrown at.*

Cuac To drive the cattle or goats to grazing lands or to the cattle camp see Cuec.

Cuak-cuak The noise that you, or one hears when chewing something, such as meat, sugar cane, etc.

Cual An Arabic language name for a sack for keeping grains (bag).see Toy.

Cuan To cause exhaustion or fatigue.

Cuancuan State of being quite exhausted or exhaustible thing.

Cuay 1. Very fat or full of fats or grown fat, see Cuath or Thiɔ̱l. 2. To get exhausted. 3. To instigate dogs or persons to do bad..

Cuaydɔk A type of tree which has strong thorns.

Cuar To miss chances or state of being unlucky in doing something. eg. Cuarɛ ni ka̱n.:He/she was missing chances.

Cuath States of being fat or very fat.see Thiɔl.

Cuath-cuath State of being quite fat and huge

Cuath piny Uncontrolled falling of anything be it a baby at delivery or when carrying it.

Cuat 1. A noise that, is heard when chewing, kissing, sucking or beating. 2. A slang for long or a falling object.

Cuat-cuat State of having such noise or being very long.

Cuäk A red meat or a meat that is not fat.

Cuäl To put a big piece of food materials into the mouth.

Cuäl-cuäl State of having quite loose clothes.

Cuäläk State of being exhausted, not active.

Cuääl Person who does not know how to dance according to tunes or music.

Cual̲ Plural of Cuääl a person who does no know dancing as explained above.

Cuän-cuän A style of walking while naked or nude.

Cuäŋ Inability to follow the tunes or songs, or difficulty in deciding, or state of confusion.

Cuääŋ The situation where one stops to do anything because of great confusion.

Cuäŋ-cuäŋ State of being hesitant in doing something or lack of taking action.

Cuäny 1. Liver of human or animal. 2. To touch something with fire or food substance on broth or stew.

Cuääny A colour of a bull or cow eg.:-Cuääny Nyaaŋ. Cuääny Bok. Cuääny Cuɔr.

Cuänycuäny The ways of touching with whatever such as tool or dog nose human body.

Cuäy 1. State of be exhausted to continue doing work. 2. To instigate or force someone or dog to attack a person or an animal

Cuäy-cuäy 1. A person who does not act very fast or quickly. 2. A person who does not stay longer in one place but on the move.

Cuär 1. Thief, Robber or Burglar. 2. An irregular way of digging a hole. 3. To be beyond the supposed line or limit.

Cuäär The other name for a lion to a certain clan which took it as their god. A Dinka name.

Cuäth 1. To set alight fire on dry grass or a hut see :Rɛp or Ruat-ruat. 2. To put something into one mouth in order to swallow. 3. A disease that causes great swelling on food or leg joints. See: Ginea worm

Cuäthcuäth State of being ready to put one hand in anything. A nickname to a person who puts his/her hand in anything.

Cuät State of being quite red or reddish or pink in colour.

Cuec 1. Right hand or side of any thing. 2. To drive cattle to either grazing land or to the marriage as dowry.

Cuel 1. The circumcision. 2. A way of sitting where buttocks do not touch ground.

Cuen Failure to swallow something which put one into hard time.

Cueny 1. The early heating when sun rays become sharp on the head. 2. To eat by touching a mouthful into a stew in a separate container.

Cuer 1. Advance or being ahead of others, eg. Ɛŋu ci cuer ɔ.? 2. Thief or one who steal things.

Cueer 1. Plural of Cuer or Cuär being the thief as explained above. 2. Stealing or stealing behavior

Cueet 1. A sound which expresses anger or disappointment. 2. That condition which delays action to take place.

Cuetni Plural of Cueet being an expression of anger or condition as explained above.

Cuet-cueetni Plural of such difficulties or constraints that hamper the duties or whatever delays any work.

Cuey Being not able to continue any longer or difficult to continue.

Cuɛ A word which means- He/she has, e.g. Cuɛ wä: *He/she has gone.* Cuæ ben: *He/she has come.*

Cuɛc State of being compact and difficult to continue.

Cuɛɛ A worm that sucks blood (leech) see Cuiy.

Cuɛk A twin baby.

Cuɛak Plural of Cuɛk being a twin child as explained above.

Cuɛl To circumcise.

Cuɛl-cuɛl Being quite little, small or short.

Cuɛy The soup of all kinds or types. It is always in plural.

Cuɛr Not well tied or state of being loose eg. Yien cɛ rɔ cuɛr: The bundle is very loose.

Cuɛr-cuɛr State of being quite loose or not properly tied.

Cuic To drive the cattle to grazing lands or as marriage cows to the bride family.

Cuiil 1. A kind of tree that is used for brushing teeth or mouth.2. To force someone to take some food,drink or whatever that he/she does not used to take or consume.

Cuil State of being quite nuisance by repeating whatever is not wanted or rejected.

Cuiili Plural of Cuiil a tree that is used for brushing teeth as explained above.

Cuiil-cuiil A hungry way of looking as when one is in need of food such as eagle, baby, child etc..

Cuin Very little, tiny or thin. Eg Gat æmœ la mucæ cuin: *That fellow gives very little.*

Cuin-cuin State of being quite little, thin or small.

Cuiny To put or dip a piece of bread or whatever into soup so as to chew and swallow.

Cuiiny A state of weather condition which becomes extremely hot particularly in the morning hours.

Cuiny-cuiny The food which is eaten by dipping pieces or small quantities into soup or broth.

Cuiy Plural of Cueeë a type of worm that sucks blood from human body when one crosses pool or water pond.

Cuir State of being straight forward shape such as spear, leaf etc.

Cuir-cuir Style or condition of being in a straight position such as thin leaves, spears or knives.

Cuit A sound of whipping with a ring or string.

Cuit-cuit Such noise of whipping or beating someone or animal.

Cuoc 1. State of being tired or exhausted of having done hard job. 2. Having been so closed to someone when fighting or walking. 3. To force someone to do anything very fast.

Cuoc-cuoc State of being very tight or lack of wide space.

Cuok 1. To strengthen wooden poles or walls by pushing in soil with a stick. 2. A certain bone that connects the elbow with shoulders. 3. State of being short and fat. 4. To collect together in order to sing war songs as in marriage or at war.

Cuok-cuok An adjective for a very short and fat person.

Cuom 1. To make final touches of a wooden works or whatever that makes final end of a work. 2. State of having good taste,tasteful or delicious.

Cuom-cuom State of having good taste or delicious food materials.

Cuon-cuon A mixture of mud, dead grass and whatever in a water pool or pond.

Counh To enter or to come into the room or the country etc where the speaker in. eg Kua counh.: Just enter. see Cuoth.

Cuoŋ 1. The right in a court of law where one is found not guilty or is right. 2. To stand up or to raise up something.

Couny To bend or to hold someone hand wrongly or to the wrong side.

Cuor Vulture or that bird which feeds on dead animals or human being **corpses** in wilderness.

Cuor-cuɔr State of being decayed or rottened or decomposed.

Cuoth 1. To appear,to go through an opened space such as door,open wall, among woods, trees etc. 2. A smell of a burning feathers, hairs or bones.

Cuɔc To be closed and not very far from each other.

Cuɔc-cuɔc State of being quite close or very tight in terms of space or distance.

Cuɔŋ To fold up or to collect one limbs as when suffering of cold.

Cuœŋ-cuœœŋ State of being in a folded manner or way.

Cuɔk 1. To collect together in order to sing war songs as in marriage dance or at war time.2. To press luggage,grains,and whatever into the container to take.

Cuɔɔk 1. The songs which are sang by young ladies to praise their boyfriends in drum dance. 2. A type of wild trees.

Cuɔl 1. The Kujur which is a result of a burned dead person, killed by lightening or thunderstorm. 2. To compensate the lost, be it a baby or something. 3. The name Cuol is compensation for lost baby. see Nyacuol for female. 4. State of being dark.

Cuɔɔl The rituals which are performed after mourning days, where the family of the diseased person are shaved and could wear nice clothes.

Cuɔl-cuɔl 1. State of being quite dark due to lack of light. 2. Being dark skin as with people or cattle.

Cuɔɔny The trained shape of bull horns.

Cuɔr 1. Plural of Cuur being the smooth skin fish with long tentacles. 2 Plural of Cuœœr a Vulture aœ explained above.

Cuɔr-cuɔr State of decaying or rottening manner.

Cuɔt A piece of intestines filled with some fat meat which is left to decomposed before being cooked.

Cuɔɔt State of giving or paying back whatever one got or received from someone when relationship is severed.

Cuööli Plural of Cuööl a piece of dirty or useless piece of cloth that is used for covering the wall opening that lets in mosquitoes.

Cuc 1. A long stick connected with Bith spear for fishing along the river banks. 2. State of being quite dark or black eg. cuɔlæ cuc: *Is quite dark.*

Cukkut Hiccough or that quick sudden movements of breathing for short period of time.See Hiccup.

Cuk 1. That part of cow rope which is tied on a peg. Eg Cuk *deep*. 2. A clay made pot for cooking, boiling things or for serving water. 3. To put on clothes. 4. To organize together to make good dancing team or group. 5. Plural of Cok a layman or woman in Ñundeng's doctrine verses.

Cuk-cuk A fat and with huge muscles person.

Cul 1. Penis or the male genital organ. 2. To have blackened due to exposure to much heat or smoke. 3. Plural of Cul a penis as explained above with stress on (u).

Cuul 1. A piece of cloth or whatever that is put on room door to keep away mosquitoes. See Dök. 2. State of having much to do with Cul eg Ca yœt cuulæ: *He got hit on the penis.*

Cuŋ 1. Plural of Cuoŋ being the right in a court. 2. To stand up something or oneself or whatever. 3. Straight forward eg. Duop mi cuŋ.

Cuŋ-cuŋ State of being quite straight no bending such as a piece of wood, road, or a human being.

Cun To pull something or someone out of something such as mob or troubles.

Cun-cun 1. State of being quite short.2. A slang for a short person.

Cuny Very short like a piece of something.

Cuny-cuny State of being quite small or short in size.

Cup A sound which is heard when a heavy object falls into the water.

Cup-cup The continuous noise or sound of falling heavy objects into water.

Cur To go deep into something such as spear into the body or the rain water into the soil.

Cuur A smooth skin fish with a relative big head with long tentacles.

Cur-cur 1. That have power to go deep into, such as rain water or spear. 2. A style of walking very fast towards one direction.

Cuth To make a hole on bull horn in order to hang some ornamental objects eg. Dhur kiæ Luëa.

Cuthcuth The smell of burned hairs, feathers, hoofs etc.

Cut 1. State of being alone eg. Ci duoth dueel æ cut: You remained in the hut alone. 2. Compensation of whatever lost or murdered.

Cuut 1. A device made of horn for sucking bad blood from the paining parts of the body. 2. The chimney which takes off smoke.

Cuw The noise of hot or a burning object thrown into water.

Cuw-cuw State of such noise of burning or glowing object thrown into water.

D

Da A suffix meaning :Ours eg. Wecda, gatda inœ :.Our country, our son etc.

Dä 1. A suffix meaning : Mine eg. Gatdä, kɛɛtdä, my son, my stick. 2. Once more is a prefix meaning mine eg. Dämaar, Däguar my brother or son of my mother, son of my father. Here Dä as a prefix meaning son, eg. Dämaar son of my mother.

Dak 1. To give nothing to someone as when distributing something. 2. Part of local pipe. 3. Not well cooked usually grain flour food. 4. Not enough or scarce.

Dakdak State of being very scarce, not enough, not in plenty.

Dakdaak 1. Plural of Dakdak being the scarcity as explained above. 2. State of little quantities.

Däk 1. To untie a bundle or rope. 2. To devoice a wife or a husband. To break the unity or relationships. 3. To demolish a building or whatever one made or built. 4. Disaster caused by wars, flood, fire etc. 5. To break grains by pounding with grinding stone.

Däklààtni State of being in disorder or no arrangement been made.

Dääk Division or the art of dividing something.

Da̱a̱k 1. He/she who divorces, destroys or divides ete.

Dàr 2. Plural of Dääk he/she who divorces or divides as explained above. State of being greedy to own anything that comes across.

Dal 1. Playing at the river sandy beach. 2. The young boys or children game of playing by rolling along river beach.

Daldal 1. State of such game of playing by rolling on the ground as explained above. 2. A person who does not take quick action and keeps on playing.

Dääl A grass or herpes bundle believed to be powerful in the traditional society.

Däli Plural of Dääl being a grass bundle as explained above.

Dam To pick up or catch something quickly such as a stick, stone, speech or talk.

Damdam A person who quickly catches or picks anything in conversation or discussion.

Dämdäm To move very fast in order to round up things or issues.

Dämdääm 1. Plural of Dämdäm being a quick move as explained above. 2. Foot prints on the muddy soil which is followed by others to avoid mud.

Dan 1. Suffix for speakers as in ours eg. Mandan, Gua̱ndan: Our mother, our father. 2. Part of nose or mouth of human being,animal or fish. 3. To pick a topic in conversation very quick or very fast. 4. To hold someone roughly.

Daan A rough way of holding someone or something.

Dandan 1. A person who jumps into any talk or conversation.
2. A person who keeps on begging or asking even when rejected.

Dany The style of horns shape to the back, or the way of expressing surprise where the hands are turned backwards.

Danydany State of having horns tilted behind or bended backwards..

Danyany State of being in backward bending position such as trained horns.

Daŋ 1. Iron or metallic tool or rod with decorations on, which is carried **by** a Kujur man eg Daŋ Deang. 2. To feel pain severely eg;: Cɛ ro daŋ: He is severely suffering. 3. A piece of meat cut from the skin when being prepared for drying.

Daaŋ Plural of Daŋ a piece of meat as explained above..

Daŋdalɛ A plant, which its routes are used as herps for curing stomach troubles.

Dääŋni Plural of Daŋ being the iron rod as explained above.

Däŋdäŋ A type of plant which yields a lot of fruits.

Dap 1. Deliver or to give birth. 2. To be quick in doing something. See mal ben, or ŋal ben.

Daap Ear or nose ornament,or any iron ear or finger ring. It is originally Arabic word for gold.

Däp A quick light setting or flash light.

Däpdäp 1. Bright color of flash or dazzling light in darkness. 2. Slang for appearance and beauty of gold.

Dar A greedy person who likes to eat or own everything.

Daar 1. State of greediness to own everything. 2. Plural of Dar being greediness as explained above.

Där 1. Centre, middle or that comes between. 2. A pain as that is caused by hitting one own elbow or hand on object.

Däär 1. A pain which affects when one teeth are hardly hit or when chewing hard thing. 2. Being in the centre, between or in the middle.

Därdär That causes pains by feeling or touching.

Därnɛy A kind of fish that electrifies when touched in water.

Dat A baby or bull noise of crying or weeping continuously for quite a long time. 2. To tie some ropes or pegs on a cow or bull neck when on a journey or a move.

Dät Cattle hooves disease which prevent or does not allow a cow to graze.

Däwdäw The appearance of a red cut on the body or the lightening at night.

Däw The appearance of the red cut on a flesh or the light in darkness.

Day Treeless opened area, land or ground.

Dayni Plural of Day being the treeless land as explained above.

Dayday 1. Style or behavior when one chews something in opened space. 2. A large treeless or an opened area or ground.

Däy To warm something as water or food on fire or in sun rays.

Däydäy State of being quite warm as a result of fever or a rise in temperature.

Dec Soldier. It is an Arabic language word.

Decni Plural of Dec a soldier as explained above.

Dedeer State of being short such as trees or plants.

Dek 1. A style of filtering white stuff beer to be the first class. 2. A fish cooking style with little water. See Dekɛ kie Dɛakɛ.

Dekdek 1. Style of running as when one is quite exhausted. 2. State of being quite short and not growing very fast eg. Grass.

Dekɛ A thick filtered white stuff with little water.

Dɛal A surprising plural for Dɛl. see Dÿ̈t.

Deel Part of the thatching grass on hut roof. It is put first before the grass.

Deeli Plural of Deel being a grass bundle in thatching as explained above.

Del 1. Big or an elderly person according to age. 2. Being thick or huge in size.

Deldel 1. State of being very thick physically. 2. State of being elderly in age or being thick not light.

Deldeel Plural of Deldel both a person or thickness as explained above.

Demdem 1. State of series movements up and down as when one is very busy or playing. 2. State of series movements during the day.

Den To borrow or credit. It is a borrowed word from Arabic language.

Deen A person who is fond of borrowing money.

Deeny State of curved back bone due to a shooting stomach.

Deenyni Plural of Deeny a curved back as explained above.

Deny deny State of having a feeling of pain which makes one to curve his back bone as a result of that pain.

Deŋ 1. State of movements when one is feeling pains. 2. State of being worried of what to do.

Deŋdeŋ 1. Situation of worry as when things become difficult. 2. A feeling of severe pains.

Deerdeer Style of walking while the tail is raised up as a case with animals and reptiles.

Dep A type of ropes which is used for typing up cows,goats,dogs etc.

Der 1. To wash a gourd Guey or Diar with hot or cold water to clean it. 2. To survive a danger of falling when one stumbles on a stone or hit by stick.

Det Plural of Dɛl being a goat as explained below.

Deet State of having much to do with goats.

Deth State of having what to do with Dɛy being iron, metal or the blacksmith tools.

Dey 1. Iron tool for forging iron pieces into useful tools. 2. Slang for a big problem that has fallen on someone for being heavy. 3. The slang for the main part of anything.

Dɛ Is a suffix meaning his/her, eg. Gatdɛ, his/her son. Ciekdɛ his wife.

Dɛa An opened treeless ground or space.

Dɛani Plural of Dɛa being treeless or opened area as explained above.

Dɛc 1. Impact of heavy load on the head or body. 2. To have a piece of meat, bone or whatever got stuck along the throat. 3. To kill by hanging where one ties a rope around his/her neck or by someone with intention to kill by tying rope around the neck.

Dɛk 1. State of being very tight or tightly connected. 2. A style of cooking a fish or meat with with little water.

Dɛl Goat or Ram.

Dɛm 1. A footstep in a muddy road after a heavy rain. 2. Relationship, connection or linkages, see Wat. 3. Early formation of butter which is whitish. 4. The falling or pouring of rain water drops as when raining.

Dɛmdɛm. Signs of butter formation on fresh milk.

Dɛmdɛɛm Little or few drops of rain water or showers.

Dɛny To curve the back as a result of shooting stomach.

Dɛɛny A person whose back is curved as explained above.

Dɛnydɛɛny State of having a curved back bone.

Dɛŋ 1. The heavenly God among the Nilotic tribes of South Sudan. 2. To level by hitting with heavy tool simultaneously.

Deŋdeŋ State of being well built, not so fat or thin but well balanced body.

Dɛɛp Having much to do with Dep the rope which is used for tying **cattle** eg. Cuk Dɛɛp.see below.

Dɛp 1. A fishing or trapping animals or birds using both nets, snares or traps in regards to animals or birds. 2. A whitish substance which forms butter out of milk. 3. To aggress or cause troubles with someone among boys.

Dɛpdɛp A behavior of drinking water very fast as when very thirsty.

Dɛɛr 1. Deep brown colour usually pink or reddish.

2. A kind of grains that gets ripened in short time or period than others.

Dɛr 1. To involve. 2. To tie very tightly.

Dɛrdɛr Involvement into someone troubles.

Dɛtdɛt 1. A noise which is heard when some food is getting cooked. 2. A noise of a motorcar.

Dɛth 1. To involve people or some one into one own troubles or problems. 2. Plural of Dɛy iron tool as explained below.

Dɛthdɛth To involve others into troubles or conflicts.

Dɛy Calves, germs of fruits, ammunitions, gun shots or piece of iron.

Di A suffix which is used for questioning as how much or how many. eg kæ di ? *How many or how much?*

Dicaar A type of beads which is of violet colour.

Dieer 1. A type of games Hockey. 2. To get worried.

Diew 1. State of being not satisfied by the court ruling. 2. An appeal against the decision taken.

Dik 1. A type of grass which indicates the fertility of soil. 2. A heavy noise caused by a heavy falling object. 3. Being not well dried but still wet.

Di̱kdi̱k 1. State of being not well dried or still wet. 2. State of having the best ornaments,clothes,beads,shoes etc. 3. Slang for a person who cares very much of what he/she wears or put on.

Dil 1. The main founder of his/her clan. 2. A little animal or game. 3. To close up some opening gaps or holes with a cover or mud. 4. To select a person out of many to cause troubles with. 5. State of having no opening or being opaque as a stone or a log. 6. A lost of hearing sense after a heavy sound as that of gun shot, jet engine etc occurred.

Diil 1. Plural of Dil the founder or the main family of the clans, tribes etc. as explained above. 2. Being or having much to do with being the founder of the clan or tribe. 3. What is used for closing the hole or opening.

Dildil State of being opaque as that of a log or stone.

Dim 1. One of smooth skin types of fish which stays at the bottom of a river. 2. A fatty yellowish spot which appears on the top of soup. 3. A slang for a bull color which has two or more colours.

Dimdim State of such fatty yellowish spots on soup.

Diimdiim A secret way of talking specially when people are many or very close or around.

Din 1. State of having much to do with songs or birds (Diit) eg.Ɛŋu ti rɛy din?: *Why are you among birds?* 2. Suffix as in Gua̱(r)din, Maa(r)din etc : *My father, my mother.*

Dindiini Just now or immediately or at once.With other Nuer section is pronounced as Dindiinä.

Diŋ 1. A colour of a cow, bull or whatever w a hich is a mixture of whitish and reddish colours.2. To refuse not to answer a question or react of a statement. 3. To go fishing by spearing the suspected areas along the river or water pool.

Diŋdiŋ 1. A sound or noise which is heard of engine, drum, bell etc hit, in a distance. 2. A slight rain or few drops usually after a heavy rainfall. 3. A bull colour which is a title or nickname for a young Nuer in cattle camp. See the colour Diŋ.4. To be in silence when one tells whatever you do not want to reply.

Dieny A large container made of wooden sticks and strings, for carrying babies, grains etc.

Dienyni Plural of Dieny being a wooden container as explained above.

Dinydiny A type of grass which grows or is found in marshy land.

Diony To open wider, as with flexible container.

Diɔk Three (3) the third or number three.

Diɔkdiɔa̱k Statement for naming things or actions that happened in threes eg Ci kɛ riŋ diœkdiœakni :They ran in threes.

Diɔkni Plural of Diɔk being three or number three as explained above.

Diɔl State of being too long to stand alone without support.

Diɔldiɔl That is too long or soft to stand alone. See Doldol.

Diɔɔl State of being fearful due to a terrible threat.

Diɔm To cheat or to take much than what one deserves.

Diɔŋ 1. A kind of wild vegetables. 2. To add butter, fat or oil to a food staff.

Diɔp To steal from someone secretly.

Diɔɔp A person who practices cheating or stealing people properties. see Wään.

Dir 1. To alivate a low land by dumping some soil or clay. 2. A fishing site across a water way where fishes are to be monitored while moving so that they are speared at. 3. To sew a part of cloth several times, so that it does not get torn again or easily.

Dirdir State of being half deaf, see Jaŋthëŋ.

Dirɛ Statement for recalling something in memory.

D̠ird̠ir State of being compact or solid.

Diir 1. Final stage of common cold or flu. 2. A statement which is said to one who does not get satisfied and who eats whatever comes before him. Eg. Cɛ bi diir: *He/she will not get satisfied.*

D̠i̠i̠r A game which is played by young boys in an opened ground using special sticks.

Dit 1. Bird.The flying creatures that have wings. 2. Song. The poetry works which are composed by poets. 3. Stage of being old,big or huge. 4. The thatching of a hut with grass.

Diit 1. Plural of Dit being a bird as explained above. 2. A statement for saying this one is quite big,huge,old or aged eg. ɛ gat mi diit, Kɛ wut mi diit: A big child and a big man or an old man. 3. A person who thatch a hut roof with grass. 4. A slang for a problem or difficulty. Eg Ti kæ mi diit: *You have got a big thing (problem).*

Ditŋu Which bird is? It is a question for a little or small thing. It is equivalent for what is this? Eg: æ Ley ŋu?:*Which animal is this?* For a big thing.

Diw State of being not yet convinced, satisfied or sure.

Diiw State of being dumped or unable to speak due to sickness or illness.

Diwdiw Lack of being fast in hearing anything due to sickness.

Diöny Ability to open widely a thing due to being plastic or flexible.

Doac 1. To put something under sunrays to get dried a little. 2. The way one is accustomed of doing thing or enjoying it.

Doak State of being quite thick and not watery.

Doal 1. State of being sleepy. 2. The mud which sticks on the feet during rainy days.

Doam A single ornament made of iron for dancing purposes.

Doar 1. State of being fool or with foolish behavior 2. Plural of Dor being the wilderness as explained below. 3. A dog that lost its master. 4. Plural of Dœr being wilderness as explained below.

Doce To bend something such as stick or iron rod.

Docdoc State of being flexible or that can be bended.

Doggɛal A bird that has some horizontal long feathers on its head.

Dok Stage of balancing food or mud paste inorder not to be watery.

Dokdok State of being well balanced and not watery.

Dol 1. To be sleepy. 2. A piece of dried soil or clay. 3. To laugh or **a** laughter see Tök. 4. To dry something such as a piece of wood with fire flame.

Dolol State of having things become difficult to separate or arrange.

Dool 1. State of having much to do with sleeping. 2. State of being shaky as when in series dancing

Door Lack of skills to help oneself or state of foolishness

Dom 1. To add some water in order to quench thirst or to make wet a dry soil or ground. 2. To catch something quickly, or to join easily.

Domdoam Plural of Domdom being light rain or showers with few drops.

Domdom 1. A game which is played by picking objects while catching the falling one above. 2. That can be easily attracted by simple object or thing.

Dom Plural of Dɔam being the dirt which appears on the eyes when one is getting up from bed in the early morning.

Donyping A type of grass that grows in places early attack by cattle which serves the same purpose..

Doŋdoŋ 1. A bull horn shape nickname or title being one of Nuer Native Pride which was extended to include the colonialists in the colonial period eg Keerdhuor,Jak Ñuaan, Kueybil etc. 2. State of being not sure in setting appointment.

Doɔth 1. To remain behind. 2. The name of last male twin. 3. The remnants of food or whatever left after meal.

Dor Wilderness.

Dœrdœr State of being very simple to go with any person or group usually dogs, cattle or human being. See Pap

Dordor.1. A person or animal that can not see well due to eye problem. 2. A stage where one can not resist or fight back due to being overpowered.

Dot State of meeting suddenly as when in crowded place.

Dotdot A sound of boiling broth which is heard in cooking.

Do̱th 1. To wean a child after two years of sucking. 2. To pull out a peg or whatever has been driven down. Eg. Cu gat do̱th ɛŋotɛ kɛ kuɛa. Ci yaŋ lo̱c do̱th: *Do not wean a child while still young. A cow has pulled out a peg.*

Doth 1. Difficult to hold up due to being fat or oil. 2. To remain behind when people started going away or leaving the place.

Dowdow As in "Gaak ɛ Dowdow". A child game statement where the group of children jump to the one who missed the answer to click his kidneys while pronouncing that statement.

Dɔaŋ 1. Aged or stage of being old or not any longer useful.2. Back part of knees

Dɔɔ Maybe. Perhaps etc.eg Wer kä jæ dœœ bia wä mai: *You go to him/her, you may go fishing.*

Dɔakni Plural of Dœk people of Dok Nuer as explained below.

Dɔk 1. One of the western Nuer sections who live along the river.Dɔk station is named after that section. 2. A hard clay soil which is free from sand or alluvial. 3. To frighten or threaten to do harm to someone or animal.

Dɔɔl State of being shaking as when dancing.

Dɔldɔl State of having something in muddy state that can be manipulated in any way wanted.

Dɔldɔɔl State of being shaky due to being so long or tall

Dɔm Plural of Dɔam being an early eye dirt as explained above.

Dɔŋ 1. Perhaps or may be. 2. State of being very old or aged person. 3. Plural of Dɔaŋ a part of the knee as explained above.

Dɔɔŋ 1. Having much to do with Dœñ being a part of knee. 2. Plural of Doaŋ. Being an old person as explained above.

Dɔŋpiny Ground nut.

Dɔpdɔp A type of plant that has some hairy parts which stick on things.

Dɔɔr 1. Wilderness. 2. A slang for long call in wilderness. 3. To assimilate someone or something or animal by showing great kindness.

Dɔɔt A cow with horns bending towards the middle of its head.(single)..

Dɔɔtni Plural of Dɔɔt being a cow with horns bending as explained above.

Dɔw 1. Calf or the young one such as, fruit, animal, or whatever. See Dɛy. 2. A female calf which is used as sheering sound by women in marriage ceremony as "Dɔwdɔw".

Döak Being quite thick not watery.

Döcɛ A local pipe. It is known as Köndöc.

Dɔar A dog that lost its master or that moves in wilderness..

Dɔär State of being fool or ignorant.

Dɔäär Plural of Dɔär being fool or ignorant as explained above.

Dök 1. A kind of fish with hard scales. see Diŋdo̱k. 2. Is the shape of the horns, when bending towards the back. 3. To make something watery thick by adding soil or flour, or whatever to make it sticks on. 4. To fit or strengthen by adding gum etc. to spear or axes.

Döl 1. A clay made tool for cooking purposes, usually three to stand a pot. 2. A reddish or deep red color of bull, cow or whatever.

Dööl Plural of Döl being a clay made tool as explained above.

Dööli Plural of Döl being red color as explained above.

Döl cɔɔk A desire or great need of meat or fish.

Dömpiny A night dance which starts after supper in cattle camp.

Dön Stage when water gets dried in a pond, pool etc.

Dölny 1. To step on someone foot or something. 2. The growth of the seeds, fruits or plants. 3. To press down something. 4. Dancing styles as when in a drum dance.

Döŋ 1. A temporary shelter 2. Ạ style of sitting. 3. To knock the door for permission. 4. Slang for knocking when in boxing games. 5. The back part of the knee. 6. A way of standing, or walking on one leg as when feeling pains.

Döp 1. To make a show off style in front of the enemies or dancers before fighting or drum dance gets started. 2. To set alight or aflame the fire 3. To imitate or adopt a way of doing things. 4. To start making butter for the first time. 5. To look for reasons to pick up a quarrel or trouble with someone.

Dööp 1. What is believed to be the cause for doing harm to someone. 2. A substance which is used for sticking two or more parts – Gum. 3. A string or rope which is used for tying up the hut door on a pole known as Wääth.

Dör 1. Tribe, Nation, Race. 2. Courtyard or compound.

Dördör Difficulties or troubles that come in confused circumstances.

Döör 1. Having much to do with compound or courtyard. 2. Plural of Dör being a tribe, race, nation as explained above. 3. State of having two sexual organs. The early Nuer had a belief that a hyena has two sexual organs. 4. To identify the good characters and bad ones of a person who plans to marry or to be married. 5. One of Nuer section known as Döör Nyoŋ.

Döt 1. To have got stuck in muddy soil or being overcome by heavy work. 2. Ability to endure hard, difficult work or task. 3. To tie a hook, fishing tool or whatever with string or thread.

Dööt State of failure to pull out of mud, difficult task or work.

Döth To wean up a baby or to stop a child from sucking when two years old.

Dööth Plural of Döth being the weaned up child as explained above.

Du A suffix for yours as in Gatdu kɛ Macdu: your child and your gun.

Duak A type of clouds which causes rain after the first one.

Duakduak State of sky being covered with some clouds after a heavy rain fall.

Dual dual

Dual Being coward or afraid eg. Wic woɔk ɛ dual dualɔ.:*The bald headed coward.* 1. State of fear, frightening or being afraid of anything. 2. A skin made fur by ancient people before clothes. 3. State of being soft like skin as explained above.

Duany To behave in such a way as when dancing or being possessed by Kujur.

Duanyduany State of being shaky as when standing, dancing or being possessed by Kujur.

Duaany Cattle hut wooden poles made device for closing the door or the gate.

Duanyni Plural of Duaany being a cattle hut device as explained above.

Duäc To beat, hit or to whip.

Duääc Whatever is used for beating, hitting or whipping.

Duääny A disable person who cannot walk or who walks with supporting tools.

Dua̱nyni Plural of Duääny being a disable person as explained above.

Dua̱ny To press or touch one body in order to alert him / her not to act blindly or to be careful.

Duäŋ A cool air or breath which people enjoy during hot or warm weather.

Duääŋduääŋ State of doing things quite,gently or carefully. Person who is not rough in doing thing.

Duaar Friendship or love connection process.

Duarduar State of being quite shy specially among strangers,in-laws or to be friendly to every body.

Duärduär State of being quite moderate, not hot as a case to weather or a period before the appearance of Sun-rays.

Duat To make noise, singing or crying all the time.

Duatduat State of being quite noisy or talkative all the time.

Duät May is the fifth month of the year in Nuer calendar.

Duel 1. A house of any type be it a hut of wood, brick, stone etc. 2. A plural of Duel with stress on (e) a house as explained above.

Dueel Having much to do with Duel hut, house or a room etc. Ta̱a̱ dueel I am in the house, hut, etc.

Duir The mistake,fault or guilty –eg- Cɛ duir: He has made mistake.

Duk Thick forest where branches and leaves could not allow sun rays.

Dukduk 1. Being not well dried. 2. State of being wet with oil, butter etc.

Dul Head hairs made yellowish as a result of application of soaked ashes on the head for sometimes.

Duul A container which is used for accumulation of butter.

Dum 1. Complete state of darkness particularly when light goes off. 2. Slang for complete blind person.

Dumdum State of walking or moving in darkness.

Dun A suffix for yours as in Mandun kiɛ Närun, your mother or your uncle to the mother side (Maternal).

Duny To make something rough soft by removing hard parts (skin, grass etc) so that it becomes useful.

Duuny A person or whatever is used for making such hard materials soft.

Dunyduny State of making or performing such hard materials soft.

Duŋ Belong, own as in Duŋdä: mine, Duŋdu: yours, Duŋda: ours.

Duɛk 1. A lay man or any ordinary person who is not possessed by Kujur. 2. State of being sticky.

Duɛkduɛk Being quite sticky as a mixture of gum substance.

Duɛlduɛl Being quite sticky as with muddy soil.

Duer Fault, mistake or state of being found guilty in a court.

Dueer Plural of Duer being a fault or mistake as explained above.

Duet State of being filled up with fish or whatever.

Duɛɛt Being full with anything except liquids.

Duɛtduɛt Being full with fish or lack of enough water in cooking.

Duɛyduɛy An aquatic worms which appear in pond water.

Duɛyduɛyni Plural of Duɛyduɛy the aquatic worms as explained above.

Duony Disease that affects the joints and disables human being to move.

Duonyduony State of being not able to walk or run due to such sickness.

Duop A food made out of pounded grain flour. See Nup

Duɔmduɔm A type of grass which is found in grazing lands.

Duɔl 1. The meeting,coming together, togetherness in order to discuss issues. 2. The accumulation of many things in one place.

Duɔli Plural of Dul that is head hair made yellow with cow dung aches.

Duœœli Plural of Duœl being the coming together to discuss issues as explained above.

Duɔŋ 1. Plural of Duɔɔŋ a bead like type made of ostrich eggs as explained above. 2. An operation made on He sheep, goat where testicles stop reproduction processes. 3. A dance which is played with ladies on the front in a marriage ceremony.

Duɔɔŋ A type of beads made of ostrich eggs.

Duɔɔp Foot path, road,street or foot prints.

Duɔp To pound or destroy a hard substance into fine state or dusty particles.

Duɔr 1. A milking cow that has lost its calf. 2. A person who does not see well.

Duɔɔr 1. Plural of Duɔr a cow which lost its calf as explained above. 2. Stage where one recalls something he/she lost in memory. See Dire kiɛ Ditɛ.

Dup 1. Preparation of food by pounding grains into flour. 2. Plural of Duɔ̱ɔp foot paths, road, or street as explained above. 3. To confuse, or disturb whatever is clear. 4. To play in dusty area where one gets covered with dust or ashes. 5. Slang for having been destroyed, demolished or completely disappeared.

Dupdup 1. State of confusion as to discuss something or investigate a case. 2. A sound that is heard when bitting a drum in drum dance.

Dur A period at dawn before day light where one can not see eg. Kum ɛ dur: *completely closed off.*

Durdur Early morning of the day or at dawn when things are not yet clear.

Dut 1. A panicking, sudden action of running when the news of attack is heard eg. Wii wii. 2. A sudden running in a race, a dance etc

Dutdut 1. State of sudden action of chasing someone, something or being chased. 2. A sound like that of steam engine or whatever.

Duth To dance or style of dancing or playing.

Duyduy State of short duration news.

Duypiny That can end up in vain or without achieving the goal – eg popular rioting, etc ends up very fast when chased by police force.

Dh

Dhacdhac The noise or sound of water when the container fills up.

Dhak Dangling state.

Dhakdhak State of being in dangling stage.

Dhal 1. Difficult to be manipulated or shaped as it is with bull horns.
2. Not possible to make any attempt once more.

Dham State of talking alone as when mentally disturbed or as a baby
see Ruac Jɔɔr

Dhamdhaam State of telling or saying nonsenses due to madness or being fool.

Dhan 1. Jokes or idioms, slang, words being said by closed friends or **intimate** brothers. 2. To add some grass on temporary roof to make shelter.

Dhandhaan 3. A temporary shelter of grass roof. Plural of Dhan being jokes,idioms or some nonesenses as explained above

Dhany The shallow area in the river or water pool.

Dhanydhany State of being shallow where one can cross very fast without canoes or boats.

Dhanyany State of being in shallow stage as explained above.

Dhaŋ 1. A bed. 2. A river bank

Dhaŋni Plural of Dhaŋ being a bed or river bank as explained above.

Dhaar A water container or a pot made of clay soil.

Dha̱a̱ri Plural of Dhaar a pot or a clay made pot as explained above.

Dharbalaŋ A kind of wild plants which grows in old compounds.

Dhay 1. State of having been killed after a long period of chasing. 2. To have got asleep due to being so tired.. 3. An opened shallow water of the river or any water surface.

Dhaydhay State of being shallow such as water stream or the river.

Dhä The sound of the fourth letter Dh of Thok Nath.

Dhämäm State of being in a puzzled, confused state and not knowing what to do.

Dhäny Improper way of sitting, walking or looking.

Dhänydhääny State of improper way of doing things such as walking as a case with lame person or a baby.

Dhiac 1. An already fished site of the water ponds. 2. To push some one or something aside. 3. A weed type plant that grows in a wheat or dura field.

Dhian To cheat someone when dividing something.

Dhiap State of being decayed or rotten due to being in old conditions.

Dhiat 1. A ganglion on human or animal body. 2. Cheating when

Dividing something.

Dhiay A sudden breakage of something such as an egg, tobacco etc.

Dhiec Five (5) or number five in Nuer counting.

Dhiet 1. To dip a dirty tool into food or drinking water. 2. To show your power or good things to some one.

Dhiey To break a heap or bulk thing.

Dhieydhiey A person who does not know or who does not always gives a concrete or a correct answer.

Dhik 1. A sound or noise which is heard when something or someone is moving along by night. 2. State of being not any longer oozing blood or water.

Dhiik 1. State of being not so wet or muddy. 2. The stoppage of

blood flow. Eg Ci piny dhiik. Ci riɛm dhiik: *The soil is not muddy. the blood has stopped flowing.*

Dhikdhik 1. The sound of foot steps at night. 2. State of having the soil not muddy.

Dhil 1. A state of not feeling pains or difficulties. 2. To take something for good.

Dhi̱i̱l Having ability to endure pains, difficulties etc. See Ruɔ̱t.

Dhildhil He/she who does not feel difficulties or pain.

Dhim To filter with a cotton bag. see Nyoŋɛ

Dhiim A person who filters the porridge, beer, etc.

Dhieem Plural of Dhiim a person who filters things as explained above.

Dhiŋ 1. Feeling of pains for having sat for quite a long time on one foot. 2. A disease that causes blood to flow through noses.

Dhiok State of putting dirty substance into clean thing.

Dhion 1. Muddy and sticky clay or soil in rainy season. 2. Slang for cheating someone when dividing something.

Dhior To add more water by mistake as when cooking or washing the room.

Dhiordhior State of having unnecessary additional water on something.

Dhiɔk Feeling of vomiting or disliking of something usually food.

Dhiɔɔk State of such feeling of vomiting.

Dhir Paralytic feeling due to having been sitting on one leg for a long time.

Dhiir State of paralytic feeling as explained above.

Dhiök The touching of food or water with dirty hands.eg

Jiok cæ pi dhiök: The dog has dirtified the water.

Dheel A large fish eating bird with a bag like part below its peak or neck. See Kil.

Dhɛaw To keep on making noise through out by baby or he goat.

Dhɛk To keep on talking or crying for quite a long period of time.

Dhɛkdhɛk A stage of weeping or talking or both after quarrel or fighting.

Dhɛm 1. The condition of eye shooting out appearance. 2. Talking or weeping habit when demanding something usually by children or kids.

Dhɛmɛm The ugly eye shooting appearance.

Dhɛn Very little quantity or piece given out.eg ɛ ŋu muci dhɛn ?: Why do you give very little?

Dhɛndhɛn State of being very little or small.

Dhɛŋ A minor operation where a vein is opened to allow bad blood flows out.

Dhɛɛŋ 1. A person who carries out minor operations on human body head, leg, hand, nose,etc. 2. A slang for a husband.

Dhɛr 1. State of becoming powerless after a long walk, work or struggle. 2. State of quick sleep as a result of being too tired. 3. The movements of something ups and downs as that with hairs or wigs.

Dhɛrdhɛr The movements of hairs or wigs when dancing.

Dhɛt 1. A small or little swelling on the skin as a result of insect bite or sting. 2. Any small size or weight.

Dhɛtdhɛt 1. The appearance of such swelling part on the body skin. 2. A state of giving out very little or small thing.

Dhɛw A baby or a he goat noise all the time.

Dhɛwdhɛw State of being noisy as a result of much talking, crying or when a he goat stimulates goats.

Dhoc 1. To push away someone in order to give a space. Eg ɛ ŋu lɛn ni hä dhoc œ? *Why are you pushing me away?* 2. State of having a container filled up eg.Cɛ thiaŋ ɛ dhoc.See Dhocdhoc.

Dhocdhoc The noise of water or any liquid when overflowing the container.

Dhokdhoak Plural of Dhokdhok being telling nonsense, useless statements or meaningless talk.

Dhokdhok 1. Nonsense or useless statements or meaningless talk. 2. A problem or a hard time.

Dhol 1. Slang for taking something as a whole or the whole of it.2. A boy or uninitiated young man.

Dhom A big iron or metallic ring which is worn on the right wrist for fighting with.

Dhomdhom Unorganized talk which goes on without stopping.

Dhon̠ 1. A lunatic, mentally disturbed person. 2. Ạn ox that does not stimulate cows due to reproductive problem.

Dhonon State of not knowing what is happening around.eg Nyuræ dhonon :*He/she is sitting without what is going on or happening.*

Dhony 1. Short piece of wood, metal etc. 2. A kind of tree which fruits are used for local pipe filter.

Dhonydhony 1. State of being not deep. 2. A state of being short.

Dhonyony 1. State of being not deep or not well dug properly. 2. State of being not well hidden in the bushes.

Dhoŋ 1. To kill something or someone by holding him /her /it tightly **to** stop breathing. 2. State of coming first or to report early. 3. To act before the others.

Dhop 1. A disease that cuts off limbs mostly leg, arms, fingers etc. 2. The shape of a head as when it is so big.

Dhopdhop 1. A kind of disease that causes its victims to talk a lot which ends with madness. 2. State of having a big head or large one.

Dhopop A state of having round big head. Eg Dhop wic mic ! nyuræ a bi nhiamdæ tä dhopop: Big head ! he/she sat where his/her face became big.

Dhor Home, house or compound.

Dhow To appear suddenly from deep water, forest or huge clouds.

Dhowdhow That can be seen without difficulties.

Dhɔal Having much to do with Dhol being a boy or unmarked male person.

Dhɔam Anything to do with adultery

Dhɔap Having much to do with disease Leprosy Dhœp.

Dhɔar Having much to do with Dhɔr, home.

Dhɔk 1. A ball like round organ inside certain types of fish. 2. Nonsense words or such word that is not clear to guess its meaning. 3. To pump out blood, water. 4. Difficulties in pronouncing words, eg. Dhɔk thok. 5. Well fitted as that of a ring or ivory ornamental object.

Dhɔkdhɔk 1. Difficulties in speaking clearly due to big tongue. 2. Slang for a problem. 3. Being well fitted.

Dhɔl 1. To collect a wife home after all the marriage procedures are over. 2. A young male who is not initiated. 3. To ask or to be little a young man to do you favour. 4. To aggress someone without previous confrontation.

Dhɔɔl Plural of Dhɔl or Dhɔ̱ɔ̱l being a boy as explained above.

Dhɔldhɔl State of being too long to be raised, or too tall to walk.

Dhɔlmay A type of plants that becomes greenish in mid summer where most of plants wilted due to lack of water.

Dhɔm 1. A disease that attacks goats and sheep in a hut or cattle byre. 2. Disorder or unorganized talk usually between women, children or in marriage place.

Dhɔn 1. A lunatic or mentally disturbed person,fool or silly as in Dhɔn ɛ nɔ̱ɔ̱k. 2. A piece of meat is cut to be given to a child or whoever, by a butcher. 3. An ox that does not follow cows. 4. Slang for impotent person.

Dhɔny Not deep or a rather shallow hole.

Dhɔnydhɔny State of being not deep but shallow.

Dhɔnyɔny That is quite shallow or clear to the eyes and can be seen quickly.

Dhɔ̱ŋ To come first or early before the others.

Dhɔŋdhɔŋ State of being so slow in acting, talking or even thinking. Not active.

Dhɔɔr 1. A large looking glass for seeing views in a distance by soldiers. 2. Home as when it belongs to the speaker eg. Dhɔɔra, *our home*. Dhɔɔrun, your home.Dhɔɔriɛn, their home.

Dhɔrdhɔr State of being shallow or a well raised compound which could be seen in a distance..

Dhɔt Part or an area between Male.Genital.Organs. See Dhöt

Dhɔɔt A concept that people or things are nothing, or to have a feeling that nothing will harm you.

Dhɔäär The appearance of the marine animals such as crocodile, hipopotamus or whatever out of water.

Dhɔät An insult for a male person whose genital area is thick.

Dhöc To explain great dislike by showing how you hate somebody or something by changing the way one looks.

Dhööc 1. Appearance of fish while moving in water. 2. State of such appearance of disliking someone or something.

Dhöcdhöc 1. The noise of water or any liquid when it flows into already filled container. 2. A way of walking as when fat or bulgy.

Dhök 1. A bag like membrane inside the fish (stomach). 2. Overgrown, become fat, weight gain due to good diet or food consumed.

Dhökdhök State of being fat or huge for human being, animal or a thing.

Dhöl To cut a something from the middle. See Gim.

Dhööl A young person usually a male who is not initiated or marked to manhood in Nuer culture or tradition.

Dhöldhöl The style of division or distribution where pieces look big.

Dhöm The adultery or illegal sexual game with someone wife.

Dhööm Plural of Dhoom a person who commits adultery as explained above.

Dhöömdhööm A way of walking in order to attack an enemy or animal in hunting.

Dhöny 1. A high part of the ground or floor. 2. A slang for big buttocks.

Dhönydhöny

Dhöönydhööny State of being high than any other place. A style of walking as when one has got big buttocks.

Dhör 1. Plural of Dhɔr being the home as explained above. 2. A big bull of several years since maturity.

Dhöör 1. Plural of Dhör being a big bull as explained above. 2. State of having a bull became big enough.

Dhöt 1. The area between male genital organ and anus. see Dhɔt. 2. To overlook somebody, something or to make him/her looks little. 3. A short stalk grain plants.

Dhötdhöt State of being very short or little in regard to size or height.

Dhöy State of thick lips mouth which keep the mouth opens all the time.

Dhöydhöy Having a big opening that does not fit the cover.

Dhuak Difficulties in pronouncing due to big tongue.

Dhuakdhuak Failure to pronounce words in the right way.

Dhuar State of being unable to move due to drunkness, weakness or laziness.

Dhuardhuar A person who disturbs or asks unnecessary questions, who could be a fool or a little minded one

Dhuc The pushing aside to give room. See Dhoc.

Dhuel A stage of maturity for male person.

Dhuk To practice homosexual behaviour among boys.

Dhundhun 1. State of being very small or a piece. 2. Slang for a short and small baby.

Dhuny 1. To fall upside down position. 2. To bend down where the bottom parts of the body (buttocks) open up, as when picking something.

Dhuony 1. A type of trees where its fruits are used in forging native pipe smoking part. See Juuth. 2. To throw down things one by one such as utensils,etc.

Dhuor A quick struggling in order to release one self from capitivity.

Dhuɔli Plural of Dhuɔɔl being an island or a land in middle of water as explained below.

Dhuɔ̱ɔ̱l An island or that area surrounded by water.

Dhuɔɔr Plural of Dhur being the cow, buffalo etc tail made for dancing ornament.

Dhup 1. State of having something became quite complicated or confused up and difficult to undo or handle. 2. A sound that is heard when an object falls into deep water.

Dhupdhup The sound of water when being steered up by he/she who practices swimming.

Dhur 1. A cow, buffalo etc tail made for dancing ornament. 2. A noise that is heard when a heavy object falls from high altitude. 3. To be in a hurry or state of being worried.

Dhuur A big trap for catching big games, Elephants, Lions etc.

Dhuuri Plural of Dhuur a trap as explained above.

Dhurdhur A game which is played by youth in cattle camp here they jump into deep water by turns from high river bank.

Dhut 1. A little swelling on the body as a result of injury, insect stinging or scar of an old wound. 2. Having tied up and becomes difficult to untie.

Dhutdhut An outgrowth ganglion on skin or body as a result of either insect sting or old wound. See Tɛt or Mɛɛt.

Ɛ

Ɛh The sound of the seventh letter of Thok Nath.

Ɛ 1. A suffix for the third person singular as in eg:

Gatdɛ,Dɛlɛ,duelɛ. His son, her goat, his house etc. 2. An interrogative vowel which comes before a

question eg Ɛŋu? Ɛŋa? ɛ mith? What? Who? Which?.

Ɛh An exclamation word just the same as in English language Eh.

Ɛth A word which expresses rejection to a persuasive statement.

G

Ga A short form for Gat as in Gamar: Son of my mother.

Galuak: Son of cow hut (byre).

Gaa Plural of short form for Gaat as explained above. eg. Gaa(t) mar: Sons of my mother. Gaa(t)Jio̠ȍk: sons of Jio̠k Ki̠i̠r. Gaa(t) Jaak: Sons of Jak Ki̠i̠r.

Gak 1. Trouble, quarrel, fighting, misunderstanding etc. 2. To deny something, statement or whatever.

Gaak A bead like but with different shape which is worn around the neck when put in a string.

Gaakni Plural for Gaak being the beads like ornament as explained above.

Gakgak 1. State of being so hard to dig or prepare for cultivation.2. To cause troubles or quarrels. See Gak.

Gakgaak State of having a thing or soil be continuously hard when digging it.

Gakgaakni Plural of Gakgak to cause troubles as explained above.

Gal To delay something or someone.

Gaal State of having caused much delay to people or work.

Galgal 1. Failure to take off at once. 2. That is too large which can not fit on the body, neck, etc.

Galgaal Plural of Galgal being whatever which causes delaying.

Gam 1. To chorus,to imitate a song or when swearing in or taking oath. 2. The help that is offered to a woman when delivering by midwife. 3. To collect rain water for home consumption in semi desert land where there is no river.

Ga̱a̱m 1. Plural of Gääm being a mid wife as explained below. 2. He /she who chorus songs or sing them. 3. Whatever is used for collecting rain water or any liquids for some purpose.

Gan Children as in eg Man gan: The mother of children.

Gany 1. Plural of Gaany being the reptile that resembles crocodile as explained below. 2. A night dance usually after sun set in western Nuer region (Bentiu).

Gaany A reptile that looks like crocodile.

Ganygany A bad style of walking which can not be recommended.

Gaŋ 1. A type of beads which was popular some five decades or more back in Nuer land. 2. To prevent something or someone to go through or pass. To guard, take care of animals, children and whatever from doing or making mistakes.

Ga̱a̱ŋ Plural of Gääŋ a guard or he/she who prevents people to pass any how as explained below.

Gaŋlɛc A person whose lips do not close automaticaly.

Gaŋyaŋ luaak A kind of surgheom which gets ripened in short period of time that provoked the naming as described:(That prevents cow not to come out of the hut in order to be sold to get grains).

Gar 1. A cow or buffalo tail which is used as ornament when fitted on women head in marriage ceremony. 2. A statement that have much to do with Gaar as explained below. eg. Rɛy gar: *inside Gaar plant.* 3. One mark on the face of a full grown young Nuer.

Gaar 1. A type of wild plant, which is used for cooking, when dried in cattle camp. 2. Plural of Gar being the cow or buffalo tail as explained above.

Gààr The plural of G̱ar being one of the six or seven marks as explained above. These are the six or seven parallel line marks on forehead of a young Nuer man. On normal cases they are six, but when two brothers are initiated or marked at ago or in one occaision the young one receives seven.

Gargar State of having few branches and leaves such as trees.

Gat Child, kid, baby or son and daughter, nephew, niece etc.

Gaat 1. Plural of Gat being a child, baby etc. as explained above. 2. State of being childish of babyhood etc. 3. Here also means ignorance as when stressed.

Gath A rough way of taking something very quick as when it is very little (food).

G̱a̱ath A tool that is used for smoothing the surface.

Gathgath A bad behavior of eating where food is consumed quickly by young boys.

Gaw 1. A type of dried grass which is used for cooking or roasting fish or meat. 2. A noise or sound as that is heard when sticks collide in the air. 3. To hit, spear, shoot something or bird very fast while it is still flying in the air.

Gawgaw 1. State of being dried like grass which is used for cooking as explained in (Gaw). 2. A slang for a thin and tall person.

Gek 1. A fashion or a style for shaving the hairs. 2. State of being not able to do something due to sickness.

Geek 1. The other side or part near to it, him or us. 2. A way of looking as when angry or not happy with someone eg. La liecɛ geek.

Gekgek 1. State of being not ready to accept what is told to you. 2. Being not obedient or very rough in listening to elders.

Geekgeek The way one looks whenever is very angry at someone who misbehaved to him/her.

Gel To cover or shelter in order to avoid heat, sun rays, or an attack from eagle bird or to darken a place in order to sleep by day time.

Geel 1. A slang for a person who defends his group. 2. Whatever is used to stop flow of winds, rays etc.

Geeli Plural of Geel being that is used to stop winds, rays or the eyes of passers-by.

Geŋ The baby or child that follows twins in Nuer traditional naming.

Ger Paddling a canoe to cross the river or water surface 2. Driving a car, plane or whatever. 3. The hairy back part of the horse neck, the back part of the fish or human being.

Geer A person who paddles the canoe, drives a car, pilots a plane etc.

Gerger The back part of an animal, fish or even human being.

Gew The bulls or oxen style in taking position in fighting.

Gewgew State of being not ready to carry out directives or orders.

Gɛa The great great grand father of Nuer tribe,to whom the main Nuer six desendents are known to be his sons-Gaat Gɛɛkä.

Gɛɛk Plural of Gɛk being part of the face.

Gɛl Part of the river banks that is always deep with grey soil.

Gɛm Conflict, misunderstanding between two or many people.

Gææm State of having much to do with quarrel or misunderstanding.eg æñu ci gææm kæ jæ æloñ? *Why did you become very much angry with him/her?*

Gɛn 1. A fixed hanging bed like inside cow hut for a young man to **sleep** in when guarding cattle at night. 2. Ṭo give very little quantity **of** anything to someone.3. A slang for a huge person with large chest.

Gɛaw A temporary roofless hut for nomadic boys to sleep in cattle camp.

Gɛɛl Having much to do with gɛl eg. Tææ gææL kuic kiir: He is at gɛl **At** the other bank of the river.

Gɛm Plural of Gɛam being the quarrel or conflict.

Gɛny To pull apart the legs or whatever limbs in order to deal with the internal parts.

Gɛnygɛny State of having legs and hands apart as in any game.

Gænyæny State of being in such a position with hands and legs apart.

Gɛŋ 1. The style of cow or buffalo horns shape which bend

backwards. See Döl gɛŋ. 2. State of being able to defend one difficulties before he/she asks for rescue, assistance or help.

Gɛɛr State of having the horns apart as with bull, cow, buffalo etc.

Gɛrgɛr A situation where a tree has few branches apart.

Gɛat Plural of Gɛt to cook food stuff without water as explained above.

Gæt 1. To fry meat,fish without water. 2. A part of the face.See Jaw.

Gɛtgɛt 1. Slang for a tiny or very little quantity given to someone. 2. The appearance of the teeth when parts are broken or extracted.

Gɛth 1. The cleaning of cattle hut where cow dung, urines are cleaned for the next day night. 2. To clean any dirt using sharp point tool or spoon.

Gɛthgɛth Slang for very little or few quantities of food.

Gɛthpiny 1. To deny a statement reported that one did not say it. 2. To clean a soft food material by pushing it down.

Gɛw 1. State of patriotism to one own position, principles,ideology

or country. 2. To stop someone passing or block his/her way.

Gɛy 1. To open space in the middle of the dancing circle to allow the singer to move freely. 2. To leave anything uncared for. 3. To denya thing.

Gɛygɛy State of being wide space in the centre. A state of being left alone.

Giey The last drops of whatever liquid being consumed.

Gieygiey 1. A sound of iron tools when hit together. 2. The real truth or pure one.

Giɛygiɛɛy The plural of Gieygiey being the final drops as explained above.

Giɛl Ebony, a kind of trees where its wood is used for making wooden equipments such as sticks and other tools.

Giɛɛl Plural of Giɛl being Ebony tree as explained above.

Giɛy The sound of metallic tools when hit together.

Gik 1. To investigate in order to collect final information. 2. To interrogate or question in order to dig out facts. 3. A sound of hitting one foot on a thorn in the forest. 4. Stammering or difficulties in pronouncing a word..

Giik A person who stammers or finds difficulties in pronouncing or talking.

Gïïk Plural of Giik being a person who stammers when talking.

Gikgik State of being not ready to listen to order or to abide by it.

Gil To persuade some one to accept something or do it.

G̱ilg̱il State of being huge or thick as a result of fatness.

Giliew A kind of grass which is used for feeding calves.

Giliŋ A noise of a copper bell or the school bell.

Giliŋgiliŋ That frequent noise of a bell when it is ringing.

Gilok A type of ornament bead which has different colours and is tied around theneck in ancient Nuer fashion.

Gim 1. A sound of a heavy falling object, explosion, gun shot, or shell. 2. To cut from the middle of a fish or whatever.

Gimɛ A kind of fish which stays in deep water and has smooth skin.

Gimgim 1. Condition of hard soil or wood as when digging, carving,or a hard river bed. 2. The same sound of thunders storm which itsef during rainy days.

Giny To cratch or destroy something completely.

Ginyginy A small piece of anything which is very short and not sharp.

Giŋ To cheat by giving little when one divides something.

Giiŋ 1. The person who cheats when dividing something to people. 2. State of giving someone little and own the bigger part.

Gir 1. The early formation of clouds on horizon. 2. The appearance of thick forest. 3. A great desire to eat fish particularly during harvest time in

October, or November every year. 4. The noise that is heard after thunderstorm, explosion, gun shot or lion roaring.

Girgir 1. The appearance of clouds or thick forest on the horizon. 2. The frequent noise of thunderstorm.

Giirgiir A style of movements to and fro near girl friend home in order to see you in order to come.

Girbaŋ A kind of small fish which has some grey scales.

Git 1. Collective fishing with canoes along the river. 2. To collectively speared someone till death in a fight. See Cok.

G̲i̲t To undergo rituals between a father and his children..

Giit A weapon made out of a horn that looks like spear.

G̲i̲i̲t Whatever is used for marking or smearing in clay work decorations.

Giitgiit State of being not ready to leave quickly due to anger.

Gith 1. To clean something watery with fingers or hands 2. To force someone to complete assignment or task quickly.

Giith To take the whole thing available at once.

G̲i̲thg̲i̲th 1. A way of forcing people or a person to do something very fast. 2. A person who forces people to carry out a task very fast.

Giw State of being the only strongest person or animal after having shown a series fight.

Giwgiw The noise of breaking hard things,such as wood, stone etc.

G̲i̲wg̲i̲w State of being hard and difficult to break as a case with clay, stone, brick etc.

Goa Good, well, better etc.

Goakni Plural of Gœœk that is monkey as explained below.

Goaŋ 1. A bending or curving on stick, road etc. 2. The first food or water given to a guest.

Goààr Plural of Goor being he/she who knows how to read and write as explained below.

Goar Being the edge of a thatched roof.

Goaar Plural of Goar being the edge of a thatched roof as explained above.

Goari Plural of Goor is one of fishing tools or devices as explained below.

Goc 1. State having been difficult to pull out such as ornaments or rings. 2. A noise or sound as that is heard when drinking water etc.

Gocgoc State of such sound or noise when one is drinking any liquid.

G̲o̲k To bend or the bending side of the horn, branch stick etc.

G̲o̲l 1. A fishing circle which is made by fishermen, women,boys etc. 2. A circle made up of people who may be listening or watching singers or dancers. 3. A piece of field grass or farm ready to be weeded out or cleaned. 4. The hairy part of the lion forehead.

Gom 1. To keep the cow dung fire by pressing it together. 2. A type of insects that causes diseases to goats.

Go̱m 1. Dryness of skin or wound after being washed with water. 2. A container usually a broken gourd for feeding puppies, cats etc.

Gomgom State of being quite closed on all sides.

Go̱n 1. A small animal of cat family. 2. A section of Lou Nuer around Watt.

Gongon A nickname given a young man in cattle camp whose bull's left horn curves towards the head.

Go̱o̱ny A person who has a case before the court.

Gonygony 1. State of being in continuous stage of troubles specially among boys in cattle camp. 2. To dig but not deep.

Goŋ 1. A wild hen or Guinea fowl. 2. A slang for a deformed person whose back is bended foorward. 3. To bend down in order to see or as a respect to a great person.

Go̱ŋ Bending or curving part or side of anything.

Go̱o̱ŋ A bending pipe which is used for distilling liquors etc.

Go̱ŋni Plural of Go̱o̱ŋ being a bending pipe as explained above.

Go̱r 1. To look for a lost thing. 2. Early stage of friendship building between young people (both male and female)

Go̱o̱r 1. A person who looks for lost thing. 2. To look for girls to make friendship. 3..A tobacco Nursery.

Go̱rgo̱r State of loud noise as that comes from empty barrel or tin.

Go̱t The shape of the trained horns.

Goot 1. A kind of sticks. 2. A tool that is used for shaping wooden materials

Goy Plural of Gooy being beauty, goodness as explained below.

Gooy Beauty, groodness, pleasant etc..

Gɔɔk 1. Monkey. 2. Slang for a person who looks like a monkey **or** being thin.

Gɔhk 1. To start game by making the first move.

2. To make some bundle well tied with the rope.

Gɔkgɔk That does not allow the normal passing of things.

Gɔhk gɔhk A style of walking specially before young ladies, in-laws, etc.

Gɔl 1. A kind of wild animal which looks like a horse. 2. The homestead.3. The cow dung fire place. 4. The middle of cattle hut 5. To cause someone or thing to fall down when wrestling, walking or moving.

Gɔ̱l To move very far to avoid the danger, water, inlaw contact etc.

Gɔ̱lgɔ̱l Failure to follow straight line or path.

Gɔmgɔm State of being quite thin due to starvation, famine or malnourished.

Gɔngɔn A nickname of bull when left horn curves or bends towards the face.

Gɔny To accuse someone before the court of law.

Gɔ̱ny To dig slightly a pit hole.

Gɔŋ Plural of Goañ being the bending or curving part of a stick or a branch.

Gɔ̱ŋ To bend something as in fishing method where snare or hook are used.

Gɔ̱ŋgɔ̱ŋ State of beind in bending or bended as with fruits or branches.

Gɔŋgɔŋ State of having so many bendings or curves either with tools,roads etc.

Gɔp To attack with claws such as eagle or vulture

Gɔpgɔp 1. Style of attacking behaviour with claws to snatch something by force, 2. State of fear and respect in observing the traditional norms to inlaws. 3. A way of showing aloofness due to being a new arrival or a guest.

Gɔ̱a̱r Art of writing or making marks on a surface.

Gɔɔr A fishing tool which is used for catching fish while on the move in deep water.

Gɔ̱ɔ̱r Educated person who knows how to write and read.

Gɔarjiath A kind of plant which is burned and its ashes are used for making snuff (local tobacco).

Gɔrgɔr 1. A noise which is heard when things are moved along the edges of the roof. 2. Slang for taking troubles to try to discover area, or parts in the forest.

Gɔt 1. To elbow someone from behind not to move.2. An aggression before the fight. 3. State of bullying young ones in cattle camp among big boys of different ages.

Gɔ̱ɔ̱t A bull with a leftside horn bended towards the eyes or the face.

Gɔtgɔt State of being aggressive towards little boys.

Gɔ̱th 1. A bat bird. 2. State of being quite angry – Dinka word. See Kɛc.

Gɔ̱thgɔ̱th That type of bat bird which lives in Coconut or in dark **places** under the rooves.

Gɔthgɔth Start of pulling one own stomach to pretend being hungry.

Gɔw 1. To prevent others not to participate in any thing. 2. The best things eg. Kɛ ti gɔw.

Gɔwgɔw State of feeling shy or observance to inlaw respects and norms.

Gu A word for questioning someone. eg. I̱nɔ gu? Is like that?

Gua A short form for Gua̱th which is a place or spot.

Guac 1. Failure to meet someone on the way due to so many routes. 2. Failure to understand one another in opinion. 3. To exchange things among you at least two persons. 4. Failure to identify or locate the cows according to their previous places in the hut(luak) etc.

Guäc A slip of a tongue as when one mispronounces a word that means the opposite eg.ɛ ŋu jumbuuth inɛ̈?:Correction:ɛŋu bum juuth inɛ?

Gua̱a̱c Plural of Guäc being a slip of a tongue as explained above.

Guak 1. An animal of dog family which defecates along the routes or roads. 2. Slang for insulting any person who behaves like that. 3. State of dried grass in the forest. 4. Unorganized talking in a large room Luak or under a tree.

Guakguak 1. State of such noise as that is heard when many people gather in one place. 2. Failure to pronounce words properly.

Gualgual State of being quite empty or lack of people in a certain area due to migrations.

Gua̱n His/her father only with third person plural eg. Gua̱n:. as in Gua̱ndiɛn: Their father.

Guaŋ 1. To be possessed by holy spirit or Kujur. 2. To make a hole on a piece of wood, stone, mountain.etc. 3. The signs and sysmptons of fish movements in water.4. An art of fishing depending on such signs. 5. Slang for something expected but have been delayed for cercemony.

Guaaŋ The appearance of fish heads or tails during the movements in water.

Guaŋguaŋ A hole or space made or cut on the mountain, soil, trees etc for keeping or hiding things in.

Guar 1. A young girl of teenager (13–15 years old). 2. To cut away the branches when looking for logs or poles.

Gua̱r 1. Physical condition of a sick person who is suffering of chronic disease. 2. Food made of grinding grains.

Guaar Plural of Guar being a young girl as explained above.

Gua̱a̱r My father, said by the first person singular.

Gua̱a̱ri Plural of Guäär being my father as explained above. Guääri is said by first person singular when addressing elders.

Guarguar State of a tree when the branches are stripped off.

Guat 1. State of becoming thin due to chronic disease or illness. 2. Wishing or express wishing good or bad omen to take place.

Guath 1. To pick something from a group, cluster or heap of spear, gun, etc. 2. Slang for being tall and thin.

Gua̱a̱th 1. Place, position, part etc. 2. To have recovered from sickness, pains or general fatigue.

Guathguath State of being quite talls, not thick or short.

Guay To smooth or remove parts of the clay making utensils or pottery works.

Guec 1. The Giraffe.The most tallest animal in the forest. 2. Seeing, watching or a slang for begging by watching where division is taking place. 3. A word which is used for instigating bulls, oxen etc. to fight. see Guecguec.

Guel To decorate the bead string by adding different colour beads.

Gueel The colour used to decorate the other or the main colours.

Gueny 1. To allow some one or something to pass by.2. The passing of fish from the swamp to the river where fishermen wait for them through **a** device way a long the water channels.

Guer 1. State of talking ill of someone or backbiting people. 2. To arrange or put things into their right order. 3. To clear a stem or branch of a tree by removing branches or thorns.

Guet 1. To pull out with the help of iron rod the inner contents of a gourd container. 2. Slang for defying someone statement not to be true.

Gueth 1. State of being quite brave or courageous. 2. Something associated with Guey a large gourd for keeping milk to ferment to make butter. 3. Having much to do with pulling out something Guath.

Guethgueth Being so brave person or courageous.

Guey 1. A large gourd container for fermenting milk in order to make butter. 2. Plural of Guææ being gravel, stone, and any hard substance in food, plural. See Guɛɛ. 3. To expand or make thin the thickness of the mud used in making pot by potter.

Guɛɛ 1. Having much to do with Guey eg. Ɛ guɛɛ, tekɛ guɛɛ. That

is a stone or gravel in food items or in the eye. 2. Slang for an evil eye. See Pëth.

Guɛk 1. Frog of all types. 2. Snail shell which is used for milk or soup food. See Guiik.

Guɛɛk Plural of Guɛk being a frog as explained above.

Guɛkguɛk A sound as that is made when one fails to observe stops when

Speaking

Guɛkguɛɛk State of such failure to observe stops when speaking.

Guɛl 1. State of arranging the bead grains according to colours needed. 2. A situation when the dancers are not following the tunes or the musics.

Guɛlguɛl State of being in different level of colours, heights, length or in dancing.

Guɛlguɛɛl Lack of continuity or smoothness or equality.

Guɛm State of cheating, where one takes greater part of something when dividing.

Guɛɛn State of being somehow round in shape as that with gourd or

pumpkin.

Guɛnguɛn Being in such a round shape as explained above..

Guɛny 1. To push aside someone, people or things in order to pass through. 2. The movement of fishes along water ways where fishermen moniter their movements by fixing long sticks Piiri inorder to spear them. 3. Slang for morning or the dawn after sunrise rays.

Guɛɛny State of having a lot of fishes passing along at ago.

Guɛnythar An insult to someone who lacks big buttocks.

Guɛnyguɛny State of being quite clear when darkness declines.

Guɛŋ 1. To make holes on pieces of wood or stone or soil. 2. To be **possessed** by Kujur or spirit.

Guɛɛŋ 1. Person who cuts or curves tools out of wood, stones or clay. 2. A kind of disease which affects women after delivery.

Guɛr Not so thick or cluster as with hairs or leaves.

Guɛɛr Plural of Guer being backbiting or the talks about bad deeds of people.

Guɛrguɛr State of being not thick or cluster as with leaves or hairs.

Guɛt 1. A soft grass which is put inside Juuth being one of the organs that make up To̱ny local pipe. It acts as a filter. 2..To comb hairs with hands or sharp thing like rod, wood.etc. 3. To be ahead alittle bit when racing or throwing spears.

Guɛyguɛy State of being round as that of stomach.

Guic To see or to look such as Guic tuut being a heifer that about toMate or in a mating period.

Guiic A child or an adult person who begs by looking at someone or people eating or dividing some meat.

Guicguic A type of insects which disturbs cattle and human being in the evenings.

Guiik Plural Guɛk a spoon forged out of snail.

Guil 1. To visit or pay a visit to a sick person or a newly given birth woman. 2. To give a look, glance at something or someone. 3. A certain bone on the chest of a human being or animal.

Guili Plural of Guil a certain bone as explained above.

Guiir 1. A colour that is between dark brown and deep red 2. A person who backbites people.

Guirguir 1. The early hours of the day where the shapes are not clear.

Guìr To arrange or put things or people into their right order.

Guìrguìr State of putting things or whatever into their right or in order.

Guith Slight difference in height where one appears to be a little bit taller than the other.

Guok 1. To silence a crying person or baby. 2. The checking of toich soil for a type of fish that buries itself when water gets dried in swamps and toiches. 3. To mark the end of any work you were doing.

Guol To mark or demarcate an area so as to deal with it particularly in weeding.

Guolguol A small space or spot on the body of both human being or cow that has different colour or a shape then the rest.

Guom To preserve cow dung fire by pressing it.

Guomguom State of having something well pressed and kept compact.

Guoŋ To bend down as when picking something,entering into hut door, to look or focus on something in darkness.

Guoŋguoŋ State of being in bending position.

Guor 1. A wild small animal belonging to cat family or a wild cat. 2. To make the floors quite smooth by smearing it with soft tool such as Guɛk, Muɔt or Tung.

Guɔk 1. To look for tortoise by checking the hiding places with spears Bieth. 2. To hang or tie a bell around the neck of a bull as an ornament. 3. A part of the ear where ornaments are fitted on.

Guɔɔk 1. Plural of Guuk being a person who checks tortoises as explained above.2. The human being ear particles.

Guɔ̱ɔ̱k Plural of Guk the corners of the room where things are hidden..

Guɔkguɔk A kind of a pot utensil where its opening is quite small.

Guɔl 1. Small fox diseases. 2. Slang for a bad person who stays alone.

Guɔm Stomach troubles which stop wastes or stool to pass out regularly.

Guɔn State of being very short and small.

Guɔnguɔn Very small or short baby or a child.

Guɔŋ 1. Guinea fowl bird. 2. A colour which mixes grayish and bluish.

Guɔ̱p 1. A skin or piece of it. 2. The foam of water as with soap.

Guɔr A big grass thatched hut for human being use..

Guɔ̱r 1. Elephant. 2. Elephant tusk ornament. 3. Plural of Guœr when (ɔ) is stressed.

Guɔɔr 1. Plural of Guor being a large grass thatched hut as explained **above.** 2. Plural of Gur a baby that follows the first as explained below.

Guɔ̱ɔ̱r To remove the hairs on the head or skin.

Guɔt 1. A kind of plant where its stalks are made as mats or carpet. 2. State of dark green colour.

Guɔ̱y Plural of Guuy a begger who begs by sitting near someone eating as explained below.

Guc The noise or sound which is heard when one is swallowing water, beer, milk,etc.

Gucguc Series and frequent noise or sound as when chewing and swallowing.

Guk The corner of a room or a shadow place in side the hut.

Guuk A small bird that makes systematic noise or songs on the tree.

Gul To make something round or to curve or bend it to make circle.

Gulgul State of having round shapes as that with rings.

Gum A way of lying down when in a terrible cold.

Gumgum State of having completely closed up one own limbs due to cold.

Gumut Owl, being that bird with large eyes which makes noise on the roof at night.

Gun Very small or any short piece of something

Gungun State of being quite short and small as a baby, maize bundle.etc.

Guŋguŋ To bend one head when asked to do so, not to break orders.

Gup Plural of Guɔ̱p being a piece of skin as explained above.

Gur 1. A child that follows the first one. 2. To take the hairs completely from the skin. 3. To lock up the room with heavy tools.

Guur 1. Being completely without horns. eg Cot guur : Hornless cow 2. Whatever is used for closing up a room completely. 3. To follow someone or something. 4. Second person father eg. Guur: Your father. See first person. Gua̱ndan.: Our father.

Gurgur State of having no horns.

Gut 1. The lower parts of the jaws. 2. State of being taken up by whirpool noise. 3. A stick hittingt noise.

Guth 1. To pick or pull either hairs or seeds in a nursery. 2. The flucking out of feathers or wings of a bird.

Guy To beg by watching and sitting near someone eating usually by children.

Guuy A person who goes to beg by sitting and watching a neightbour or person eating.

Gä The sound of eighth letter of Thok Nath.

Gäc A distorted Arabic language word for a belt. See L͟a͟ak.

Gääc Surprise or puzzling word meaning: what could be done after the house head death.

Gäcgäc A piece of luck which rescues one in difficult situation.

Gäk 1. Difficult to go through eg Ci dupk.œ gäk: You have closed our routes. 2. A set of cow tails made as ornament which is put on the horns of a favoured bull. 3. To close, lock or shut the door, window or a box etc.

Gääk A piece of a strong wooden stick which is used for locking hut door, by nigtht.

Gäkgäk Sound of fire flame burning or gun shots.

Gälgäl Not fitting well such as rings or wrist ornaments.

Gäm 1. To collect rain water or any liquid that is falling from above. 2. Incomplete string of beads or bead grains. 3. State of zeal or show of patriotism to country, tribe, section or even clan. 4. Not fill up cotainer.

Gääm 1. A mid-wife 2. A person who choruses the songs. 3. State of not well filled up.eg Dhaar æmæ cæ gääm : This pot is not well filled up.

Gän To preserve or rserve something for a later use.

Gängän State of little quantity of seeds or grains for next sowing.

Gängään Plural of Gängän being little quantities available as explained above.

Gäŋ 1. To protect, keep or stop usage of something, animals or human being to meet or join up in one place. 2. A traditional piece of leather dress which is worn by women around genital organs to cover secrets of the body in ancient days. 3. To bend or tilt to one side as with untensils. 4. The sun movement towards, the west.

Gääŋ A person or whatever that prevents, protects etc. anything from danger or misuse.

Gäŋgäŋ State of being in bending, continuous bending or lack of stability.

Gäp State or situation when one is in danger of drowning or when one inhales much air or smoke.

Gär Situation when anything could not get in or get out due to being quite large than the entrance.

Gäär Person who is a specialist who performs traditional marks on the forehead of a young Nuer.

Gärgär State of being so large to go through a small door or narrow one.

Gät 1. A way of walking when fat or with a problem between two legs. 2. A kind of oil or fat that is obtained when one burns a gourd utensil that had contained butter, fat or oil before. 3. A new word from Amharic language in Ethiopia which means to take people property by force.

Gätgät State of failing to sit up right due to pains between two legs.

Gäth To clean a wooden tool by smoothing the outer part with sharp device or broken piece of glass, or whatever.

Gäw 1. A type of tall grass which is used in hut roof thatching. 2. To obstruct the work to go on. 3. A noise or sound of gun shot.

Gäwgäw Noise or sound that is heard when a large hollow barrel or tin is hit.

Gäy 1. Another pronunication for Gäc being a name for a child borne after death. 2. A confused person who does not know what to do.

Gääy A state of surprise or confusion where one does not know what to do.

Gääygääy State or a situation where one does not know what to do or in state of confusion.

Guä A short form for both Gu̱adin or Gua̱r which means father or my father.

Guäc 1. Things or items of little values or importance. 2. Slip of a tongue where one says a wrong statement eg. Ɛŋu jum buuth inɛ mɛ!! 3. An unintended wound or murder in a fight

Guäcguäc State of delaying by looking for unnecessary things while people have already started moving.

Guäkguäk The noise of cooking or boiling broth.

Guäl 1. To exchange things such as animals, goods according to needs. 2. To replace someone place, duties etc as a result of a new arrangement.

Guääl Plural of Guäl being exchange of things as explained above.

Guär 1. To grind grains to make soft paste with grinder. 2. To keep oneself away from active involvement due to being a guest, stranger or being an in-law.

Guärguär State of shyness due to being a stranger or an in-law.

Guät 1. Rituals which is performed in the funeral rites. 2. State of being in bending forward or to the front.

Guätguät State of falling while running forward when hit by stick or when running to hide.

Guäth Plural of Guaath being the position or part as explained above.

Guäyguäy State of being so large and can carry a big quantities.

Guɛ̈ɛ̈ŋ A disease or sickness that affects a mother who has just given birth.

Gök 1. Prophet, person possessed by Kujur or spirit. 2. A skin or leather container or bag made out of calf, goat skin.

Göök 1. Plural of Gök the prophet or someone possessed by Kujur as explained above. 2. A rib bone of the human chest or animal. 3. Part of hut internal building.

Gökgök State of bending towards the front part.

Göl What is quite a different topic or issue. see eg. ɛ göl.

Gön 1. To carry something dangling along. 2. To catch with hook or anything.

Göön Whatever is used for carrying things.

Gööni Plural of Göön being a container for carrying things as explained above.

Göny To having a case before a court or to accuse someone to a court.

Göŋgöŋ State of having many bending or curves such as tools, roads etc.

Göp 1. To pick by force as the eagle does for children. 2. The series fishing with Bieth spear. 3. To fight with hor ns as with animals (bulls, oxen etc).

Gör 1. To look for a lost thing. 2. A noise of a heavy falling hollow object.

Göör Plural of Go̱o̱r being a young man who practices friendships with young ladies.

Göth To pull oneself up in order to reach some thing high.Eg Gœth Rœ ɛ jɛn bi jɛ cop œ: *Pull yourself up in order to reach it.*

Göy A noise of a falling big hollow object.

Göygöy 1. An object that causes loud noise. 2. Anything that can be seen in a distance.

Göyöy State of being in quite clear place to be seen very easily.

H

Ha A defying word meaning not true.eg Ha ruac æ mœ ciæ thuok:*No, this talk is not true*

Hak 1. A sound of a breakage or fraction. 2. To bother into something you are invited to.eg Cu rœ hak : Do not bother.

Haak A sound of breaking wood or a tree.eg Wia raar tæ kæ mi ci wäh haak : *Get out there is breakage sound.*

Haal A word which is used to express denial or distancing oneself from

troubles. eg. Haal cä ŋäc ni jɛ: No, I do not even know it.

Ham A sound of wood breaking in closed distance or in the forest.

Ha̱m 1. A sound which is made by elephant or gun shot. 2. A thigh or that part of leg above the knee.

Ha̱a̱m Plural of Hàm being the thigh as explained above.

Hamham 1. State of such continuous noise or sound of wood breaking. 2. Ṭhe continuous noise of elephant when very angery.

Han A great desire to eat after long illness. Eg ɛŋu cæ ji han inœ ? *Why are you in such a great desire to eat like this*?

Hanhan That great desire to eat as explained above.

Hap A series or continuous visitings of one place frequently.

Häp 1. To allow the falling of something down. 2. Slang for telling some secrets.e g wer cuɛ hap piny en wanɛ: *Go do not pour it out here.*

Har To escape by running very fast from the danger. Eg Cu kɛ jɛ har: *They start running.*

Harhar Having high deafening noise like that of elephant or airplane.

Haw Sound or noise of stones, gravels, grains when shaken in a container for soothing the baby to sleep.

Hawhaw That continuous noise a mother makes to lull or sooth her baby. See YiekyieK.

Hay Word which expresses surprise or satisfaction of information or food consumed.

Hayhay 1. That series noise of a dog when barking. 2. A person in great surprise when a thing got spoiled or misused.

Hephep Large surface of water, in a container, in a lake etc.

Her To reject someone request to do him/her some help, assistance etc.

Heer A big grain container which has eight measurements.seeThɛɛm.

Hɛc Word or an expression meaning No eg. Ɛ jɛn guath dɛ?

Hɛc ciɛ jɛn: Is it, its place? No, it is not.

Hɛk A sound or noise of breaking of utensil or chewing something **with** stones or gravels.

Hɛkhɛk A noise as that of breaking bones, clay, glass utensils etc.

Hɛl Eating alone without sharing food with any body. Not to share **anything** with people. Style of greediness.

Hɛm Whitish or bright in colour.

Hɛmhɛm State of being quite bright or whitish.

Hɛny To lie on stomach. See Bappiny.

Hɛnyhɛny State of being bulgy or clumsy shaped person.

Hɛp To consume by chewing grains when so hungry.

Hɛphɛp That noise that is heard when goats or cows chew hard grains..

Hɛpböö Bull noise or sound when hungry and needs to be released for grazing.

Hɛr Being quite whitish, clean or bright.

Hɛrhɛr State of being quite whitish or bright.

Hɛt 1. To feed or eat without stew, milk or whatever that helps eating. 2. To eat or chew grains by goats. 3. A sound of bone when touched in operation or initiations.

Hɛthɛt The noise of bone when being touched as explained above.

Hɛth 1. To eat a lot without stopping. 2. To pour out waste in big quantities.

Hɛthhɛth State of having such behavior of eating without stopping as explained above.

Hɛw A noise of grains or gravels inside a container for soothing a baby.

Hɛwhɛw The noise of gravels, grains or whatever in a container.

Hɛy Word or an expression which means No, just like that one above but of different pronunciation when suffering of severe pains.

Hɛyhɛy That noise of enduring or feeling severe pain.

Ho̱c The noise of pulling a heavy object.

Ho̱cho̱c State of such series noise of pulling a heavy object.

Ho̱kho̱k That series noise of falling heavy objects as when breaking hammering or destroying wood in the forest.

Ho̱l State of having deep shadowed eyes e. Ho̱l nyin.

Ho̱lho̱l State of having such eye shape, having deep sank eyes.eg Wer

cuah guic ɛ hòlhòl: Go,do not look at me with those

shaped eyes.

Hom High voice or argument with loud noise.

Homhom Much noise as that is caused by cars or elephant in the forest

Ho̱p The collapsing of something or whatever eg. Ci duel ho̱p wiidiɛn. *The house collapsed on them.*

Ho̱r To be quite whitish or bright after washing such as a dirty white cloth. See Hɛr.

Ho̱rho̱r The noise of beating empty barrel.

Ho̱t A hole of snake, mouse, ant etc.

Ho̱tho̱t A noise which is made by hyenas,rats,dogs etc, when scratching the soil, to make hole.

Hoy Not solid, not compact,not hard etc.

Hoyhoy State of being not compact nor solid,not hard etc.

Ho̱th 1. A local utensil made of branches for carrying luggage. 2. To raise up something heavy. 3Ṭhe growth of plant which raises the soil.

Hooth A person who leaves his/ her compound to go and live in a new place.

Hɔa Having much to do with Hɔw the world or the Universe, Globe eg. Juɛy mi te̱ rɛy hɔa.: A disease in the world. Cɛ ben rɛy hɔa. *He has come to the world.*

Hɔat State of having much to do with Hɔ̱l pounding.Eg Meer tæ hœat: *Meer went grinding.*

Hɔa̱c To warm oneself by sitting near a burning fire or flame.

Hɔ̱c State of being wet with water. See Wac.

Hɔ̱ɔ̱c To be near the fire place warming up eg. Cɛ wä hɔ̱ɔ̱c kɛ mac: *He has gone to warm with fire.*

Hɔ̱k Plural of Yaŋ a cow as explained below under letter (Y).

Hɔk 1. To push a head or aside something or someone to give way or space. 2. A way of looking.Eg Hœk ni jɛ jok :Push him back eg. Cu ha guic ɛ hœk : *Do not look at me like that!*

Hɔ̱l 1. To pound grains with a mortar to make flour. 2. A bone of thigh.

Hɔl 1. A kind of grass that is used in thatching huts. 2. Heavy smell as that with tobacco.

Hɔlɛk A rather deep part of shallow water. It is distorted word from Hɔt lɛɛk.

Hɔm 1. Trench or trap for catching animals. 2. To instigate or persuade someone to do bad.or wrong. 3. To push through accidentally. 4. The reduction of the volume of swelling when fluids are removed from wound.

Hɔ̱mhɔ̱m Shrinkage situation as when the body or wound releases fluids.

Hɔ̱n 1. To test or check the fitness or strength. 2. To examine. To try to know whether someone has known something or not.

Hɔ̱ɔ̱n 1. Temptation. 2. Word which expresses Yes, Yeah or correct.

Hɔ̱ɔ̱ni Plural of Hɔ̱ɔ̱n being temptation as explained above.

Hɔny To land, put or fall on something.

Hɔp 1. To cause bruise on the skin with finger nails or thorn action. 2. To push something through eg Cu jɛ hop thin. 3. To pound grains with a pounder. See Pi̱l. eg. Bɛl baa kɛ hɔp kɛ pi̱l.:The grains will be pounded with pounding stone.

Hɔɔphɔɔp The noise which is heard when one is itching his/her body.

Hɔr 1. To replace someone in fishing seat or in fight. 2. Noise of an opened hand blow. 3. An opened area where cattle graze far from farms. 4. State of being quite bitter as with taste eg. kɛcɛ ɛ hɔr.

Hɔ̱r To gain breath after fainting or lost breathing.

Hɔrhɔr Being quite spacy or having enough capacity to keep or contain good quantities.

Hɔt Plural of Hɔat the bending curve on the wall, frame, path etc.

Hɔ̱t 1. To pound grains to make flour. See Hɔ̱l. 2. Equalize or has the same powers or height. 3. A disease that destroys liver of animal such as goat known as Håtcuäny.

Hɔthɔt 1. Being quite tiny or small. 2. Long or tall. 3. State of being quite growing very fast, tall and slender.

Hɔ̱th To refuse to answer a call while listening.

Hɔ̱ɔ̱ath A person who does not listen to any advice.

Hɔw 1. World, Universe, Earth, Globe. See Hɔa. Having much to do with world. 2. Noisy falling object.

Hä 1. The sound of the nineth letter of Thok Nath. 2. A word which expresses mine, I, me, eg. Bia kä hä: you come to me.

Häc A bundle ready to be carried on the head.

Hääc Plural of Häc being a bundle as explained above.

Häk 1. An old piece of wood or tree. 2. A noise of a falling object such as gourd utensil.

Hääk Plural of Häk being an old piece of wood as explained above.

Häkhäk 1. An already decomposed piece of wood or whatever but not yet apart. 2. State of being weak due to decaying as a result of ageing.

Häm The thigh or that part of the leg between hip and knee.

Hämhäm That noise that is made by an elephant or gun shots.

Hän I, me or my self eg.

Hän bä wä: I will go. Eg Hän a bææni : I am coming. Bä wä hän: *I will go myself.*

Häny To put a heavy load on someone, something or on the ground or floor.

Häŋ State of being easy to be adapted.

Häŋhäŋ A person who is easy to get adapted into any way of life.

Här To open or stretch something very wide.

Härhär Widely opened or spreaded well as with piece of cloth or skin.

Hät Desire to do something which is too big or difficult for one capacity.

Häät Plural of Hät being a desire to do something as explained above.

Häthät A claim that one can do something which is quite beyond his/her capacity.

Häy A cry when in great suffering or in danger.

Häyhäy A crying word which expresses the state of severe pains or suffering.

Hök 1. A gourd forged container for carrying grains, ground nuts or butter. 2. A noise of a falling object.

Höök State of a heavy falling object noise, such as a big tree, hut etc.

Hökhöök.A series noise of falling trees in the forest.

Hönyhöny State of bulky or clumsy shape.

Höŋ An opening or a space in anything.

Hööŋ State of being quite opened. See Kuɛl.

Höŋhöŋ State of being opened or with a hole on it. eg. Piece of cloth with openings: Biiy mi höŋhöŋ.

Hör 1. A type of plant which floats on water because of being very light. 2. To prick the body in order to suck out unwanted blood. 3. To fight on behalf of someone who is either young or weak to fight.

Höth 1. To travel or migrate from place to another. 2. Part of human or animal body at the lower part of the belly and above the legs.

Höthni A person who keeps on moving or migrating through out.

Hööth Plural of Hooth being a person who keeps on moving as explained above.

Höw A male human being or animal whose testicles got removed or not reproductive.

Höwni Plural of Höw being human or animal as explained above.

Höwhöw The noise of an old dog, empty drum, barrel etc.

Höy 1. The waist part of human being or animal. See Lɛt. 2. The unknown movements of a person when he/she in deep sleep in ancient days when people used to sleep on the floor.

I̱

J

Jaa A short form for saying “Jɛn a thin” : It/ he/she is there.

Jac 1. To make charcoal pieces from cooking fire. See Jac raar. 2. A game which is played by throwing divided four pieces of sorghum stalk. See Jac jaac.

Jaac 1. The charcoal made by pushing aside some glowing pieces of wood fire and get covered up to make charcoal. 2. The foreface of a cow. 3. Whatever is put on the face as decoration or ornament.

Jacjaac The game that is played with four halves of sorghum stalk.

Jacjaacni Plural of Jacjaac being the game as explained above.

Jak 1. A cow colour which is of two colours, whitish dominance and orange on the head. 2. A type of grains that grows in winter or in cold weather. 3. State of being not well cooked or roasted properly.

Jaak Plural of Jak being a cow with that colour as explained above.

Jakɔ̱k The crow Ṭhere are two types of crows thus : Jakɔ̱k ca̱r.

Jakɔ̱k rɔ̱l :The black crow and white with black one.

Jakɔa̱̱k Plural of Jakɔ̱k being the crow as explained above.

Jak thok pur A white and brown bird with a large flat beak.

Jal 1. To make final washing of something or someone body. 2. A black feather bird that lives on snails. 3. A tuber plant that looks like onion. It is said that in history the early nations who came to Africa (Nuerland) got poisoned due to the fact that they ate it as onion.

Ja̱l 1. Journey, travel or migration. 2. The flow of water or any liquid over the edges as when the full container is moved.

Jaal Symptom of vomiting due to stomach troubles or sickness.

Ja̱a̱l 1. Plural of Jäl being a guest or a visitor as explained below. 2. To make someone walk particularly a baby, when he/she wants to learn walking or to make a sick person walks around to gain energy.

Jaljal Flowing of liquids over a full container.

Jam A kind of rope which is used for tying up a restless cow.

Ja̱a̱n Early soft hairs of a baby.

Jani Plural of Ja̱a̱n that is the baby early hairs as explained above..

Jany 1. Shallow, and not deep water well, holes etc. 2. State of having delayed very much. 3. An impolite way of answering. Eg ɛ ŋu jany i hä mœ? *Why do you answer me like that?*

Jaany State of having stayed away for a long time from home.eg ɛ ŋu ci jaany inɛ? *Why do you delay like this?*

Janyjany 1. State of being quite shallow and not deep. 2. A person who gives rough reply to an enquiry.

Jaŋ 1. Appearance of fresh wound with blood on 2. A decoration brightness, glittering colours. 3. A person who hears very little.

J<u>a</u>ŋ A person from Dinka tribe.

J<u>aa</u>ŋ Plural of J<u>a</u>ŋ a person from Dinka as explained above.

J<u>aa</u>ŋni Whatever have much to do with Dinka people or land.

Jaŋjaŋ State of shining or bloody appearance.

Jap Flooding or increase of water level due to rainfalls. See Moak

Japjap Flow of water due to flood as a result of heavy rainfalls.

Jar A style of walking.

Jarjar 1. State of such style of walking where a naked male person shows off. 2. Not deep but shallow water. 3. A person who is opened and does not hide things.

Jat Failure to get fish when one has fished for long time.

Jay To deny something, an allegation or whatever.

Jayjay State of denial, or not ready to accept what could be true.

Jek 1. To find, get, discover, locate something or someone. 2. To greet a person or meet him/her by checking hands. 3. Slang for having played sex with a girl friend.

Jer To pluck away the leaves from the stem, or to remove meaty parts from bones etc.

Jerjer 1. State of being quite thin and lacking flesh 2. A slang for being fast in running.

Jɛ Pronoun objects form of he/she/it, John eg. Wer kä jɛ: go to him/her/it John.

Jɛn 1. Pronoun for third person singular.eg Jɛn cɛ wä : *He/she/it/John went or has gone.* 2. Means woods, trees usually when cut down as logs or when in the forest as trees. 3. Plural of Jiath being a tree or a wood. 4. A round figure such as tens 20, 30, etc eg Jɛ̈n diɔk means thirty and also it could mean three poles or logs.

Jɛr Leaves of sugar canes, sorghum stalks, grass etc.

Jɛrpiny To cut or peel the leaves of sugar canes or surghom stalks.

Jɛth 1. Deep sadness or sorrow. 2. To cross water surface,ditch, river etc. 3. Part of the rope which is tied around animal neck cows, goats etc.

Jɛy To let or allow someone or something goes eg. Aa jɛy: Let him/her/it Joh goes. See Jiɛn.

Ji Pronoun for subject or object eg. Ruacä kɛ ji: I am talking to you. It is a short for Jin which means you eg. Jin ber kɛ: You come.

Jiaac Having started or moved to command. State of movement for action in drum or marriage dances. Eg Wia ci kuen jiaac : *You go, the marriage has started.*

Jia̱c The belly or stomach see Jic.

Jic 1. A kind of small bluish bird. 2. A carbon that appears on cooking utensils when subjected to fire and smoke. 3. Stomach or belly. See jiàc.

Jiic State of having absorbed water as clay utensil or stoppage of blood flowing.

Jicni Plural of Jic being the small and bluish bird as explained above.

Jicjic That has the capacity to absorbs water as clay utensil.

Jiec 1. To get up from sleeping or when one is lying down. 2. To rise up or to take one position in adulthood.

Jiekjiek Plural of Jikjik a state of being clean as explained below.

Jiel The dirt parts or wastes that are left when grains got separated.

Jieŋ State of getting little or smaller due to sickness or whatever.

Jieth Plural of Jith being scorpion as explained below.

Jiew Well.or pit hole or laterine.

Jieew Having much to do with well, pit hole etc eg. Rɛy Jieew :

In the well or in pit hole.

Jiey To feel electrified or shilling with cold in winter.

Jieyjiey Having electrical power.

Jiɛn Having much to do with wood. Eg Rɛy Jiɛn.: In the trees or wood.

Jiɛɛn.1. To move or leave from one place to another. 2. To become active or strong such as alcoholic substance.eg Ci koaŋ jiɛɛn:*The beer has become active.*

Jiɛr Grass or surgheom stalks leaves eg. Kɛ jiɛr bɛɛl: *Those are surghom stalk leaves.*

Jiɛrjiɛr State of being skinny, thin or lacking flesh on the body.

Jik A type of black, dark soil or clay for smearing hut floors or walls.

Jikjik State of being quite clean and careful of one own out look.

Jikäny People of Sunrise. It is fully known as Ji käny cäŋ. It is a collection of three main sections of Gaatjaak, Gaatjio̱k and Gaatguang of Eastern Nuer people who originated from Bentiu Area in Western Nuer.

Jin Pronoun You, being the second person singular. See Yɛn.

Jio̱k 1. Dog. 2. To tell something to someone. Jiok ni kɛ bia: *Tell them to come.* 3. A colour of black and white. 4. To make a black mark on something. 5. Mark that is made when one crosses water surface.

Jio̱o̱k Plural of Jio̱k being a dog as explained above.

Jio̱klɛc A kind of fish that has sharp teeth for attacking its enemies.

Jio̱k nyapɛc Wild dog that lives in the forests.

Jiol The first thing or action that one starts with.

Jio̱m 1. To give food or whatever to one mouth or to a child. 2. A feeling as when one is sick or fearful.

Jio̱mjio̱m State of feeling fear when one is moving in the forest or **in** a dark night.

Jio̱ŋ 1. State of being powerless to do anything or action. 2. A four stands or more device for storing sorghum at harvest.

Jio̱ŋo̱ŋ Powerless state or being without powers.

Jio̱ŋjio̱ŋ State of being rough as a restless cow.

Jio̱p The axe. That metallic device for cutting wood or trees.

Jio̱rjio̱r State of being quites large such as wound wound or a crak.

Jio̱w A bull which was first left to be ox but later was casterated.

Jio̱wni Plural of Jiow a casterated bull as explained above.

Jiɔm 1. The dry season or winter. 2. Wind, air or storm.

Jiɔam 1. Plural of Jiœm being the dry season or wind as explained above.2. State of having much to do with wind.

Jip State of being equal in height, in racing, in jumping or in swimming.

Jirjir State of being very angry, unhappy, annoyed or disturbed.

Jith 1. Ear being part of human being or a plant leaf such as sugar cane or stalks of plants. 2. Scorpion.

Ji̱th Plural of Jith being human ear, stalk or leave as explained above.

Jithlual A kind of plant with red leaves.

Joac 1. State of being visible or very clear to the sight. 2. A slang for a plenty of food materials or free meals.

Joak 1. Plural of Jɔk being a disease.eg ɛ wec mi tɛɛ joak: *A town with diseases.* 2. Later on, in a later time or to be in last action. 3. A ghost person. Nuer believe that the dead people are living some where and called them Jɔɔk.

Joakni Plural of Jɔk being a name of a baby borne after many dead babies as explained above..

Joakjoak State of movement towards the back while looking in front.

Jol. 1. To start doing something for the first time.See Jiol. eg

Jol rœ kɛ wä: Just start going. 2. To add some water to the cooking or boiling broth.

Joŋ State of being not attentive to what is going on before you.

Joñjoñ State of being not attentive.See Jooñ.

Joñoñ 1. Being not relax but in a series tension. 2. State of being difficult to get relax.

J̱oŋj̱oŋ State of being quite restless and difficult to be handled

Jòñòñ State of being quite restless to be handled.

Jɔk 1. Disease, illness or sickness for both human and animals. 2. The behind or back part of anything including human being. 3. A name of a baby borne after several dead babies. See Wiyual, Jul, Wicjuac etc.

Jɔɔk The ghost people or the dead persons.

Jœœñ State of being not attentive to whatever is going on around.

Jɔm 1. Winter season when people refer to it.eg. Bɛ tuok ni jœm: *It will happen in winter.* 2. Having taken something with hand or with container.

Jœñjœñ State of being ready to show off in drum dance or in combating.

Jɔr 1. To throw a spear when fishing in shallow water. 2. One of the methods Nuer use in fishing in the river. See Thar raar.

Jɔ̱ɔ̱r A suffice which allows things to happen without notice. eg. (i) Päljɔ̱ɔ̱r: To allow oneself be mistreated. (ii) Bänyjɔ̱ɔ̱r: To make someone not to be included. (iii) Yorjɔ̱ɔ̱r: To throw something or someone away as when useless. (iv) Ruacjɔ̱ɔ̱r: To talk alone when one is sick or feverish..

Jɔ̱th A place near fire place for keeping native pipe materials such as tobacco, charcoal etc.

Jɔ̱thni Plural of Jɔ̱th being a place near fire as explained above.

Jɔw The sound, the noise, the voice of anything see Jiööth.

Juac A dried piece of grass.

Juaac Plural f Juac being a dried piece of grass as explained above.

Juak To take the greater or bigger part as cheating when dividing **something.**

Ju̱ak 1. The part of the bull or cow meat around testicles or udders. This type of meat is consumed by elders or aged persons. 2. The act of taking the great part of something.

Juäl 1. Tail of any kind animal, fish etc..2. A slang for a problem **eg.** Tɛɛ kɛ juäl :He/she has got a tail.

Ju̱al 1. The plural of Juäl being the tail as explained above. 2. To pour water on oneself when the weather is quite hot.

Ju̱alɛ The collective hairs of the forehead being one of the ancient styles **after** Dul.

Ju̱aljio̱k A type of short grass. See Bɔk.

Juan 1. State of looking difficulties where one pulls eyebrows muscles. 2. An under wear or inner wear cloth. 3. To cause wrinkles on the face, cloth etc.eg Cu nhiamdu juan: *Do not wrinkle your face.*

Juanjuan State of having a surface of anything not smooth or straight due to up and down on it.

Juaŋ To grab or take hold of something suddenly and cling on it.

Juaaŋ A name of someone whose father practised such harsh way of doing things.

Juaŋjuaŋ 1. State of catching or grabbing things. 2. Being ready to grab things.

Juar To take as much as possible from things without permission.

Juarjuar A person who takes or who is always greedy of any thing she/ he finds.

Juat To clean soup or milk food container with fingers. See Juet.

Ju̱at A feather of birds or insects.

Juath Plural of Juey that is sickness as explained below..

Ju̱ath Plural of Juäth a kind of fish which is delicious when roasted.

Juc 1. The chasing of a defeated group in war, fight, games or racing. 2. State of being quite equal in height or sharp as with figure.

Jɛn diɔ̱k ɛ juc : Thirty sharp.

Juuc A person who runs or chases in such a way eg. Juuc Buɔl, Juuc nath, Juuc cɔ̱ɔ̱ni :He/she who chases drum, chases people and licks bones.

Juek State of having been grabbing things or always do that action. See Juak.

Juekjuek State of being quite fat where it becomes difficult to see the other parts of the body.

Juel State of having become matured or manhood. See Dhuɛl.

Juen State of pulling one eyebrow muscles.

Jueeni Plural of Juen being a style of pulling eyebrow muscles most frequently as explained above..

Jueeny A large swamp north of Ulang and Luakpiny counties where fishermen and fisherwomen collect a lot of fishes between April and July every year.

Juet To clean the container of soup or milk with figner. See Juat.

Juey State of being sick, ill, not well or feverish. See Jua̱th.

Juɛk Part of the neck below the jaws.

Juɛɛk Plural of Juɛk being part of the neck as explained above.

Juɛŋ State of having grabbed or caught something firmly. See Juaŋ.

Juɛr The taking of something without permission. See Juar.

Juɛt Aggression or troubles shooting behavior amongst the boys or children

Juɛɛt A kind of plants which grows along the river banks or in side water in marshes or lowlands.

Juɛtjuɛt A person who is aggressive and looks for troubles.

Juk To ejaculate by playing sex with hands among matured boys.

Jul 1. A baby born after several dead babies. 2. A kind of fish which lives in swamp water or Toc. 3. To add fresh milk to sour one. 4. To add cold water to hot one.

Juljul State of being sick, feverish or ill.

Juny State of being quite short. See Junyjuny.

Junyjuny Being quite short, very small in height or body.

Juoc 1. To chase someone, something or animal. See Juc. 2. To have defeated. 3. To suck out some fats or soup from bone components by mouth eg. Juoc ɛ cɔ̱w or cɔ̱w ti juooc.:To lick bones or lickable bones

Juooc That can be sucked by mouth as explained above.eg Titi kæ juooc käpæ kæ:*These are suckable take them.*

Juok 1. A group jumping show before young ladies in a drum dance. 2. A slang for taking a big mouthful of food by hungry person.

Juol 1. The green plants or grass that covers the farm or garden which is cleaned or weeded. 2. To swallow food or something.

Juoli Plural of Juol being the green grass as explained above.

Juopjuop A disease, traditionally believed to infect different cults in different clans or sections through sharing utensils etc.

Juor To have got lost completely and difficult to be traced.

Juoor State of having got lost completely. eg. Gat ɛmɛ cɛ juoor.:*This child has completely got lost.*

Juoot State of having testicles shrunk into their bags.

Juɔk The seven days of the week.

Juɔl Slang for whatever is swallowable.eg.Thilɛ mi dɛ juœl ? *Is there what I can swallow?*

Juɔɔl 1. State of having the farm full of grass. 2. To have much hairs on the head. 3. Plural of any swallowable materials (food items).eg Kak ɛmɛ cɛ juœœl: *This farm is full of grass* eg. Ci widɛ juœœl: *His/her head is full of hairs*. Eg Tɛɛkɛ juœœl? *Are there swallowable materials (food)?*

Juɔp To have shrunk or got burned a little bit

Juɔr State of being in a distance or very far.

Juɔɔr State of having gone far a head and the others are to follow.

Juɔ̱r A foreigner, stranger or from a different tribe or nation.

Juɔ̱th Whatever have much to do with Juuth the smoking filter part of the great Native pipe.

Juɔ̱thni Plural of Juuth being the smoking filter part as explained above.

Jup To cut a small piece out of a big or long one. See Yup.

Jupjup A short piece cut from something a cloth, skin, meat etc.

Jur 1. State of having much to do with foreigners eg Wia raar jur: *Get out foreigners.* 2. Plural of Juɔ̱r being a foreigner as explained above.

Jut To disturb, to become nuisance to someone or people.

Jutjut The behavior of always casusing disturbances or unrest to some one or people.

Juuth The filter part of traditional pipe which is a part of Tony,.

Jä The sound of the eleventh letter of Thok Nath.

Jäc Benefit or good looking face as when you say: eg Thilɛ jäc kiæ Tee jäc :*That does not attraction or has attraction.*

Jäcjäc 1. The sound or noise of boiling grains. 2. A sound or noise of water flowing from high ground.

Jäk 1. To send someone to take,call someone or bring something. 2. The arts of producing or making butter by shaking frequently the gourd container.

Jääk 1. A person sent to collect, inform, take something or someone etc. 2. The person who moves the milk container to make butter.

Jäl A guest or a person who just arrived from a journey.

Jääl A person on journey or traveler.

Jäm To paint with big colour as when decorating walls.

Jämjäm State of having bright colours such as black and white.

Jämbiɛl Bright colour – Title of God in Nuer religion.

Jäny 1. Delaying in coming. Failure to make a quick follow up. 2. Impolite way of answering people when called.

Jääny The failure or delay to come quickly. Eg. Cia jääny: *You delayed a lot.*

Jänyjäny 1. A rough way of answering people 2. A person who answers people in such a bad manner.

Jäŋjäŋ State of being quite rough and restless like cattle or horses.

Jäw State of being quite tall and thin.

Jäwjäw A person who is tall and thin.

Jääy A person who denies whatever he/she said or accepted before.

Jiäc Stomach or belly particularly the intestines.

Jiääc Plural of Jiäc being a stomach as explained above.

Jiäk Plural of Jiääk bad one or not good as explained below.

Jiääk Bad, not good or ugly. Eg Nɛmɛ ɛ mi jiääk: This one is bad or ugly.

Jiäkjiäk State of being bad or ugly in shape or appearance.

Jiäkjiääk Plural of Jiäkjiäk being bad or ugly as explained above.

Jiöl To add some water while cooking when water component is about to run short.

Jiöm To take a mouthful or take anything from a great quantity grains, food, water etc.

Jiöny 1. To mark someone with bad statement or answer. 2. To scratch with fingers the itching parts.

Jiööny A person who scratch or who is suffering of skin disease.

Jiönyjiöny He/she who has a rough way of answering people

Jiöp To cut wood with axe.

Jiööp A person who cuts trees with axe.

Jiöör 1. A large ulcer wound. 2. A large area or part of swamp.

Jiöt Difficult to overcome, cross, jump etc.

Jiötjiöt Being difficult to do, overcome, cross etc.

Jiööth Plural of Jɔw being the sounds, noises or voices of anything.

Jiöwni Plural of Jiöw being a casterated bull as explained above.

Juäh Yes or ok being an old pronunciation which is still being practised in Western Nuer Region.

Juäk 1. Chicken pox disease that infects children. 2. The genital organ of both male and female. 3. A way of holding a stick in the middle of it.

Juäkjuäk State of becoming fat as with the bull,ox etc.

Juäl Tail of any type including feather of birds.

Juäŋ To have rough behaviour with people particularly children rough or women.

Juäŋjuäŋ A person who behaves in that rough manner.

Juäñäñ State of being quite difficult to be handled or controlled.

Juät Plural of Jua̱t being a feather of a bird as explained above.

Juäth 1. A kind of fish which is eaten when roasted. 2. A part of the hand or arm between wrist and elbow.

Juäthjuäth Any thing or whatever like hand size.

Jöl State of having added water to the cooking utensil in order to get cooked.

Jöp Having much to do with cutting of wood with axe eg. Jöp jiɛn ɛ lat: Wood cutting is a task.

K

Kac 1. To jump up or over something. 2. To lie or to tell untrue stories or message. 3. To bite with teeth as when eating or fighting some one. 4. The situation of cow mating where an ox jumps on a cow.

Kaccik A donkey in Western Nuer Muul in other parts of Nuer land.

Kackac 1. State of telling lies or untrue stories.2. State of having something becomes quite difficult to operate or undo.

Kak 1. Farm, field or garden. 2. A small animals of cat family with whitish tail. 3. A sharp pain as that happens after a fresh wound. 4. The collision of two spears as when thrown at ago to one direction. 5. To open a guord in order to make utensils.

Ka̱k To spit dirty substance after coughing.

Ka̱a̱k Plural of Kääk it is either a person who goes hunting or who looks for troubles as explained below.

Kal 1. Fence of both wood, stalks, bricks etc. 2. A place where people go in order to eat meat, fish or whatever except milk. 3. A person who lacks cattle.

Ka̱l To go to visit the bride or bridegroom, before or after the settlement of marriage.

Kaal 1. Plural of Kal those people who either go out to eat meat or who lack cattles as explained above. 2. State of having what to do with place where people go to eat meat or fish. eg. Cɛ wä kaal: He has gone to eat meat or fish.

Ka̱a̱l One who visits bridegroom Ka̱L as explained above.

Kam Distance, space or an open ground.

Km? 1. Plural of Kam being the distance or space as explained above. 2. A device which is used for torturing the criminals or wrong doers. 3. State of becoming hard like a dead log of wood. 4. Slang for a powerful person.

Kamkam A poverty way of life or living with difficulties where one **depend** on begging here and there.

Kamkaam Having much to do with poverty life. eg Næy tœtœ täkæ kamkaam ni thaar: *These people were in poverty life* oæ *begging since last year.*

Kampiny To be in between two legs, two people or buildings etc.

Kan To hang something or place it against a strong body or a pole..

Kán Plural of Kaan a kind of large leaves plant as explained below.

Kaan A kind of plant which has large conical shape leaves.

Kankan State of being in great need of assistance or help.

Kankaan A situation where someone is always in need of help or assistance..

Kaŋ 1. To deceive someone or to tell something which is not true. 2. State of deception or to make someone believes wrong thing.

Kaaŋ 1. A bugle or whatever that produces sounds. 2. A fishing device built in water where fish are traped by allowing them in and get closed in to be caught.

Kaaŋni Plural of Kaaŋ being either bugle or fishing device as explained above.

Kaŋkaŋ A deeper part of the water surface that is considered to be shallow.

Kaŋkaŋni Plural of Kaŋkaŋ being the deeper part of water as explained above..

Kap 1. To hold or carry something on the head, horn or whatever. 2. To help someone to put something on her/his head to carry. 3. Raise or lift a hut thatched roof to be put on the mud wall.

Kar 1. Plural of Kaar being a branch, descendent or tributary of water as explained below. 2. Feeling or sensing the bitterness of salt. 3. To carry or hang on the shoulder etc. 3. To have branches or buds as a sign of growth or reproduction..

Kaar 1. A branch, decendent or tributary. See Kar. 2. Sickness usually fever of all sorts.

Ka̱a̱r Plural of Kär to cut fish or meat into long thin pieces in order to dry as explained below.

Karkar 1. A sort of feeling about salty taste. 2. A feeling of pain as when sick. 3. A kind of shoes that does not cover the foot.

Kartum The real or original name of present Khartoum, the capital of Sudan. It is a combination of two parts Kar and Tum the first is the tributaries as explained above. The second is the confluence or the meeting point of any two, three or more different things eg. water routes, branches or decendents. See Tum.

Katɛ Salt.

Kath 1. Plural of Kaw being the newly married woman as explained below. 2. Plural Kaw that is the chest organ of both animal or human being.

Kaath Stage of being young wife or newly married woman.

Ka̠a̠th Plural of Käth that is a foot step as explained below..

Kathkath State of walking or talking any how as when one is not well in mind.

Kaw 1. The chest organ of animal or human being. 2. A newly married woman or young wife.

Kaway 1. A person who does not cultivate food even for himself. 2. A small bell which is hanged on the waist.

Kawayni Plural of Kaway being both human being or bell as explained above.

Kay 1. State of having got satified by taking water when thirsty. 2. An opened forest or area where people go for along call or defecating wastes. 3. The first born child or the child born first to the family.

Kaay The outer scale of Thow being an Acacia Nilotica fruit.

Kayni Plural of Kay being an opened area in the forest as explained above.

Kek Embankment or building a bank of wall to stop flood or any water.

Kekni Plural of Kek being embankment of wall stop flood as explained above.

Kem The way the blind person moves about.

Kemkem 1. The state of the blind person moves about. 2. A state where one says anything.

Ken A cow bird which is whitish in colour.

Ke̠n Plural of Ken being the cow bird as explained above.

Keŋ The frames or borders of the wall or whatever.

Keŋkeŋ A place at the fire place where native pipe charcoal and tobacco are kept.

Kep State of weeping, talking or singing all the time.

Keer The edges of anything that hold or occupy an area. Eg Keer Buol: Edge of drum dance.

Ket 1. A small bird of the Luɛtluɛt family. 2. To compose song criticising someone. 3. A cow or cattle attending turn to take them to grazing.

Ketket The same name for such a bird as explained above.

Keth A taste of food material about to go bad or decay.

Kethketh State of having such taste as when eating or drinking.

Kew 1. To involve or implicate someone into troubes. 2. The appearance of ears on the head, see Kew Jith.: Having his/her ears standing up vertically.

Kewkew State of being troublesome or troubles shooter.

Kɛ A suffix meaning with eg. Bia wä kɛ jɛ. You go with him/her/it.

Kɛa 1. A divorced woman. 2. A first born child or baby eg. Nɛmɛ a ciɛk mi kɛa, kä nœmœ a jɛn kɛa mandiɛn: This is a divorce woman,and this is their mother first born. 3. A seed of gourd or pumkin etc.

Kɛat A small or bushy type tree.

Kɛaw A small game.

Kɛc 1. A small bird which acts as a pest and feeds on grains. 2. Anger, bitter feeling or annoyance. 3. Bitter taste of anything eatable. 4. A kind of trees which grows along water ways, rivers and distches. 5. A measurement for grains or whatever in the market.

Kɛ́c Plural of Kɛc being a bird or whatever except the taste as explained above.

Kɛɛc Having much to do with Kɛc as in eg Tææ rɛy kɛɛc. : *He/she is inside bushy trees.*

Kɛcwaŋ A kind of fish.

Kɛckɛc State of having quite bitter taste.

Kɛdi 1. A word which is said to he/she stands on the way to let a path. Eg Kædi gweny ni gat :Let him/her a path. 2. How many or how much? Eg Tœtœ kæ di? : How many are those?

Kɛk 1. Reputation, fame or whatever that keeps memory alive. 2. A scar or a light wound on the skin. 3. To cancel something by crossing.

Kɛak Plural of Kɛk being a scar or to cancel as explained above.

Kɛl 1. Figure one(1). 2. To fry meat, fish or whatever.

Kɛlkɛl One by one, or one after another.

Kɛlkɛɛli Plural of Kælkæl being one by one basis as explained above.

Kɛlɛk nyaŋ A kind of fish.

Kɛliw The whole of or all of it but not part or a piece.

Kɛm 1. A kind of trees which is used for making good sticks for spear. 2. State of very bitter taste.

Kɛ́m Plural of Kɛm being that kind of trees as explained above.

Kɛɛm State of having much to do with Kɛm. eg Rup kɛɛm : Being a village near Ulang town.

Kɛmɛ It is bitter taste.

Kɛn 1. They, being third person plural.eg Kæn a ni ? Where are they? 2. To hit or beat some grain bundles in order to separate grains from the stalks. 3. To beat, lash, whip with stick or whatever as a punishment. 4. Negative as in Kæn kæ (n) ben : They have not come.

Kɛɛn The newly ripened grains which are struck by beating the grain **bundles.**

Kɛnɛ A word meaning he/she with. Eg Cæ ben kænæ man : He/she came with his/her mother.

Kɛnykɛny A short live pain which effects or attacks both human beings and animals.

Kɛaŋ The moon light in darkness.

Kɛɛŋ To have fire starts glowing, giving energy or burning up. Eg: Cɛ mac kɛɛŋ.The fire is burning.

Kɛŋ To have fire glowing seriously for cooking, warming or lighting etc.

Kɛŋkɛŋ 1. A state of having something is full of water as in flooding. 2. State of being very feverish when sick.

Kɛp To take liquid food such as milk or soup food using a spoon or any other eating devices.

Kɛpɛ A piece of a bright colour skin of a goat, or a monkey that is worn around the legs above the feet during drum dance.

Kɛpkɛp State of frequent drinking much water when one has eaten good food or when sick.

Kɛr 1. The first rains after long dryness. 2. A colour of a cattle eg. Kɛr riaal. Kɛr jio̱o̱k. Kɛr dööl. 3. Single of Kɛɛr being divisions of a byre by lines of poles in order to accommodate cattle or cows at night. 4. To search by checking water or any liquid with fingers, spoons or sticks.

5. A decorated piece of iron or metal which is put in a hole on the lower lip. 6. A piece of iron or metal device for cutting or decorating the iron or metallic tools of black smith. 7. To stir cow dung in order to get dried for the evening Smoking which scares the insects. 8. To make or show the boundaries of a building or a fence. 9. A mark or scar on the body or on the ground. 10.To start a topic as when talking with a friend most probably a girl.

Kɛɛr 1. Along stick which is used for stiring cow dung so as to get dried. 2. A disease which affects the legs, etc. see kɛrkɛr.

Kɛrkɛr 1. A disease which affects the legs as explained above. 2. A sound of a small fish that is hit in fishing pool.

Kɛt 1. A song composed for abusing someone when rivaling over a lady or whatever dispute between clan, section or tribe. 2. To swim or the art of swimming. 3. To sing a song. 4. The art of decorating metallic or gourd utensils. 5. Plural of Kɛat a kind of small or bush tree as explained above.

Kɛɛt 1. A stick of any type or height, size or length. 2. Having much to do with bushy tree eg. ɛ kɛɛt mi tah ræy kɛɛt: It is a stick in bushy trees.

Kɛtni Plural of Kɛɛt being a stick as explained above.

Kɛth 1. Iron or metallic rusting with water. 2. Pancreas, that gland which releases insulin to help the body uses food. 3. A ritual which is performed when one murdered someone or killed him.

Kɛɛth 1. State of being quite rusted eg. Cɛ kɛɛth ræy juaacni :.It got rusted in the grass. 2. Cow or bull urines etc.eg Wia gamæ kææth:*You go and collect cow urines.*

Kɛw 1. State of standing up for long time.eg Guicæ cuñæ kæw: Look he/she stands up for long time. 2. To fry some food, usually meat or fish in a pan. See Kæl.

Kɛɛw Plural of Kɛaw being the small game as explained above.

Kɛwkɛw 1. Style of walking along in shallow water. 2. A person who causes troubles with anybody near him /her.

Kɛy 1. A water plant that exhibits colourful flowers where its seeds are eaten in hunger or famine. 2. Plural of Kæàh being both first born baby, seed and as well divorce woman.eg Næmæ æ kæah, kä titi kæy bææl kænæ män: This is a first born and these are sorghum seeds and a divorced woman. 3. The borders of each farm or field to its adjacent ones.

Kɛyɛ A kind of plants which is eaten as a wild vegetable.

Kic 1. A disease which affects human being and his animals. 2. A type of beads which has green bluish colour. 3. Meaning nothing or minute as in Kic. Eg Cɛ thil lɛ kic : there is nothing at all.

Kìc Plural of Kic being a type of beads as explained above.

Kickic 1. Being quite minute or meaningless. 2. Ạ slang for a helpless or hopeless item.

Kiɛl To cough or coughing disease.

Kik 1. To mediate in love or friendship making between young people. 2. To add some grass to already thatched roof. 3. To put on something In a shrine.

Kiik 1. A person who helps or mediates in love making or friendship

between two or more young people. 2. A person who does not pronounce words easily–stammer. See Giik.

Kikkik State of being quite stout, short and fat.

Kil 1. A large huge and short animal with two horns on its nose or Rhino. 2. A large fish eating long legs bird with a long beak and a bag like dangling part below its head.

Ki̱l Plural of Kil being that bird as explained above. eg. Ruoc Ki̱l luo̱th.

Kilkil A whooping cough which affects young ones.

Kim 1. Doctor, a distorted Arabic language word for a doctor of medicine (Hakim). 2. To start the topic as in Kim piny.

Ki̱m A silence deep weeping condition of unhappiness.

Kimkim State of being quite stable or stability of anything.

Kin A sound which stops cow, bull or cattle after showing restlessness. Ịt is made by tuisting one tongue and force air out.

Kinkin A state of body shaking as when one is fainting or feeling cold.

Kiny To press the itching part by hand or fingers.

Kinykiny A sort of series itching on the body or eyes.

Kip 1. To cut with an axe, knife, spear, spade etc.Eg. Wer kipni rony ræy

Kakä : You go and cut stalks in the farm. 2. Whatever is used for cutting or chopping down things.

Kir 1. A type of wild trees which has very strong long thorns. 2. The water way or river. 3. To beat the drum in early morning as an indicator or announcement. 4. To offer sacrifices to the dead or ghosts offering goats, cows, tobacco or beer.

K̲i̲ir 1. State of having much to do with Kir as a tree eg. Kuok k̲i̲ir: Kir thorn. 2. God of river or of water where many Nuer of Jikäny descend from. Eg Kœn gaat Kììr täh næy thin: We the sons of Kiir are there.

K̲irk̲ir The feeling of fever, sickness or fear.

Kit 1. To start the song to be chorused by people. 2. To make holes when sawing seeds. 3. The bright colour of cow, cloth or whatever.
4. A crocodile or an alegator tail. 5. Failure to go on swimming in the middle of water, or river. 6. To become clear after pollution. 7. The appearance of fats on the soup.

Kiit The person who starts the song or verses of Ŋundɛng Bong Doctrine. * Kiit palä : He who starts prayers. * Kiit Buɔ̱l He who sings drum songs. * Kiit Cio̱kä: He who starts war confrontation songs. * Kiit Diit He who starts a šong.

K̲i̲it 1. Plural of Kiit being he who starts prayers or songs as explained above. 2. State of much or series laughting eg. Cɛ kiit kɛ to̱k: He/she overwhelmingly laughter. 3. State of not being able to continue swimming any longer.

Kitkit A series or continuous laughter.

Kith To throw something such as flies,or fishing net.

Kiith Slang for trouble shooter that forces him/her to cause troubles eg ɛ jæ cɛ kiith: Do not allow him/her to be a trouble shooter.

Kithkith That is any how or any way of movements.

Kiw 1. To start digging, show the frame or the borders of a building, fence etc. 2. A sound of spear or metallic tools. See Gim. 3. To pass stool as when with diarrhea.

Kiwkiw 1. Weeping that goes on for quite a long time(children or babies). 2. The noise which is heard when digging, milking or beating drum.

Ko We/us eg. Ba̱ ko wä. Bia kä ko: We will go. Come to us.

Koah Dry piece of cow dung in wilderness. See Kɔw.

Koac Whatever is sewn by hands not ready made.

Koa̱c 1. Stage when a human being female releases menstruation as

a sign of maturity. 2. To become cold or cool as when sun sets or when the fire is put off in cold weather or in winter.

Koak 1. Whatever is bought not natural product or home property. 2. A crack on the dry soil or clay. See Bak. 3. A grave, where dead body is buried.

Kohààl Plural of Kɔhàl being the calf as explained below.

Koam 1. Having much to do with Kɔm being a chair, any seat or throne. 2. Slang for much talk where participants talk a lot.

Koa̱m 1. To beat in order to separate grains from bundles.2. Continuous whipping or beating for quite a long time.

Koap 1. A type of smell such as soap, perfume etc.. 2. Ạ water plant that floats on water.

Kopkop A state of having powerful smell such as bathing soap or perfume.

Koar 1. A type of trees that has long whitish thorns. 2. Plural of Kɔr being appendage to someone who may be a chief, and Member of Parliament etc.eg æ raan koar kuär: *He/she is an appendage to a chief.*

Koat 1. A kind of trees which fruits are soaked to make soft drink. 2. That is climbable or to be reached by climbing. 3. To put or place something somewhere to hide.

Koc 1. State of being quite cold either in winter or rainy days. 2. To be hard due to being dried.

Kockoc State of becoming quite hard due to dryness.

Kok The arts of buying and selling of goods or whatever.

Ko̱hk State of being broken such as a utensil, pot, skull, canoe etc.

Kol 1. To start grinding grains or grain particles to make food. 2. A type of plant that is weeded out of the farm. 3. To dodge something such as a spear or stick.

Kom The back or outer cover of anything tree, maize bundle, stalk etc.

eg. Kom jiaath kie Kom rɔɔny:The outer part of tree or the outer part of stalks.

Ko̱hm Slang for any helpless being such as babies children and even adult.

Kööm A person who has long, which implies being giant or huge.

Kömköm 1. State of involving oneself in troubles for sake others. 2. Being quite huge or high to sit on or to lie on.

Komkom State of being poor or poverty state where one lives in great shortages of food materials.

Kony The state of heavy rainfall which destroys the sown seeds in a farm.

Kop 1. To talk a lot as when angy as with a child when beaten.eg ɛŋu kopi mo? *Why do you talk alone?* 2. Plural of Koap a kind of water plant which floats on water as explained above.

Kopkop 1. State of being happy and laughing throughout. 2. State of being very small, short and fat.

Ko̱r Fighting, war, quarrel etc.

Kornyuot The month of June or the six month of the year. See Nyuot.

Korwaay A plant that has seeds with thorns.

Ko̱t A shield, a piece of hard skin of crocodile, buffalo etc. which protects from sharp points such as spears,swords etc in a war.

Ko̱th 1. Plural of Köth being a type of marine grass which is chewed by children as explained below. 2. Ạ type of grass which is used for making utensils see Pät. 3.Plural of Kööth being the release of air or gases as explained below.

Kohw Th plural of Kɔah being the cow dung when dried in wilderness as explained above

Ko̱w 1. A wooden device or utensil for pounding grains etc. 2. Having nice smell or taste.

Kowkow 1. State of being shy as when with people you do not know or in-laws. 2. State of being not well fixed or fitted. See Kɔtkɔt.

Koay A wooden pole that is used for roofing a hut or a byre.

Koy Plural of Koay being a pole which is used for making hut roof as explained above.

Kɔha̱l Calf of a cow.

Kɔŋ The behavior of a child to welcome his/her father or mother back home.

Kɔaaŋ Plural of Kœaŋ being beer or alcohol as explained below.

Kɔaŋ Beer, alcohol, whatever causes intoxicant.

Kɔap A type of marine plant that floats on the river or water surface.

Kɔar A type of trees that has long whitish thorns.

Kɔ̱a̱th Plural of Kɔ̱th being kicking of one foot on a stone while walking.

Kɔth To kick one foot on a stone,wood or iron when in a hurry.

Kɔc 1. Cold, cool not hot. 2. State of being quite hard.

Kɔɔc Being quite cool or cold eg. Ɛŋu cɛ kɔɔc inɛ? *Why it became cool like this*?

Kɔckɔc State of being very cold or cool as that with ice.

Kɔackɔaac Plural of kœckœc being cool or cold as explained above

Kɔk 1. To sell something or somebody. 2. Late stages of cow conception to deliver calf.

Kɔhk 1. To up root, to take away the shell from main parts (nuclear or nut). 2. Having much to do with the hole or grave Koak. Eg Tɛr mi wäät

kɛ raan kohk:.A hatred which amounts to digging out a dead person from the grave.

Kɔ̱hk Slang for an aged person or a broken container or skull.

Kɔ̱hkkɔ̱hk 1. State of being quite broken as with utensils. 2. To please people in order to gain respect or to be accepted.

Kɔ̱l To fan air in order to cool or to make energy for heating up.

Kɔl 1. The hard fat meat of the cow or animal. 2. A type of plant that is weeded out of a farm or a field.

Kɔhl An air bag for fanning characoal fire in Black Smith Forge.

Kɔhɔl A cow tail device for fanning or waving during songs or verses of

Ŋundeng Böŋ.

Kɔhɔli Plural of Kɔhɔl being cow tail as explained above.

Kɔ̱lkɔ̱l A kind of worm which has several leg like parts for movements.

Kɔ̱lkɔ̱li Plural of Kœlkœl being a worm that moves as explaine above.

Kɔlkɔl A slang for a person who denies whatever he/she says..

Kɔlpiew A kind of creeping plants,where its fruits are used for playing games of spearing training.

Kɔ̱hm 1. An insect of any type or kind.2. A slang for slippery person.

Kɔm 1. A seat, chair, stool etc. 2. A slang for power, authority, and governance.

Kɔn We, first speaker. Eg Wanɛ kœn dial: we all go or let us go.

Kɔ̱ɔ̱n A kind of disease which attacks both human and animal's feet or hooves.

Kɔnykɔny State of being not very smooth surface or ground.

Kɔŋ 1. The others eg. Tin kɔ̱ŋ ɛni? Where are the others? 2. To show respect to one father or mother brothter or sister or whoever, by running to him/her when she or he comes to one sight particularly when coming from a journey or a visitor guest, newcomer etc.

Kɔŋkɔŋ State of rather high or big object or very fast growing thing.

Kɔhp Stage of swelling due to decaying, fatness or when very angery.

Kɔr After, to follow or to come behind. Eg Wia kœr morun: Go after your mother.

Kɔ̱hr 1. To open hot food to have it cooled so that one can eat it. 2. To separate any wet substance in order to have it dried eg. Cow dung, flour, grains etc.

Kɔhr The waste part of the newly prepared skin for sleeping.

Kɔɔr A sickness which Nuer believe it is caused by having had sex with one father wife.

Kɔrkɔr The part of skin which is cut off from the main skin eg Guicɛ ɛ bi widɛ cie wic yakä mi kap kœrkœr: look at him,his head is just like the head of a hyena which carrying such cut off edges of skin.

Kɔ̱rkɔ̱r State of being less compact soil, and easy to break.

Kɔryɔm The early stage of locust when it moves in swarms to attack fields.

Kɔht 1. A kind of creeping plants that climbs a strong stem.or tree 2. A piece of skin or a small animal fur which is used for sitting. 3. Plural of Kɔ̱t being bird wing as explained below.

Kɔt 1. Plural of Kɔat a kind of tree which has fruit that have bitter and sour taste. 2. A tuisted or a knitted feathers which is used for fanning or scaring away flies. 3. To hide something such as stick, food materials etc. 4. State of having food got burned in cooking process such as meat, fish etc.

Kɔ̱t A wing of a bird.

Kɔtkɔt State of having something not well fitted such as roof or whatever.

Kɔ̱th Kicking of one foot on something unknowningly when walking.

Kɔ̱hth To check the fire by stiring it with a stick

Ku 1. An article which means just. eg. Ku ben. Just come 2. A suffix of second person belonging eg. Gaatku, Kuaku, Biiyniku etc. your children, your property, your clothes etc.

Kua You (at least two) for just eg, kua wä, kua ben, kua riŋ: *You just go, you just come, you just run,*

Kua̱ First person speaker eg. kua̱ wä?, kua̱ ben?, kua̱ riŋ?. *I just go?, I just come? I just run?*

Kuac 1. Leopard. 2. Leopard skin court where cases of argument are decided according to rituals or traditional belief. 3. Scales of a fishs, human skin or whatever is cleaned out from a tree or wood.. 4. To scale a fish or remove the scales of the fish. 5. To clean a wildland to make a farm. 6. A colour of a cattle or animal eg.– Kuac riaal – Kuac thia̠a̠ŋ – Kuac nyaaŋ

Kuak 1. Property, luggage, tools or whatever of personal belongings. 2. To hold one own hands around the chest in cold weather. 3. To walk with hands on the shoulders with friends.

Kual 1. To steal, take without permission someone property eg cɛ wä kual.ça̧ lœ kual.: He/she went to steal. I̧ was after stolen. 2. Stolen property or things or loots.eg Titi kæ kuak ti kual : These are stolen property.

Kualkual State of stealing habit or style of taking without permission. See Kuel.

Kuan 1. Let us. eg. Kuan mi̠th.: Let us eat. 2. Plural of Kuän being the food of grain flour, but now it has become any type of food materials.

Kuany 1. To pick from the ground. 2. To get or find a lost item. 3. To choose or select from many items. 4. Anything that is found after it got lost. 5. Slang for a child that is got without paying dowry.

Kuanykuany State of poverty or poor condition. See Kuany :That is living by collecting whatever food left or thrown away by well to do families.

Kuaŋ 1. To be shy when one with new or strange people to whom one shows respect. 2. A game which is played while swimming in a river, as in Kuaŋ Lɛɛk

Kuaŋkuaŋ A person who keeps himself very shy in respected places of in–laws, guests etc.

Kuar To separate whatever items from the source, eg. milk,weeds etc. in water eg. Kuar lieth, kuar bɛl, kuar juac, kuar etc.

Kua̠r Plural of Kuäär being a chief or anyone who is responsible as explained below.

Kuaar 1. The substance that get formed on the top of hot milk. 2. The weeded grass from the farm or field.

Kuat 1. A chain of iron which is worn around the neck. 2. A chain that connects two pieces of traditional pipe eg. Kuat Tööny. Traditional pipe chain. 3. A disease that attacks or affects goats and human beings. 4. State of being not knowing what is happening around you.

Kuatkuat Stage of trembling for fear or when feverish.

Kuath 1. To scare insects from one own body or food materials. 2. State of having cooking fire escalated out side the cooking area. 3. Slang for having paid no notice of what is happening around you..

Kuathkuath State of nothingness to stop or not available at all. Eg ɛ caŋɛ kuath

kuath : Nothing remains in the place.

Kua̱w State of being vulnerable to disease or whatever. Eg ɛ puœny kua̱w.

Kuay Plural of kuɛa being descendants, off springs or seeds.

Kuuk Itching or whatever cause itching eg. Kuuk ɛ hä kie ta̱a̱kɛ Kuuk: *I am itching or I have itching disease.*

Kuc 1. When referring to the cattle or skin separation eg. Ta̱a̱ kuc hɔ̱ɔk: *I was separating cows.* 2. Plural of Kuoc a kind of tree species as explained early under singular.as kuoc.

Kuec To stay alone in the wilderness. To clean a wild land for a farm.

Kueec The tool which is used for cleaning the rough surface.

Kueeh A colour of a cow where black dominates with whitish on the head.

Kuel 1. To steal,to remove or take things with out permission. 2. A type of trees with large leaves. 3. A copper ring usually red or yellowish in colour. See Läŋ. 4. A line which is drawn to separate two warring factions not to cross. It is marked by Earthen Chief. 5. A kind of smell which is a result of burning hairs or feathers.

Kueel 1. A person who steals, a thief or a burglar. 2. Having much to do with "Kuel" tree eg. Thar kueel :Under kuel tree.

Kueem A stick like wood which is used for ordering grass when thatching.

Kuen 1. Stomach troubles or constipation. 2. To clean a bone by picking meat parts. 3. State of having much to do with marriage. eg Wà guäth kuen : *I am going to marriage place.* 4. To count whatever available.

Kueen Bridegroom.

Kueny 1. State of being quite restless such as cow. 2. A bone of tortoise. See Kueny kuët.

Kueeny State of being quite clean where water runs down very fast when bathing.

Kueŋ 1. To put something on or down. 2. To escape falling down as when hit with a stick.

Kuer 1. An opened plain ground without trees and tall grass. 2. A tall log sticks like for pushing a canoe in water full of grass. 3. State of throwing a spear, stick or shoot bultet, at some one or something. 4. To produce fruits such as trees or vegetable plants.

Kueer To wrestle or wrestling game.

Kuet To remove the testicals from a male calf or goat.

Kueth 1. An insult, rebuke or a court decision that one of the two is guilty or has no right. 2. Plural of Kuey being both the bird and cow that share the same colour.

Kueeth 1. A name of a person borned after a series insults between the parents or clan. 2. Plural of Kueth as explained above. 3..A person who lost his upper teeth.See Nya̱a̱r.

Kuew Whistling by tuisting lips to make such noise or sound, usually among the nomads. See Luou.

Kuey 1. A colour where the body is dominated by one colour except the face,or the head of a cow or a bird, which is always whitish. 2. A bird that has the same colour which feeds on catching fish from water surface.. 3. State of being very little,small or being few quantities.e g Titi kuey

kɛ:These are few.

Kuɛa A seed,off spring or descendant. See Kuay.

Kuɛak To have eyes developed after birth such as puppy or young dog.

Kuɛar To go and collect fire wood for cooking purpose.eg Mama cæ wä Kuæar: *My mother went to collect fire wood.*

Kuɛat Tortoise.eg Pal jàlæ kæ kuæat: Pal is carrying a tortoise.

Kuɛc 1. To clear wild forest or soil for cultivation. 2. To clean woods to make useful materials. 3. To prepare a log to make sticks, pegs etc. 4. Very strong and hard. Eg Næ mæ kal mi kuæc : This is a strong fence.

Kuɛckuɛc State of becoming strong or hard.

Kuɛk 1. The young locust swarm where its attack of fields was used For naming a generation in Eastern Nuer people as a memory of that year. 2. To peel or separate maize grains from the bundle or fruits, to clean the outer cover before use. 3. To pull off one own hands after greeting a friend or when holding something tightly.

Kuɛl 1. Plural of Kuël being the star as explained below. 2. An opened hole on the roof or whatever that allows rays or light to enter into dark room or space.

Kuël A night star that appears in the dark night.

Kuɛɛl Plural of Kueel being he/she who steals as explained above.

Kuɛlkuɛl The appearance of decoration in a special patterns or manner.

Kuɛm 1. To hit something continuously when one is to shell the nuts .2 To level grass or to unify it when thatching a hut. 3. To break big stones to make small pieces of stones to suit the building purpose.

Kuɛɛm A disease that affects human limbs by causing sharp pain.

Kuɛn 1. Marriage, 2. To count or read, 3. Style of thatching a temporarily shelter.

Kuɛɛn Countable or what can be counted.

Kuɛnkuɛn A temporary hut, shelter in cattle camp or makeshift.

Kuɛŋ Jogging or to slow down running.

Kuɛŋkuɛŋ State of being quite active and not idle.

Kuɛr Plural of both Kuer being an opened ground,a log or a tall stick for pushing canoe in watery grass.

Kuɛrkuɛr The line of back bone of human being or animal.

Kuɛt 1. To kick with foot or legs as with human being or cattle. 2. A rejected calf due to being big enough to continue sucking. 3. A crack on a wooden, bone or a tool. See Tool.

Kuɛtkuɛt The movement of goats or calves when tied down.

Kuic 1. Lack of knowledge or ignorance of events or news. 2. The other side of anything eg. River bank, food container, hut etc.

Kuie Small, tiny. See Mi tɔt.

Kuik A type of vulture or eagle eg. Kuik Cuɔr.

Ku̱ik A sound of gas when being released through anus.

Kuil Smell of burning feathers or hairs.

Ku̱il Constipation or stomach troubles

Ku̱i̱il Severe stomach pain or constipation.

Kuin 1. To give very little of something. eg ɛ ŋu la muci ɛ kuin œ? : Why do you give very little that? 2. To make something strong and straight such as a string or rope. 3. To clean by picking and eating the meaty parts of a bone.

Kui̱n To make ready to shoot an arrow from a bow.

Kuinkuin 1. A person who does not give big quantity, but very little. 2. A small fish that does not swallow the snare but eats bits by bits from it.

Kuiny 1. A sudden jumping either for fear or in a dance.2. State of being restless.

Kuiiny Restless cow that refuses to get milked or to be tied down.

Kuinykuiny State of being restless when being milked or handled.

Kui̱nykui̱ny State of being quite clean from dirts.

Kuiŋ State of being means or he/ she who gives very little.

Kuir The art of throwing a weapon,stick, spear, gun shot etc.

Kui̱r A kind of disease which attacks goats or sheep.

Kuit Having much to do with Kuɛt castration. eg. Gac cæ wä kuit: Gac went to castrate.

Kuiit A person who is an expert in removing animal testacles such as goats, rams, bulls or male calves.

Kuith 1. To throw very far, to jump very high. 2. A sorghum bundle thrown off by wind as in Kuith thuɔ̱l.

Kuk 1. Persuasion or to force someone to do what he does not want to do. 2. A sound or noise of something hits an object very hard. See Kuok. 3. State of being very short and fat as with cow tail eg. Ɛ dhur me Kuk kie kukkuk : A compact short tail.

Kuuk A disease which causes itching on the whole body.

Kukkuk The continuous sound of hitting or shooting in a distance eg. Ɛŋu ta̱ kukuk ɔ?: What makes such sound or noise?

Kul 1. A piece of well carved bone which is worn around the neck, as an ornament long time ago. 2. To close up fingers or hands when hiding something. 3. A kind of animal known as warthog or wild dog.

Kulkul State of having hands closed up. eg. Palɛ ɛŋu tee kulkul kɛ baŋ ɔ? Leave him why does he/she close up his/her hands for nothing.

Kum To close or cover up something with lids or whatever. eg. Kum thokdu. Kum pi. Kum thɔ̱ŋ. Kum kuän etc.: Close your mouth, close water,close soil grinder device, close food.

Kuum Whatever is used for covering anything or human body. It can be a lid for container. It can be a piece of cloth or blanket for human being.

Kumɛ 1. Government, a distorted Arabic word Hakumɛ 2. A magical worm like organism that is forced out by a witchdoctor.

Kumɛni Plural of Kumæ being such organism as explained above..

Kuumni Plural of Kuum being whatever is used for covering as explained above.

Kumkum 1. A noise that is heard when people or whatever is running about inside a room.corridors or verandas eg. Ɛŋa ta̠a̠ kumkum ɔ ?: Who is making such noise? 2..A section of Burun tribe.

Kun 1. Mouse – rat. 2. A suffix which shows people belonging eg. Kuakkun.: Your property. Bɛlkun: Your grains. Duelkun: Your houses etc. 3. A slang for a very clever woman who keeps things usually food in a clever way for quite along time.

Kuny Plural of Kuɔ̠ny being burial of human body or whatever. eg. Tee Kuny nath: He was in people burials.

Kuŋ To start or the first sign of luck as when fishing eg. Cɛ kuŋ kɛ yiew.

Kur 1. Plural of Kuɔ̠r being figure 100 (One hundred). 2. Nodes of stalks of sugar or sorghum. as explained below. 3. A colour of a cow which is dominated by whitish with black spots on the head and back parts. 4. A powerful delicious taste.eg Kurɛ kur.: It is ever delicious. 5. To lull or soothe a baby in order to sleeps.

Kuur State of being clean hands in doing something eg. Ciek mi kuur. *Cleaned hands woman.*

Kut 1. A small dog or a puppy. 2. To take hold of a baby in cold weather.

Kutkut 1. A rolled crude tobacco which is smoked by natives who do not have manufactured ones. 2. A maize bundle which is put in fire before peeling it.

Kuut He who behaves in chivalry like bridegroom.

Kutdɛɛt A type of plants which covers the farm soil as weed.

Kuoc 1. To separate things or animals. 2. The lower part of the leg. 3. To remove the skin of the penis.

Kuok 1. Persuasion to do something,or make it fit. 2. A noise when one hits something or releases gases through anus. 3. The back part of human head

Kuook 1. A great need to smoke tobacco, when one is addicted to it. 2. A Nuer leader who had disappeared long ago where many think and belief to be the present Luou tribe of Kenya.

Kuokkuok The noise of hitting something hard.

Kuol 1. To go on raiding to collect animals from enemy. See Kuel – 2. To change or disway someone in order to tell him/her something alone or secretly.

Kuool He who goes and collects cattle by raiding neighbours.

Kuòòl Plural of Kuool being a cattle raider as explained above.

Kuom 1. Murmuring due to injustice or mismanagement done to someone. 2. Very short, fat and thick cow. 3. State of being exactly done as in Ɛ kuom inɛ.

Kuomkuom 1. A dried grass which the cattle chew in marshes during grazing. 2. State of being quite short, fat and thick.

Kuon To abstain oneself from someone belongings or property.

Kuoon State of having taken an abstention decision eg. Pälɛ cɛ kuoon: Leave him/her for he/she has abstained.

Kuonkuoon State of behavior where one looks unconcerned or being aloof.

Kuony 1. Too much rainfall that destroys crops. 2. To bury someone or something.. 3. Sunset, moon or any other star (s).

Kuonykuony A style of walking when one is suffering of legs or foot pains.

Kuot A taste of food or smell.

Kuotkuot 1. Having that delicious smell or taste.2. A noise which is made by a cat, dog or a human being very angry.

Kuoth 1. God, Almighty. See Cäk.eg Ruac Kuoth : God message. 2. To blow air in order to make fire burns.eg Wer kuoth mac: Go and blow the air to the fire. 3. To whistle bugle or horn to alert people or as music.eg Ber kuoth Kaaŋ : *Çome and whistle the bugle*. 4. To cool hot food so as to eat it properly. 5. To blow in air through cow genital organ to stimulate it to release milk. This Nuer device is and still proves useful.eg Kuuth ber kuoth yaŋ : Ëxpert of cow blowing come and blow the cow. 6. State of anger where one blows out much air as a sign of anger.

Kuooth 1. Godliness or state of being Godly. 2. State of having a wed thing got dried a little such as clothes, hairs, body etc.

Kuow State of being allergic to diseases

Kuɔc The plural of Kuoc being separation of cattles or the lower parts **of** the legs as explained above.

Kuɔɔc 1. The lonely wild buffalo. 2. Slang for aperson who likes to stay alone. 3. A kind of trees. See plural Kuc.

Kuɔk 1. To force or persuade someone or something to accept doing something or let it fit in. 2. The back part of the human head. Plural with stress on (ɔ).

Kuɔ̱ɔ̱k A short live sort of hunger which affects young and aged people.

Kuɔl 1. A type of creeping plants which seeds or fruits are offered for sacrifices, as part of rituals in Nuer social settings. 2. A cow colour where the body is red but with some whitish spot on both sides of the belly. See Köl. 3. To do a minor operation to get out a thorn from one own foot or someone foot.

Kuɔ̱n Having much to do with Kun as a second name eg. Wal Kuɔ̱n. Gac Kuɔ̱n Jok Kuɔ̱n etc.

Kuɔ̱ɔ̱n Plural of Kun being mouse or rat as explained above.

Kuɔny State of getting difficulties in walking.eg Deng cɛ kuœny baa kap

: Ɖeng is already not able to walk,he is to be carried.

Kuɔnykuɔny Walking with difficulties due to sickness.

Kuɔŋ A maggot. See Gatkuœŋ

Kuoŋkuoŋ A size of middle height for cattle and others.

Kuɔr 1. One hundred. 2. A delicious taste food.

Kuɔɔr Dried local food which is prepared for long journey. It is also known as Mankuɔɔr.

Kuɔ̱t 1. Become fat due to well and regular sucking or feeding such as baby or calf. 2. State of chivalry behaviour of bridegroom.

Kuœœt Plural of Kuut being he who shows chivalry behaviour such as bridegroom as explained above.

Kuɔt Delicious smell of food.

Kuɔth A type of fish.

Kuœœth Plural of Kuœth being a type of fish as explained above.

Kä 1. The sound of the twelfth letter of Thok Nath. 2. A suffix which ascertains what you are thinking or intending to eg. Rialikä, Pälikä, Pärikä: Adjust, forgiveness, sudden attack. 3. Means "to" as in "Wa̱a̱ kä Yomding": I am going to Yomding. 4. Means "can" as when one says. "Kä dee wä bä" I can go also. 5. Means "that" as in "Kä ruac ɛmɔ gɔa ɛ " : That talk is good.

Käc 1. Plural of Kac to jump up frequently when in dancing as explained above. 2. State of biting with teeth or the wound made as a result of a bite. 3. The cow condition pains at delivery.

Käckäc Style of walking as when suffering or when in hurry to catch up.

Kääckääc That same style of walking with long strides when in hurry.

Käk 1. The art of opening guord to make utensils. 2. To recall or mention one own ancestors, eg.Käk Lual: Are Chany Choul Geng Walɔk, Lindiit……… Kiir. 3. To go hunting animals for meat, skins ivory tusks etc. 4. The dirts you spit off after coughing.

Kääk 1. A person who goes hunting for games. 2. He/she who opens guords to make utensils 3. Slang for a person who looks for troubles or problematic person. eg. Cu rɔ kääk: Do not hunt yourself to a problem.

Käl 1. Plural of Kal being the fence as explained above. 2. A line of trees in bushy forest.

Kääl A person who visit his/her wife or husband home as marriage rituals and traditions.

Käm To hand over or give something to someone. Eg Käm ni jɛ mac: Give him/her a gun or fire.

Käpiny 1. To put or place something that is being carried on the head down. 2. To take hold of passerby by force.

Kän 1. To miss something or someone. To escape the danger narrowly. 2. To take or pick something. 3. Slang of sexual intercourse. 4. A name for a person who was born where someone missed death or danger marrowly.

Känkän State of being quite shaky or weak as when walking.

Käny 1. The rising of the sun. 2. To ask for the debt (s). 3. To jump towards the speaker(s) 4. Gross misbehavior of a person eg. "ɛŋu ci käny i̱ nɛmɛ?": *Why did you misbehave like this?*

Käŋ Plural of Kääŋ is a short expressive statement as explained below.

Kääŋ A short expressive statement between young men in cattle camp which is said to explain a particular meaning. eg. Tut ɛmɔ, mɔ cɛ riaŋɔ la tharɛ a yienyɛ nikɛ thilik nikɛ thilik.That fellow when satisfied he places his buttock on an iron pole

Käŋkäŋ State of being quite shaky or weak due to sickness.

Käp 1. To take hold of someone or something. 2. The tail of a big fish which is given to a child to roast.

Käpkäp A state of being in great confusion when talking. A person who does not frame what he/she wants to say or tell.

Kär To prepare a fresh meat or fish into long pieces as to get it dries very fast. A long piece of dried meat or fish.

Käär A badge that is worn by chiefs as a sign of authority.

Kät Plural of Käät being eagle bird as explained below

Käät Eagle or that bird which takes by force from people particularly children who do not know much of it.

Kätkät Difficulties in walking particularly with children, babies, sick or aged people.

Kërkër A lizard.

Kërkëri Plural of Kërkër being a lizard as explained above.

Kɛäh A first born baby or child.

Koäy A monthly period or menstruation of human being female.

Kuäk 1. To take or grab as much as possible, usually food, meat,land etc. 2. A type of plants which is used for fermenting milk before making butter.

Kuäkkuäk 1. State of being quick to take something such as food or mother breast. 2. A behavior which shows great love to one mother, father etc.

Kuäl State of having something hidden or to hide it.

Kuäläl State of being in closed condition or wrapped up.

Kuän Food made of grain flour.

Kuähn State of having much to do with flour cooked food eg. Cak kuähn: Food milk

Kuähnɛ The grain flour food substance.

Kuänkuän Ear lobe or that soft fleshy part of the ear.

Kuäŋ State of being not so harsh or difficult in dealing with something or someone.

Kuääŋ To do something very slowly not in harsh manner.

Kuäär muɔn Earth chief.

Kuäär 1. Chief, president,minister etc, or an elderly person. 2. Chieftency or presidency.

Kuät A noise of foot steps heard outside the room at night.

Kuätkuät State of such noise of foot steps by night.

Kuäth 1. Bone marrow. 2. To cover something with either grass, cloth or paper.

Kuäthkuäth Style of behaving where one appears covered up with clothes.

Kuäw To add something usually water, soup etc on dry material.

Kuäwkuäw State of being quite shy or not series in doing something.

Kuäy Early stages of food material decaying smell.

Köc 1. To sew whatever or join two parts with needles and string. 2. To prepare the hut roof by putting poles. 3. To start spearing or shooting someone or something.

Kök 1. A hole on a tree trunk. 2. Selling and buying. 3. Bribing someone to give you what you do not deserve. 4. A sharp pain which is felt in the bone. 5. To make noise or sound when in drum, war, marriage ceremony or happiness.

Köhk Reputation, well known widely or by many people.

Köök A kind of disease which causes sharp pain on the bones.

Kökni Plural of Kök being a hole on a tree trunk as explained above.

Kökkök State of being pure and not mixed with any other blood except one father eg. Gat mi Kökkök: Pure son or child.

Kökköök Plural of Kökkök being pure in blood as explained above.eg Titi gaat ti kököök: These are pure children.

Köl 1. Dominantly brown colour with whitish spots on the belly. 2. To dodge a blow, spear, stick etc. when in fighting. 3. A skin of animal which the early people use for sleeping or sitting on. 4. A slang for any sleeping materials now. 5. State of having got frozen due to much cold temperature, or having sat down in one place for quite a long time.

Kööl Plural of Köl to dodge anything dangerous as explained above. eg Titi kɛ kɛn kööl yiööni :These are the experts who dodge spears.

Kölköl A brown ant that move in group in a long line.

Köm To carry a baby on the hip bone when his/her mother is busy.

Kön 1. To hang up one hand or leg when is paining. 2. State of having the body or part of it becomes stiff due to cold.

Könkön State of being quite hard or stiffness due to series cold.

Köŋ A style of running to welcome someone home being a mother, Father, relative, in-law etc.

Kööŋ Running for a race.

Köp 1. Local food which is made by frying sermented flour of grains. see Gæt. 2. Slang for series walking or running.

Kör 1. Ripening of gourd, pumkin etc. 2. To play sex with male friend. 3. Plural of Köör being the edges of the farmland as explained above. 4. The scale of the horn, tree stem which indicates the ages.

Köör 1. The edge of a farm, skin etc. 2. A fishing device tool that looks like a harpoon.

Kööri 1. Plural of Kör being the scales of horns, trees etc which indicate the age of the animal or tree.2. wars or desputes.

Köt 1. To climb anythingsuch as wall, a ladder, a tree etc. 2. State of putting something out to dry.

Kööt 1. Draught or lack of rains. See Rɛath. 2. What is used for climbing trees, walls etc. 3. Money given to someone to pay as transport in buses,taxis etc. 4. A slang for anything one uses to let him /her to get what she/he actually needs or wants. 5. He/she who climbs, walls etc.eg Wer kööt käli : *Get out fences climber.*

Köötni Plural of Kööt being a device that helps to climb tress or walls as Explained above.

Kötköt Ever dried subistance such as a shell.

Köth 1. A kind of water plants that is chewed by young people in marshes. 2. A kind of water plants which is used for making utensils such as Pät a filter which separates flour from grains particles. 3. State of frequent release of gases or air through anus.

Kööth The actual releasing of air or gas through anus.

L

La 1. An article which is used for specifying or identifying someone or something eg. la ŋa? la mi̱th?: who? Which one? 2. An article which is used for repeating action eg. La wee lät: he/she goes to work. La pɔakɛ. He/she bathes.

Lac To defecate or long call diarrhea. eg Lac cow:: Meaning short call of passing urine.

Laac A person or animal who frequently defecates due to diarrhea.

Lak 1. To wash hands,body or whatever to become clean. 2. A small section of Nuer tribe which lives along River Zaraf in Great Upper Nile Region neighbouring Gaatwaar section. 3. A word that is said for having covered a long distance very fast or quick then expected.

La̱k 1. The liquids or fluides that come out from mouth while one is sleeping or from mouth of a child or baby. 2. A leather belt which is tied around the bull neck or dog neck as decoration.

Laklak Slang for little quantity of water, milk etc. in a container.see Laklaak.

Laklaak Plural of Laklak being little quantity of milk,water etc as explained above.Eg Ci duoth ti laklaak :*Only little quantity that remains.*

Lal A child or baby way of talking meaningless words or sounds.

Lallal A person who keeps on asking for something even when rejected. See Dandan.

Lam 1. To call God, ancestors and spirits to bless the sacrifices or to influence quick recovery of a sick person or whatever that needs recovery or blessing. 2. A type of taste or smell of food items that about to decay or spoil.

La̱m 1 A kind of a smooth skin fish. 2 A word which is used to test the luck, in the second round result.

Lamlam The taste of food that about to decay or spoil.

Lan State of failure to manage, use or handle anything.

Laan State of having failed to manage or handle as in this statement: Ci wec ku laan : The nation, country or home has been mismanaged or mishandled.

Lanlan A person who does not do his/her assignment quickly.

Lany A distorted English word for decline in considering what was decided or agreed early.

Laŋ 1. To hang oneself on a branch of tree or whatever while playing. 2. Plural of Läŋ a copper ring that looks yellowish in colour.

La̱ŋ To pray while asking Almighty God to forgive one sins, or answer one needs.

Laŋlaŋ A game where children particularly boys hang themselves on tree branches.

Lap 1. To beat or lash with a stick or whip. 2. To lick milk, soup or water by animals such as dogs, cats etc. 3. Slang for human being taking soup. 4. The placenta in a wormb after birth.

Laap Having much to do with the placenta.

La̱a̱p 1. A container that is used for giving a dog soup, milk or water. 2. A type of grass grains that looks like rice.

Làr State of being milky or with enough milk.

Lààr Plural of Làr being a milking cow as explained above.

Laplap 1. State of being so weak and hungry. 2. A song which goes on for several hours or long period of time.

Lar 1. Aimless way of walking or lingering. 2. To have told or reached the message to the right person (s).

Larɛ 1. A village which is known to have plenty or enough food. 2. Tell or say it.

Larlar Aimless walking or lingering at leisure time.

Lat 1. Talk, discussion or whatever negotiable. 2. Work, assignment or anything to do.

Laat Plural of Lat being a talk, information, statement, problem. As explained above.

La̱a̱t 1. A small stick of wood or comb that is used for ordering the hairs. 2. Plural of Läät being a servant or he /she who does the task as explained above.

La̱a̱tni Plural of Làààt being a device stick that is used for putting hairs in order as explained above.

Lath 1. Cotton, string or thread made of cotton. 2. Quake or earth quake. 3. State of being shaky or trembling due to fear, cold or sickness. 4. To separate the flour from grain particles with utensil see Pät. 5. To linger or to go around aimlessly to enjoy walking.

Laath 1. State of aimless way of walking around in the evening or morning. 2. The nineth month of Nuer Calendar.

Lathlath State of being afraid, trembling or frightened.

Law 1. A device stick which is used for paddling canoe to cross the river or water. 2. To pull out something such as weed grass from water or flood.

Lawlaw A state of making a hard item (food, soil,local beer) soft by adding water, soup or milk.

La̠wla̠a̠w State of having something dangling down while hanging or tied up with a rope or whatever.

Lek 1. To close the door, window or whatever.2. To cross the river without using hands in swimming.3. State of bending towards one side or the other as when not steady.

Lekleek State of being in shaking position as with hanging object.

Lel 1. A group of coconut trees in a thick forest.2. A device or art work container made by tying up pieces of certain types of wood for hanging utensils.

Leel 1. Having much to do with Lel as a container for keepimg utensil while hanging.eg Bia wä tœw leel: You go and store it in lel. 2. A way of doing thing Eg Thilæ leel gatmaar :There is no way my brother or son of my mother.

Lem To join or to come near a group in such a slow motion.

Leny To be ahead either by running, walking, singing etc.

Lenyleny State of being naked (nude) while walking.

Leŋ 1. State of having a stick or a log not straight. 2. A stage when a heated cow failed to get a bull or ox for mating.

Leeŋ A series insulting, abusing to one another in joking way

Lep A piece or part of something which petrudes from the main body.

Leep 1. Whatever is used for opening such as key or any device.2. Prestated words or talks (Tongues).

Lepleep State of such parts that hang downwards from the main body.

Ler Prostitute or common woman who plays sex with any person. See Ria̠r

Leer 1. To change the solid material into liquid such as ice,fat etc. 2. Prostitution see Ler.

Let To gaze or look from a distance to see something properly.

Leet Plural of Lɛt being the cannibal or a man-eater as explained blow.

Leth 1. Sweating or to sweat. 2. State of hot weather or being so hot.

Leeth Having become quite hot or warm. eg. Cɛ leeth: It has become hot.

Lethleth Being quite hot.

Lew 1. Flame. See Böl. 2. Great desire to smoke, eat meat etc.

Ley 1. Tooth. See Lɛc. 2. Plural of Ley being an animal as explained below. 3. An animal with the same spelling,same pronunciation but with stress on the vowel (e).

Lɛaw A tuber plant that is eaten or consumed during starvation in Nuer land. It is very bitter and healthy.

Lɛc 1. Plural of Ley that is tooth as explained above. 2. Whatever looks like teeth such as gears in a machine.

Lɛk 1. A tall stick which is used for pounding grain to make flour. 2. A kind of fish with large scales. 3..Having closed the door or whatever.eg Cuæ læk thin: Do not close it in. 4. To move away from the path or road.eg.Lɛk ni ro jok: Move backwards. 5. To swim without moving one hands or legs. 6. To disclose the secret specially after being tortured or threatened eg Cu lɛk ba ji nak: *Do not disclose the secret you will be killed.*

Lɛɛk Plural of Læk being both, the wooden pole for pounding grains and a kind of fish.

Lɛklɛk A position that can not allow anything to stand properly.see lekleek

Lɛl To do, to carry out the task or assignment.eg. ɛŋa biɛ lɛl œ? : Who will do it ?

Lɛm 1. Has become big a little bit. 2. Has come nearer and nearer. 3. A kind of birds that makes noise at dawn to alert travellers to start off.

Lɛany 1. A local kujur stick. 2. To lose the skin as a result of burning

Lɛny 1. Over flow of water or whatever over edges. 2. To be ahead of the racing team or walking. 3. Being completely naked. See Lenyleny. 4. To clear one hairs off to be bald head.

Lɛɛny The over flowing of water or whatever liquids over edges in continuous manner eg Ci pi lɛɛny: The water has overflown edges.

Lɛnyjɔ̱ɔ̱r To have liquids over flown to the ground.

Lɛŋ 1. To relate the bad events whether bad or good. 2. To tell bad events about someone in his/her presence. 3. State of being very narrow and about to cut off.

Lɛɛŋ 1. Plural of Lɛŋ being the art of telling or relating all bad events of someone or people. 2. A gathering where young people exchange insulting words to each others.

Lɛp 1. Tongue. 2. To open anything, or to address the meeting. 3. The clouds movements which allow the sun rays to reach the ground.

Lɛplɛɛp State of being quite opened.eg ɛŋu ta duel lɛplɛɛpä mœ? Why the room is in opening state?

Lɛr 1. A district in Dok Nuer section in Western Nuer. 2. To escort a young, an aged person or a calf.

Lɛɛr To roll over from high to low ground.eg Wer piny ægoa cu bi læær : Go down good do not roll over.

Lɛrlɛr Having a slopping manner or character.

Lɛt 1. Man-eater or cannibal. 2. That part above the hip and bellow the belly or stomach.

Lɛɛt Plural of Lɛt being man-eater as explained above.

Lɛtlɛt State of being not clustered but in separated positions

Lɛw 1. Plural of Lɛaw being a kind of plants as explained above. 2. State of walking while naked. 3. To add much water or milk to porridge.

Lɛwlɛw 1. State of walking naked and thin. 2. A slang for a poor type or light food.

Liah Death. See bath, tɛth, thil: All are slang words for death.eg Liah bæcæ loñ :*Death is painful.* Guandœœñ cæ bath : *Grandfather got lost.* Nàran cæ tææth kiæ cæ thil : *Our uncle has fallen or not there.*

Liac 1. Pregnant for human, a cow or whatever with a baby or calf in

the womb. 2. Dried fish or meat eg. Liac lɛɛk.

Liak To praise something or someone.

Lial 1. An insult which refers to anus see Liel. 2. An angry look at someone you hate very much.

Liaŋ To make a calf or a baby to take water, milk or drug.

Liap State of having an area overcome by flood.

Liat 1. Very tiny fish. 2. State of being very thin. 3. A slang for a helpless thin person.

Liaw Sickness or chronic disease.

Liáw Plural of Liaw being chronic disease as explained above.

Liec 1. To look at or to give a look at someone or something. 2. Having much to do with conception about an animal.

Liel Anus. see Cot for animal anus.

Liem To beg or ask for something.

Lieem 1. Plural of Liim being a persom who begs for something or whatever. 2. A person who is sent to spy out the enemies' movement before attacking them.

Lieny 1. A big harpoon like device which is used for hunting Hippopotamus. 2. To select from the mass of people or things.

Lieny Calf dung.

Liæt The sand or gravel particles which are softened in water runways.

Liew 1. To add much butter or milk to a food see Kuän or Köp. 2. A kind of maize grain which looks yellowish in colour. 3. Straight forward matter with no bendings. See L̲iwliw. 4. A type of beads which is yellowish in colour.

Lieth State of being grey in colour or when it is a name. see Lieth Deang and Lieth Gac :Where the first is a name while the other is a generation.

Lien A suffix which comes as Manlien kie Guanlien aunt (maternal) or uncle (paternal).

Liic Whatever is used for cleaning the ears and teeth.

Liicni Plural of Liic being the device that is used for cleaning ears or teeth.

Licliec A kind of disease that affects human joints.

Lik 1. Complete silence or dead silence. 2. A game which is played by touching sensitive areas of the body which provoke laughter. 3. A sound of a heavy falling object.

Likni Plural of Lik being a game where a person is touched on the stimulating parts in order to make him/her laughs.

Liklik A kind of birds that lives in cow byre Luak which is black in colour.

L̲il A small water way that flows into the river. eg Næmæ æ lìl mi bäär: This is a long water way.

Lil To drink all at once. eg Lil piiku gatmaar: Drink all your water son of my mother.

Lim 1. State of begging or asking something. See Liem. 2. State of being very sweet or sweetness of a taste

Liim A beggar or one who lives on begging others.

Limlim 1. A continuous begging for something without stopping.

Liny 2. State of having very sweet or sugary taste. To select the best from a heap of junks or whatever.

Linyliny State of being quite careful of what one wears, eats, drink etc.

Liŋ 1. Hearing sense. 2. Sickness or chronic disease. See Liaw.

Liiŋ A person who spies in order to get information about enemies CID.

Liŋɛ You listen (ɛ) for second person singular.. eg Ber liñæ gœa : Come to hear well.

Liok A part of human buttocks. It is always in plural.

Liook An insult to a person whose buttocks developed such characteristics see Liok.

Liom State of being mixed up or a mixture.

Lioy Whatever can show symptoms of sickness or disease that had affected the body.eg Tææ kæ lioy baa rialikä : It has some defect will be put right.

Liɔm A mixture of human beings or things in one centre or in a container.

Liœœm A state of great mixture of so many things in one place.

Lip 1. The upper hairy part of the human being genital organ. 2. A noise as that is made by a falling heavy object. 3. A marine bird which lives on fish.

Liprɔ Needle. A distorted Arabic word Ibra being a needle.

Lir To cut off the unwanted parts of nails or parts of animal skin.

Liir 1. A disease which affects the neck below the ears (Cancer). 2. A certain new fashion of dancing in Eastern Nuer Region. 3. A cool air which blows after heavy rainfall. 4. A device which is used for cutting nails or finger nails.

Lirlir A wave of cool air which blows in hot weather.

Ḻit 1. Dark brown colour. 2. Slang for having eaten the great part of the food eg Lit kuan ɛ mɛ camɛ jɛn:*the greater part of this food is eaten by him/her.* 3. A frozen fat or butter. 4. Plural of Liæt being the sand as explained above.

Liit Cloud formation or early stages of clouds formation.

Ḻitḻit Tiny or very small in size such as sand, sugar etc.

Lith 1. Connected with death Lia̱h eg. Cɛ rɔ jiɛc lith.: He raised up from death 2. Grey colour which is a mixture of whitish and dark colour.

Liw Death –dead. See Lia̠h. eg Cɛ liw :He/she is dead, or passed away.

Liwliw State of being quite straight forward or stiff.

Loat Plural of Lɔt being a kind of worms as explained below. See Lœt.

Lo̠c A peg or a piece of wood hit on the soil for tying up a cow or a goat.

Lo̠o̠c Having much to do with tying up cows down for long period. Eg æñu ci hœk buut lòòc œ? Why the cows remiand tied up on pegs like this?

Lok The flow of air or wind.

Lo̠k 1. To hate, dislike, unwanted etc. 2. A bee hive which contains honey.

Lo̠o̠k Severe pains of a wound with pus.eg Löökæ ciökä : Severe pain on my legs.

Loklok 1. As in Gaak ɛ loklok a game which is played by young ones where a person is touched on his./her sensitive organs that force laughter. 2. State of being quite light to be moved by winds.

Lo̠klo̠k State of being in a dangling or hanging state.

Lo̠kcio̠k Whatever follows one foot prints or steps in order to kill or eat him/her up. The real word is Luk cio̠k.

Lol 1. A feeling of vomiting due to sickness.2. A depression, valley or water stream. 2. The deepest water bed in the river or whatever.

Lo̠o̠l 1. A piece of wood which is used for thatching roofs 2. A piece of wood which is used for removing food or whatever from cooking utensil or cow dung fire.

Lohl Whatever makes attraction to people appearance in drum dance.

Lom 1. To play sex or sexual intercourse. 2. A sexual friend woman or man

Lonh A tuber plant that looks like potato.

Lony 1. Lion. 2. To untie or release a cow or whatever to be free. 3. Plural of Lony being a lion as explained above. 4. Slang for when eats without chewing the food.

Lo̠o̠ny State of being flowing, oozing, bleeding of any liquid eg. Bi riɛm lo̠o̠ny: *Blood will flow.*: Koaŋ ɛmœ loony ɛ jœœr: *That alcohol is licking out*.

Loŋ 1. Deep and narrow.eg æ pul mi caa tæt æ loñ : A deep narrow dug hole. 2. To get away without telling anyone.

Loŋloŋ 1. State of being deep and narrow hole. 2. A person who does not tell people what he wants to do.

Lop 1. Manoeuvring or lobbying for something. 2. State of being cold all over.

Loplop Being very cold or soft such as a piece of cloth or skin.

Lor 1. A metallic part of a traditional pipe which is used for smoking. 2. To welcome home a visitor, guest or to go to escort the cattle home after grazing in the evening.

Lot Direction or to show the direction when asked.eg Lot Yomding kä Majok : The direction of Yomding from Majok.

Low To make a stick or a pole straight forward.see Lowlow.

Lowlow State of being straight forward as a stick a pole a road etc.

Lɔ̱ A suffix, meaning after or later eg. Bia lɔ̱ ben: you will come later or after.

Lɔa 1. A person from Lou Nuer section of Wat or Akobo. 2. Having much to do with Lɔw the Bamboo plant eg. Taŋ lɔa : A Bamboo stick.

Lɔac Having much to do with heart.See Lœc. Eg Thil lœac æ bœar :

Lack of heart is a shame. Nuer belief that people think with their hearts.

Lɔc Heart eg. Dit lɔc.: Big heart, is a slang for a greedy person.

Lo̱c 1. Plural of Lɔc being the heart as explained above.2. A peg or that piece of wood which is used for tying down cows or goats.

Lɔguotɛ A kind of trees which is used for making shrines and other rituals..

Lɔk 1. Flow or air blowing on water. 2. Movements of something when put against the wind. 3. The art of separating or filtering grains, using the winds or air. 4. To keep on talking for long time when angry.

Lɔklɔk To keep on talking due to anger or sadness.

Lɔl To cause vomiting by putting one own finger into the throat.

Lɔ̱hm To hand over something in a neighbouring distance.

Lɔm A woman or a man friend or the concubine.

Lɔn The tip part of the penis.

Lɔɔp 1. State of maneouvring or lobbying for something. 2. Cold or cool wind as that of winter or after rainfall.

Lɔ̱t Worm which lives in decaying meat or flesh.

Lɔtlɔt State of being quite tall and thin.

Lɔth 1. A long string or thread which is used in fishing arts. 2. State of being quite dirty.

Lɔthlɔth 1. Being tall and thin. 2. State of being fast in growing such animals or plants.

Lɔw 1. Dark grey. 2. A colour which is a result of dirts. 3..Plural of Loa being a Nuer section in Akobo and Wat as explained above..

Lua An informal pronunciation for Luak eg. Wä lua(k) Gatluak: Iam going to Gatluak byre (cattle hut).

Luac 1. Gum. 2. The gum like substance that affects the growth of plants in a farm. 3. State of bending down as with buttocks, tails, horns. eg Luac piny. Luac thar: Bending state.Bending buttocks. 4. Slang for heavy rain fall state.

Luaac 1. Plural of Luac being the gum as explained above. 2. State of continuous flowing of rain water. eg. ɛŋu cɛ luaac inɛ mɛ? *Why it continues flowing like this?*

Luacluac State of heavy rain fall flowing water or whatever such as fat.

Luak 1. Cattle hut Byre which is larger than human being sleeping one. 2. To modify or forge a metallic device to fit the purpose.

Luaak Having much to do with Luak.eg Tɛɛ luaak: He/she is in luak.

Lukluak 1. State of being quite tall and thin. 2. Ģrowing very fast.

Lua̱a̱k Plural of of Luääk being the person who renders assistance, support, supply etc.to people or helpless ones.

Lual 1. Red. See Dɛ̈ɛ̈r etc. 2. Being pink in colour.

Luál Old grass from hut roof which became brown due to smoke.

Lualduɔt A kind of games from Tiang family.

Luan State of being physically weak due to sickness.

Luanluan A person who is physically weak.

Luany To take as much as one can,from free substance.

Luány Being overcome by talk, disease, pains or hunger with stress on (á).

Luanyluany State of being talkative, or great singer who does not repeat songs.

Luaŋ 1. Common house fly. 2. Ģeneral pain or fatigue. 3. A state of having energy to carry out heavy task.

Luáŋ Plural of Luaŋ being the house fly as explained above with **stress** on (á).

Luaaŋ State of being in general fatigue.

Luaŋluaŋ 1. A person who feels such general pain or fatigue for quite along time. 2. State of being completely weak or helpless.

Luar Not pure, state of being a mixture such as human races or food items.

Luarluar 1. A person who does not keep his/her statements, ideas, opinions, positions. 2. A person who of mixed background, and not pure.

Luat State of being physically weak due to chronic disease.

Lu̱at Slang for what one get without difficulties.

Lu̱a̱t 1. The cold winds or humidity after rainfall. 2. The simplicity of pulling out something from the soil or whatever without difficulty.

Luatluat State of being so weak due to sickness.

Lu̱a̱tlu̱a̱t The feeling of softness of the soil or cotton mattress.

Luath 1. A pickable type of food such as fish, meat etc. where spoons or whatever are not needed. 2. To pick whatever of one choice be it food or anything from a set of items. 3. State of having grown up very fast.

Luathluath 1. A person who grows up very fast. 2. State of picking whatever she/he admires from so many items available.

Luay 1. A long line of people moving in drum dance. See Dep. 2. To pull the string or thread when fishing in the river. See Luey. 3. To wonder or move aimlessly in order to avoid work.eg: ŋak jalɛ ni luay:X is moving aimlessly.

Luayluay 1. Having much to do with length of string, thread etc. 2. The newly developing fruit such as Beans etc.

Luayluayni Plural of Luayluay being the newly developing fruits as explain

Lueath A string that is used for tying down eg.Næmæ æ lueath yœœkä: *This is a dancing device string.*

Luek Advice or to give advice to a person.

Lueek 1. A person who advises people to take the right decisions. 2. Plural of Luak being the cows hut as explained above.

Luel To exchange things such as cattle, food, grains etc.

Lueel 1. What is used for exchange or barter. 2. A person who exchanges goods etc. 3. State or stage of showing up before combating between bulls or oxen etc.

Lueŋ Deep part of water.see Luŋ.

Lueŋlueŋ State of being the deepest part of the water.

Luer 1. To reduce the tight state of a rope. 2. The decrease of flood water level.

Luet 1. To pluck out a tooth from child teeth to avoid tooth ache. 2. The style of fish way of eating from a fishing snare.

Lueth 1. To suck whatever by mouth such as liquids, breast etc.. 2. The style of taking a mouthful when eating fish or meat.

Luey 1. A kind of trees which is hard and tall. 2. To select or choose one from many items.

Lueyluey 1. A wild bird that makes a lot of noise along water pools or banks.. 2. A small bell which is tied on a string around the waist of a child to alert the parents about his/her movements.

Lueylueyni Plural of Lueyluey being either a wild bird or a small bells as explained above.

Luɛa An accumulated cow tails ornament that is put on bull right horn.

Luæani Plural of Luæa being an ornament of bull tails as explained above.

Luɛak State of being shaky or shaking as a spear, pole, peg, etc.

Luɛk 1. State of being shaking and not stiff. 2. Snails.

Luækluæk State of being not fitting, loose or tight.

Luɛɛk Plural of Luæk being the nails as explained above.

Luɛl 1. To slaughter an old animal or human being in war. 2. To pick the gum substance from the tree. 3. To take or remove fish from the hook in fishing game.

Luɛny To pull back the penis skin as when ready for operation or action.

Luɛɛny State of having the skin pulled back the penis.

Luɛnyluɛny State of such practicing the pulling of the skin off the penis.

Luɛŋ To poison by giving poisonous substance.

Luɛɛŋ 1. What is used for poisoning.2. To have got satisfied at last. Eg Gat nyieeti keni luææñ? : Son of sisters you are not yet satisfied?

Luɛt One of the two parts of the face with few hairs.

Luææt Plural oæ Luæt being one part of the face as explained above.

Luɛtluɛt The movements up and down inside tall grass.

Luɛtluɛat A small bird which moves while shaking its tail.

Luil Grey colour of a cow,type of grains or whatever.

Luiny The appearance of dim light or fire in darkness.

Luinyluiny State of being very tiny objects.

Luinyluiiny Plural of Luinyluiny being very tiny as explained above.

Luir To go straight to something, someone or a spot.. See B̠ir.

Luirluir 1. State of going straight to someone, something or a place without stopping or asking. 2. Being quite narrow in size.

Luit To pull out a thorn or whatever from narrow place.

Luitluit Being so tiny or little in size.

Luith 1. To pull out from a narrow space such as thorn. 2. A sharp pricking pain which is caused by thorn or needle. To disappeare very fast in crowd without informing people eg Cuæ wä luith piny ni bakä: He/she disappeared very fast at dawn..

Luithluith 1. A sudden feeling of pain on the foot as a result of thorn or needle pricking. 2. A person who is fond of slipping away.

Luoc 1. To reply, response or appeal. 2. Plural of Luc being impotent as Explained above. 3. State of being quite high as with ground. 4. To return or go back eg. Luoc jɔk : To go back or return.

Luooc 1. Cases of appeal in the native court. 2. Plural of Luuc being the murderer.

Luocluoc High ground or raised soil.

Luok 1. Having much to do with case or accusation. Eg Biel cæ wä luok :Biel has gone to court. 2. To keep on talking very angrily among women folk or children. 3. A colour between red and brown.

Luokluok 1. State of being reddish or brownish in colour. 2. A sound of some liquids in a container when moved from side to side.

Luol The deep part or spot of a river or any water serface

Luom To play sex or intercourse.

Luonh To come early in the morning or at dawn.

Luony 1. To untie the knot of string or rope. 2. To have water or flood over flown the river banks 3. To swallow without chewing some food item. 4. A group of cows or cattle when released for grazing. See Luny. 5. To release cattle for grazing at around 9:00 or 10:am.

Luoŋ 1. To leave without telling or informing people around you. 2. A very tight narrow pit hole or entrance.

Luoŋluoŋ 1. A person who leaves without telling people. 2. A narrow tight deep hole.

Luooŋluooŋ A stilthy way of walking ready to hit, shoot or spear an enemy or a game in hunting.

Luop 1. To manoeuvre or lobbying for something. 2. The movements of grass leaves due to winds.

Luopluop Movements of grass or plant leaves as a result of wind blowing.

Luor 1. To welcome or to go and welcome home a guest. 2. To go and bring home cattle from the grazing. 3. To assist or help a person when he/she is doing some work. 4. To go and help in bringing fish when people come back from fishing. 5. To go and assist or help someone hands when carrying something heavy. 6. An iron part of the large native pipe Töny

Luoor Plural of Luur being a person who goes to bring fishes or escorts cattle home as explained below.

Luorluor The flow of water, blood or whatever from the source.

Luori Plural of Luor being a native pipe smoking tool as explained above.

Luot 1. Position, status or function of something. 2. To pull out liquid or pus by mouth. 3. State of having something fit, good, well such as clothes,shoes etc.

Luoth 1. Departure or taking off at dawn, when on a journey. 2. Food which is served to a person on a journey in the early morning. 3. Having much to do with Luoth the top part of the head. see Luɔth.

Luow 1. To whistle by tuissting tongue and lips to force air out to make sounds. 2. Being straight as a stick. See Thiew luow.

Luowluow State of being quite straight and no bending.

Luoy Good things or best results. It is always in plural.eg Duol æmœ thilæ jæ luoy:That meeting has no good results.

Luɔk Slang for ripening of fruits where their colours change from green to either brown or red. see Loar.

Luɔ̱ɔ̱k Plural of Luk the case before the court or judge as explained below.

Luɔl 1. A kind of guord utensil which has deep bottom that is used for eating.2. Plural of Luol being the deepest part of a river or any water surface as explained above.

Luɔm A man or woman friend or concubine.

Luɔ̱ɔ̱m Plural f Luum being a girl friend or boy friend.

Luɔɔm Plural of Luɔm being a woman or man friend or a concubine.

Luɔ̱ŋ 1. Being upside down or bending downwards. 2. To look downward.

Luɔ̱ɔ̱ŋ State of being with out horns or with horns bending downwards. See Cɔ̱t.

Luɔ̱r A kind of savanna trees with reddish bark and whitish thorns

Luɔ̱ɔ̱r 1. Plural of Luur being one who escorts the cattle from grazing or people from fishing. 2. Plural of such Savanna tree that has reddish bark and whitish thorns.

Luɔ̱t A shirt. See Ruony or Lutlut.

Luɔt 1. Direction of a place. 2. The intention.eg Gööri luœt Yomding, kä luœti ni ŋu? You want direction of Yomding and what is your intention?

Luœœth The top part of the head, or the peak.

Luœth Plural of Luœœth being the top part of the head as explained above.

Luc 1. Impotent person who does erect or reproduces children. 2. To murder or kill secretly anything be it animal or human being. 3. Slang for whatever is done secretly be it discussion, agreement etc.

Luuc A person who carries out whatever actions secretly.

Luk 1. The case before the judge or court. 2. To follow the foot steps, or the case history. 3. The movement of something on one body or surface. 4. A noise of a falling heavy object.

Luuk Having much to do with such continuous noise.eg Tɛ kɛ mi luuk pɛɛk ɛmi: There is frequent heavy noise in that area.

Lukluk 1. Such noise of a repeating action. 2. Early stage of a frog.

Lul 1. Weeping, wailing, mourning and even crying when in deep sadness. 2. A name of a baby born, when sad event took place or happened.

Lum 1. Plural of Luom that is to play sex as explained above. 2. A type of grass which is used in huts building. see Gäw.

Luum Boy or girl friend.

Lumköör A kind of wild vegetables in Nuer land.

Luny 1. To cut off all leaves or branches of a tree. 2. To come back home Eg Ci luny jok :You have come back. 3. A cattle releasing for grazing.

Lunyluny State of having a tree branches or leaves cut off.

Luŋ To bend down or to look down.

Luŋluŋ State of being bending or bend down.

Lurlur A state of being so fat, to look as if swelling.

Lut 1. A disease that affects human body back part. 2. To hit, beat or lash continuously.eg Ba ji lut mi wi jaany jɔɔr: you will be lashed or beaten if you delay. 3. To bend down in order to dodge a stick hit eg Bi kɛɛtdä lut: You will dodge my stick. 4. To clean the weeds after the sorghum stalks become high. Eg Nyariak Cæ kaa(k) dæ lut :Daughter of Riak has cleaned her field.

Lutlut 1. State of being extraordinary huge due to fatness or swelling. 2. A way of walking in the forest where one goes bending under bushy trees.

Lutwäär A worm that lives in cow dungs.

Luth A kind of fish that buries itself in mud in dry season.

Luuth 1. Plural of Luth being that type of fish as explained above.

Luuth 2. A game which is played with twelve parallel lines of holes By two persons or players.

Luur 1. A person who goes in the evening to escort cattle home after long day grazing.2. A person who goes to assist the father or mother carrying fishes home from fishing pool, river etc.

Lä The sound of the thirteenth letter of Thok Nath.

Läc Menustration or monthly period of adult human female.

Lääc Having much to do with Läc eg. Riɛm lääc: Menustration blood.

Läk 1. Having much to do with cattle grazing in the marshes. 2. To make goats, calves etc graze while tied down with a long rope to Avoid escaping. 3. Dream, night mare. 4. Plural of La̱a̱k being the belt that is tied around a bull neck. 5. The fluids that come out when one is in deep sleep or that flow Out from a baby or a child mouth.

Läkläk Being soapy substance like spitow etc.

Läl 1. A big ring shape metal with sharp points (teeth) used for fighting among boys., see Nyuɛny 2. Plural of Làl a water way for fishing as explained below. 3. A man made small stream for fishing or trapping fishes.

Lääl Having much to do with Làl eg. Tæ wic lääl: *He was by water stream.*

Läm Luck, the actual luck where the owner of a thing is judged or known in the result of the second round.

Läny 1. State of being far a head of a person or people. 2. A state where the skin looses hairs due to sickness. 3. To add water into flour to have it fermented. 4. To paste the hairs with a mixture of ashes and water to change the colour yellowish or brownish.

Lääny 1. Mixture of pounded grains soaked in water to ferment. 2. State of having distance between people walking eg. Caa rɔdien lääny : *They are walking apart.*

Läŋ A copper ring which is yellowish in colour.

Läŋläŋ Having bright yellowish colour or golden colour.

Läp 1. To have eaten something very fast. 2. Slang for having exhausted sex action continuously.

Läpläp A large piece of something which is still hanging and not yet cut off from the main body.

Lär A milking cow.

Läär 1. Plural of Lär being a milking cow as explained above. 2. Information a message or report.

Lärlär A milky cow or which produces enough milk.

Läät An employee, labourer, servant or worker.

Läth 1. To put on or wear anything cloth, shoses, rings etc. 2. To put down, place, or hang something. 3. To score a goal in a game. See Yur.

Läw 1. To tie down a goat or calf in grass land with along rope to allow it moves freely in order not to escape. 2. To walk or linger, aimlessly.

Läy 1. A sudden passing of watery stool when sick of diarrhea. 2. Cow or female animal genital organ.

Läyni Plural of Läy being an animal genital organ as explained above.

Liäp To make or terrify someone by telling terrible stories.

Liääp 1. To mix food ingredients soup, meat or butter for a meal. 2. A mixture of sand with cement for building purposes..

Luäc 1. A type of spear or hook that has no teeth on it. 2. A person from Dinka section –luäc.

Luäk 1. To help, aid or support someone,oneself or something. 2. The aid or whatever is given by donors to victims of any cause. 3. To allow a heavy load reaches down very quickly due to its impact. eg, Kuɛ luäk piny: Just put it down.

Luääk A person who supports, renders services,assists etc.to people in need..

Luäl 1. To change the morning tastes of the mouth with food or whatever. 2. Plural of Luääl being a kind of trees as explained below. 3. To change the bitter taste by adding water, sugar or fresh milk.

Luääl A kind of trees that has long dangling fruits.

Luäny 1. To add some water, milk, soup etc on dry substance in order to make it soft, wet by soaking. 2. State of being wet or soaked.

Luääny Having been made wet, soaked to maximum stage.

Luäŋ Ability or power to do something.

Luääŋ Whatever makes or helps something to be possible.

Luär 1. Lack of endurance, weakness to sustain hardship or difficulties. 2. Slang for giving in or surrendering.

Luäär Having much to do with Luär is weakness to do something.

Luärluär A person who is weak to face hard job, or work.

Luät 1. Great show of deep love or chivalry. 2. State of being over cooked such as meat, tuber food (potatoes etc).

Luätluät State of being quite soft such as soil for sawing seeds

Luäth 1. State of having not got what one targetted, such as in fishing or whatever. 2. State when one gets something without much talks or difficulties.

Luäy To release gas through anus without making noise or sound.

Luäyluäy A slang for very simple or easy to go without much persuasion.

Lëër 1. Prostitution. See Ria̱r. 2. To change the solid material into liquid form as that with Fat, Ice etc.

Löc Plural of Lo̱c being a peg as explained above.

Lööc State of being tied on peg for quite a long time. Eg Tah hok Lööc ni wen œ? Why the cows tied on pegs since then ?

Lök 1. Reject whatever,be it a statement or an offer to marriage. 2. To clean sorghum grains by stirring it in the air.eg Man gan cæ wä lök bææl: The mother of children has gone to filter the grains.

Löök Plural of Lök to clean the grains as explained above.

Lööl A colour which is a combination of brown and black.

Löny Flow or oozing of water, blood or whatever liquid.

Löŋ 1. To repeat with high, loud voice as Gam lo̱ŋ. 2. To call someone with high or loud voice from a distance.

Lör Whatever is handled or used by many hands.

Löör 1. That part of the spear or gun that is not covered with wood. 2. A peeled maize bundle.

Löt State of being quite dirty with fluids as in wound, nose etc.

Lööt Being so dirty with such fluid etc. eg. Gat ɛ mœ ci wumdɛ lööt ruothɛ jɛ:This child or baby his/her nose is dirty clean it?

Löth 1. A big native bell which is tied around a bull neck. 2. To have extended a messge or whatever to some one else. 3. To raise something so that it is not to be reached by children, dogs etc.

Lööth 1. Plural of Löth being a native bell as explained above.. 2. Whatever have been into so many hands. See Lör.

M

Ma 1. A short form for the word (Mama) which is mother. 2. An additional word which precedes the first word of the statement e.g. Ma bia wä: That you will go.

Ma̱a̱h A word for addressing an age mate or younger ones among boys or men.

Mac 1. Fire of any type. 2. Gun of an type. 3. To take someone property by force. 4. Collection of bee hives for honey.

Mac To take something by force.

Macmac 1. Behaviour where one takes by force. See Mac. 2. To cheat when selling goods with unnecessary high prices or when correcting an examination paper where you give failed results.

Mactap Maize grain which grows in place of tobacco. See Manytap.

Mak 1. Launching an attack to someone or people in their place without notice. 2. Water increases or flooding in the river due to heavy rainfalls. 3. To push back someone or something with both hands.eg Cuɛ hä mak jok :He/She pushed me back. 4. To change the direction of canoe by pushing water forward. 5. A food which is made from not yet dried grains.

Mal 1. Peace.eg Mal yɛndial gaatmaar? Are you all in peace, sons of my mother? 2. Be quick in doing something. e.g. Mal be̠n: Come quickly. See Ŋal. 3. A weapon made out of animal horn. See Giit.

Malɛ Greeting, meaning peace be with you.

Malmal State of being well or in peace. See Mal.

Malieth Eagle or that bird with greyish feathers. Mam Sudden or that happens by chance or unprepared for. eg. Riali rœ ikä ɛ ji ca bi mam :Prepare yourself before you are caught up.

Ma̠a̠m To make sudden blows,to overpower someone before he/she could prepare.

Ma̠a̠mni Plural of Ma̠a̠m being an attack before someone prepares as explained above.

Mammam A state where one does not know what to do.

Man His/her mother. eg Nɛmɛ ɛ man Nyaŋ Lual : *This is Nyang Lual's mother.*

Maan State of having nice, beautiful or good looking face or structure.

Ma̠a̠n State of having good attraction to people or things.

Mandan First person speaker about mother, our mother see Mara

Mandun Second persons,your mother. See Morun.

Mandiɛn Third persons plural, their mother.

Manpalëak Hen. See Nyante̠e̠r being the name of a hen in Western Nuer.

Many Stage of when one talks alone due to anger.

Manytap Adistorted name for maize plant which yields yellowish grains. The correct name is Mactap.

Maŋ 1. Waves or tides of water in windy day. 2. To be overcome by sickness that can not allow him/her to get up.

Maŋmaŋ A bad condition where one is either sick or tired.

Maŋpiny Bog down or being overcome by pains or whatever.

Mar 1. To answer the puzzling test questions. e.g. Mar cäär kook wec? :Tell the black which makes noise in the village? 2. Plural of Maar being the blood relationship. Eg Ti kæ mar ti ŋuan: You have many relationship. 3. State of looking very sick or not well.

Maar 1. My mother, first person singular speaking eg Maar ɛ ni? *Where is my mother?*. 2. Blood relationship. 3. Anyother relationship that ties two or more.

M̲a̲a̲r State of being confused and forgetful.

Mara Our mother, being first person speaking.

Marmar A cow mentioned in the marriage discussion or settlement w hhich as not been given a colour or value, to be given in near future.

Marmari The plural of Marmar being a cow to be given as explained above.

Mat 1. Union, meeting, assembling, gathering together. See Duɔl. 2. To add 2 + 5 = 7, to collect or put items together. 3. Concentration in one place as that of cattle camp.eg. Mat Burjuok :Burjuok cattle camp concentration 4. To pound some grains in order to make flour for a quick food paste. e.g. Matnim kiɛ matnom, both have their Dinka language origin where the general meaning is to put heads together by pounding.

Ma̲t Depression or low land.

Ma̲tma̲t Heavy noise of rain thunderstorms or plane engine noise.

Ma̲th To drink or smoke. We only make difference by adding either water or tobacco.

Ma̲a̲th 1. Plural of Määth being a great smoker or drunkard as explained above.. 2. Whatever is used for smoking or drinking

Maw Fat or butter, which is a borrowed word from Dinka language.

May 1. Art of fishing in the river,pool, water ponds etc. 2. To check what the other person is about to say so that you protest.eg ɛŋu mayi thokdä thin œ? Why do you check me?

Ma̲a̲y 1. Plural of Määy a fisherman as explained below See Balaaŋ. 2. A tool which is used for fishing.eg snares, fishing net, harpoon etc.

Maayni Plural of Maay being whatever is used for fishing as explained above.

Maymay State of being not ready to do something quickly.

Meny Style or manner of sitting. See Mɛny.

Mɛ Meaning this. It is a short form for Mɛmɛ.

Mɛɛ 1. Goat bleating. 2. Means that.Eg Kä mææ lat kœnæ jaani ?: *What we talked about where is it?* 2. Before or that day. eg Mɛɛdan : Before,Once upon a time or that day.

Mɛk 1. To select or choose from many or more than two items. 2. Choice or selection.

Mɛmɛ This one, while pointing or touching the item.

Mɛn 1. To prepare thread, string, or rope from the raw material substances. 2. Means this one e.g. Mɛn mɛn: This this. 3. Is a statement for threatening as in eg Bæ pät a bi mɛn du : He/she will slap you until you get it.

Mɛnmɛn State of having a thing very stickly which causes difficulty in handling or swallowing.

Mɛny A bad way of sitting for a shooting stomach or full with food.

Mɛnyliɛl A kind of insects which opens its bottom while moving or stopping.

Mɛnymɛny An ugly manner way of walking.

Mɛŋ To bend to one side or state of bending something.

Mɛɛŋ Having been bended to one side, such as bull horns shape.

Mɛŋmɛŋ A bended shape stick, path or road.

Mɛr Deep or dark brown.

Mer 1. To use a torch or whatever in order to see whatever you are looking for in darkness.2. The tears.

Meer Plural of Mer being the tear as explained above.

Mermeer An angry or hungry way of looking ready to attack something.

Mɛrmɛr The appearance of something inside water.

Met 1. To taste something. 2. To smoke big pipe. see Töny.

Mɛt To deceive someone by telling untrue news or stories.

Mɛɛt An out growth on the skin as part of the body.

Mɛtni Plural of Mɛɛt being an out growth on skin as explained above.

Mɛtmɛt State of being not well growing due to lack of water or fertilizers.

Mɛtɛt The appearance of eyes when having eye sickness.

Mɛth A type of trees which could be teak.

Mɛthni Plural of Mɛth being a type of trees as explained above.

Mɛthmɛth State of being simple or thin.

Mɛy Plural of Mɛay being the root or where a person comes fromIn terms of birth. see Kar.

Mɛymɛy The smallest or thinnest part that holds two things together. See Nɛynɛy.

Mi If, unless as in eg Mi Choul a thin a bä : If Choul is there let him come. Ɛmi wi̱ jɛ päl: Unless you leave it.

Miak A kind of creeping plants.

Mic An angry statement meaning, what a?

Miey To press someone with fingers to have him/ her be careful or to listen to you.

Miɛk A kind of plants which produces powerful nice smell when burned to scare flies.

Miɛy Plural of Miɛɛy being a single hair of giraffe as explained below.

Miɛæy Single hair from horse or giraffe tail eg Næmæ æ miɛæy juäl gueec:This is a giraffe tail hair.

Mil To combine some ingredients to make local beer stuff.

Mi̱l The smell of roasted meat or fish.

Mi̱i̱l A condition which affects someone after having eaten heavy meal or meal with butter.

Milɛ The mixed substances that when filtered makes white local alocoholic drinks eg Koañ æn bor : White stuff beer.

Milmil A delicious sharp smell of food from either meat or fish.

Mi̱m Hairs of all types or sources..

Mim Charcoal from fire wood.

Mimi That one or that. See Ni̱mi.

Min An article for that e.g. Mindan, mindœŋ:That one before, or the other one..

Minmin 1. He/she who does not do any work quickly.2. She/he who does not talk openly.

Miŋ 1. Deaf or lack of hearing sense. 2. To add a heavy load or yoke on someone or something. 3. Plural of Miŋ deaf as explained above.

Miiŋ The state of being deaf or lack of hearing senses.

Miŋmiŋ Extraordinary heavy load or weight.

Miɔt A hoof of an animal

Miœtni Plural of Miœt being the hoof of animal as explained above..

Miɔr Style or a quick way of drinking milk..

Miɔɔr A very thin type of fish or whatever.

Mir 1. Sunset, evening or dusk. 2. To recall one sense of memory.

Mi̲r Plural of Miir the turtle as explained below.

Miir 1. State of becoming dusk, evening or sun set. 2. The turtle. 3. A tiny grain beads which is put in the string and worn on the face or forehead as traditional ornament.

Mirmir State of becoming not clear to the sight.

Mirmiir State of seeing things with difficulties or faint shapes.

Mi̲i̲t 1. Rainbow. 2. Having very colourful, such as black and white. 3. That insect which exhibits light in darkness.

Mi̲tmi̲t The other name for the same insect that exhibits bright light in darkness.

Mith The food, food materials or a meal.

Mi̲th 1. Meaning which one of the many things.eg Gööri ni mi̲th? *Which one do you want?* 2. Tentacles of a fish, cat, rat etc. 3. Plural of Mith being the food as explained above. 4. A sound which is made by human being or cow to alert her/ its young ones to enjoy sucking or whatever.

Miith 1. To feed young one. 2. What is used for feeding a kid.

Mìthmìth 1. The pepper plant. 2. Slang for he/she who eats a lot of food.

Mìw The movements of eyelids.

Mìwmìw Series movements of eyelids. Eg ɛŋu tä waŋdu mìwmìw œ? *Why your eyelids are moving like that?*

Mo 1. A word which expresses expected bad results when someone was advised before not to do something.eg Mo kuɛ nɛn !: *You just see it !* 2.A short form for Momo eg Ku momo päl lɛni wä kä mo: Leave that, just to go to that.

Moa Drowning in water, but Nuer added smoke which causes what like drowning (suffocation).

Moa̱c Plural of Ma̱c to call one bull colour, horns etc when in showing off, in danger, among age mates showing off or in surprise scene.

Moak Flood which is a result of heavy rainfalls.

Moa̱l 1. To crawl or walking on kneels as a baby or when sick. 2. Plural of M œl being the leg joints as explained below. 3. State of becoming not restless such as a milking cow,a rough person etc.

Moaŋ Plural of Mɔŋ that is chatting and joking gathering.

Moar The sound which is made by cattle or cows when about to cross water, river or when on a journey.

Moɔ̱c To give a gift or present to someone.

Mok 1. A child conceived without menstruation or monthly period. 2. To feed or eat raw grains.eg Bia mok kæ bæl : You eat raw grains.

Mo̱k The buffalo being one of wild tough animals.

Mo̱o̱k A situation where one feels sleepy in the morning due to lack of proper sleeping in previous night..

Mool Overwhelming flood which covers large areas in a short time.

Mom 1. One of big wild game in the forest. 2. To grab something or to take hold of whatever comes before you.

Mon 1. The state of fainting when sick. 2. A type of plant which is used for making sweeping tools. 3. To put or throw food into the mouth very fast.eg Cɛ dhœn mon thookdɛ: *He/she has put or thrown a piece of meat into his/her mouth.* 4. Just like that Mɔ as explained early.eg Mon, kua nɛn : *That is,you just see.*

Mony 1. Got dead, passed away, lost, see Joak being the ghost person .eg ŋak cɛ mony :X had passed away. See Thil, Tɛth, Bath etc. 2. Nothing, very little or of no value.eg Biel la mucæ æ mony : Biel just give nothing or very little.

Mo̱o̱ny A person who makes messages or rubs paining part of the body according to people belief to cure pains.

Monymony Little or tiny thing of less value.

Monymɔɔny Plural of Monymony being very little or tiny thing as explained above.

Mormor 1. State of being warm as with body, water, soup, milk etc. 2. A kind of brown colour ants.

Mot A cow dung fire that is kept closed to keep fire for long period.

Motmot State of playing with fire.

Moth 1. To eat or chew food, e.g. dry bread, grains or a dog way of dealing with bones. 2. State of being sharp as with a knife,a spear, a sword etc. 3..To lash, beat a child or a woman. See Lap or Duäc.

Mooth 1. Whatever is chewable, not soft food. 2. A type of grass in the compound.

Mɔc 1. To get sprayed by a boiling pot in the cooking process. 2. To offer something

Mɔɔc Plural of Mo̱c being the gift as explained above. See Möc.

Mo̱l Knee joint or being the joint of leg and thigh bones.

Mɔl 1. To kneel down.eg Mœli ɛn tämɛ : Go on kneels now. 2. To creep, crawl on chest or lower part of the body. 3. A name or a slang for creeping animals, particularly snake. 4. To bury or the putting of soil on grave.

Mɔɔl Plural of Mɔl being the creeping animal as explained above.

Mɔlä Next tomorrow in Eastern Nuer version.

Mɔlɛ Next tomorrow in Western Nuer pronunciation.

Mɔli Plural of Mul being a donkey as explained below.

Mo̱lmo̱l A cow or a person who is not restless or troublesome.

Mo̱lmo̱a̱l Plural of Mo̱lmo̱l being not restless or troublesome as explained above.

Mo̱lmo̱a̱li Plural of Mœlmœàl being state of moving on knees or crawling like a child or a baby.

Muo̱n 1. Plural of Mun grave yards or burial areas. 2. Residential plot As explained below.

Mɔnmɔn A person who does things secretly or in isolation. See Muœnmuœn.

Mɔŋ Time passing gathering where jokes and laughable stories are told or related

Mɔɔr 1. To bathe with some boiled or warmed water usually a sick person or a recent delivered woman, a wounded person or a baby. 2. Your mother when said by first person. eg. Mɔɔr: for single,Mɔɔrun for more than one person. 3.A type of bird pest which feed on sorghum. See Kɛc. 4. A type of plants that looks like tobacco.

Mɔrmɔr A kind of insects known as red ant.

Mɔt The hot ashes of cow dung fire.

Mɔ̱t.1. To shave the hairs or to cut it off. 2. A slang for ritual which is performed by cleaning or clearing the hairs of bride on brideday celebration. 3. Yearly ritual which is performed for the death of the Family head.

Mɔ̱a̱th To disclose or to tell a secret to someone in a low voice.

Mɔ̱a̱thmɔ̱a̱th The state of telling or disclosing secrets in low voices.

Mɔth Sharpness of spear, knife, razor etc.

Mɔ̱th To tell a piece of information to someone as quickly as possible .eg Gatmaarlen ɛ ji måthä mɛ : Son of my aunt let me tell you this very fast.

Mɔthmɔɔth State of being so sharp as explained above.

Mɔymɔy State of being shy in front of people where you can not express

yourself or decide. Muc Plural of Mɔ̱c being a gift eg. Ba muc thöp. : To pay gifts as explained above.

Muk 1. To take hold of something or someone with both hands. 2. To tie the main wooden poles that form the hut roof.

Muuk The main pole of wood which holds the hut roof.

Muukni Plural of Muuk being the main pole which holds the hut roof as explained above.

Mul Donkey. It is a borrowed word. See Kacik.

Muul A ganglion or out growth on the knee joint or any other part of the body.

Muuli Plural of Muul being that ganglion as explained above.

Mulmul Situation when something or someone lost shape due to fatness.

Mum Confusion state of mind where one does not know what to do after the death of important person in the house.

Mummum State of much confusion as explained above.

Mun 1. Soil, mud, land, ground, plot or earth. 2. Grave or cemetry.or plot. 3. To hand over something. see Ŋun.

Muny To take part of a tobacco bundle or package.

Muɔ̱n Having much to do with soil as grave.eg Kuär muœn: Earth chief.

Mur The female genital organ or vagina.

Muor Plural of Mur being the female genital organ as explained above.

Muur 1. Having much to do with Mur eg. Nɛmɛ la tɛɛ muur: This is always inside vagina.2. A person who bathes a newly Delivered woman or sick person with warm water

Muɔr Having much to do with vagina or Mur. Eg Bia jek thok muœr :You will get it at vagina entrance.

Mut 1. Spear or swearing ceremony of a clan such as Mut wiiu of Gaat kiir.. 2. To prick ears, lower lip or nose in order to put or hang on an ornamental device.

Muœt Being witchcraft.

Muœœt Plural of Muœt being the witchcraft as explained above.

Mutŋëac A kind of plants which grows in the field or a farm.

Muth 1. The period of fifteen days of no moon light. 2. Darkness or a state of black out.

Muɔ̱th 1. A type of grass which is very strong and difficult to weed in a farm. 2. Yellowish copper steel rings. See Ci̱k i muɔ̱th : a copper steel ring.

Mä The sound of the twenty seventh letter of Thok Nath.

Mäc 1. The early pains or symptoms that preced the delivery of a baby. 2. Plural of Mac being both, the fire and gun as explained above. 3. The action of collecting Bee hives. eg. Tɛɛ mäc tuari : He was collecting bee hives for honey.

Mäl To show peaceful and no roughness.

Mälmäl 1. State of being peaceful, calm and not troublesome or rough. 2. A slang for a person who does not beat, shout or fight children or anybody.

Mäm 1. An action which happens by chance or sudden. e.g Bɛlä jɛ Kɛ mämdɛ kɛ hä : *I blame: him because he/ she surprised me*. 2. A rather surprising or stupid way of looking..

Mämmäm To be in a surprising state or to look thick or clamzy.

Män 1. To overcome the condition usually the taste, and colour. 2. Plural of Ciek a woman as explained above.

Mään Having something to do with women eg La tɛɛ kut mään.: He/she used to stay near women.

Mäŋ Not so sound in mind or rather foolish.

Mäŋmäŋ State of being either fool or of little hearing sense.

Mäy 1. Summer season in Nuer land which starts at the end of February to May. 2. To be in fishing process. e.g. Tɛɛ mäy: He/ she Is in fishing processes. 3. To spend summer season eg Bia mäy ni ɛn waalɛ ? *Where will you spend summer this year?*,

Määy Fisher man/woman.

Mär Thunder storm, explosion sound or noise.

Määr 1. Plural of Mär being the loud noise or explosion Or thunderstorm as explained above. 2. The beginning of creation eg Nimɛɛ bä naath ni määr: As the coming of human being from creation.

Märmär 1. The puzzling questions for testing general knowledge among youths as part of folktales. 2. State of not appearing well in water.

Märmääri Plural of Märmär being the puzzling questions as explained above.

Määth 1. Friend. Eg Wàh dhœr määth dä: I am going to my friend house. 2. To do something very slowly and not in a hurry. Bia piny ɛ määth: Come down very slowly.

Mök Plural of Mo̱k being a game Buffalo as explained above.

Möm A mouthful of food material.see Dhuœn.

Mööm Plural of Möm being the mouthful of food as explained above.

Möny The rubbing of someone stomach as when it is paining or conception purposes.

Mööny A person who carries out such activities as explained above.

Möt A style of sitting where the chin rests on the knee joint when one is in great or series need of food or whatever.

Möy The drowning of animals in water as sacrifices for Kujur of water.

N

Na The sound of the fifteenth letter of Thok Nath.

Naa Short form for word Naath which is people, nation or tribe etc.

Nac A cow heifer. see Guic tut.

Nak 1. A shelf like wall built place which is used for storing food and utensils. 2. A set of upper teeth or lower ones or both.

Na̱k To extract something such as tooth, teeth out, the tail, tusk or tongue.

Na̱a̱k 1. Whatever is used for killing, wounding, harming such as gun shot, spear, stick and lastly the disease. 2. Plural of Näk being the killing or murdering as explained below.

Nam 1. To escort a person on journey, a guest etc. 2. To pick a word or statement from someone before finishing talking.

Na̱a̱m Plural of Nääm being he/she who escorts as explained below.

Namnam Slang for a person who behaves as explained above.

Na̱n Distance which is far from a certain point.

Nan To pick a word very fast as when two persons are talking.

Nannan A slang for a person who behaves very quick in saying something.

Na̱nna̱n State of being very far from a certain point.

Naŋ To take someone or something. Eg Naŋ gat : Take the baby.

Na̱ŋ State of taking something or someone.eg Täh nàñ gatä : I was escorting a baby.

Nar My uncle first person singular. Eg Wäh dhor Nar : I am going To uncle home.

Naar State of having slowed down as that of heavy rain, dust or bird pest.

Na̱a̱r The sour milk which is mixed with fresh milk in order to make fresh milk gets fermented for special purpose.

Na̱a̱ri Plural of Näär being the cow that is given to uncle in marriage

of his niece as explained below.

Nath 1. The real human being or stock who is known with long face and middle height.. 2. To take out food from the cooking utensil such as fish or meat. 3. Ạ state of getting very angry due to provocation See Loaw rec:Get out the fish, Kuɛr guiiyni: Getting out the stones, kɛac.ni jin :You got angry.

Na̱th 1. To take hold of someone as when wrestling or fighting 2. Having taken position for both wrestling or fighting, e.g. Cikɛ na̱th or cikɛ ka̱p:They, each has taken position or they have taken hold.

Naath Plural of Nath being the real people or nation or tribe as Explained above.

Nay To tie up with a piece of string, cloth or rope.

Naynay A creeping plant which twists itself around a stem of a strong tree, wood or a pole.

Naywal The same plant which is used for building huts as explained above.

Nen Seeing, watching or looking at someone or something. See Guic, Nɛn.

N̠e̠e̠n Spectacle, glass, mirror or a spectator.

Ne̠r To honour, greet a young man or lady by hailing him or her according to his/her bull colour, horns or whatever as follow: Biel riaal, colour Tuŋ gɔɔr, shape of horns Luëah nyaaŋ, *ornament which is hanged on the right horn of a bull.*

Neer Plural of Ne̠r being the honour of a young man according to his bull colour or horn shape as explained above.

Ne̠e̠t A bushy wild tree, its leaves are boiled and eaten as wild vegetable.

Ne̠tni Plural of Ne̠e̠t being such bushy tree as explained above.

New To take something by force without consulting the owner.

Newnew State of being very thin where it can get cut very fast or easily.

Nɛ This as in eg ɛŋu nɛ? what is this? See Nɛmɛ: This. Nɛɛ Short form for Nɛy before suffix, being people eg kɔ, kiɛn,Ku, kun, kɔn, kɛ, kä, etc.

Nɛɛkɔ = Our people

Nɛɛkiɛn = Their people

Nææku =Your people

Nɛɛkun = Your people

Nɛɛkɔn = Our people

Nɛɛkɛ = His // her people

Nɛɛkä = My people etc.

Nɛm 1. To hold something from the edge. 2. To miss narrowly by touching part of the body with spear or gunshot.

Nɛmɛ 1. This one, while pointing at or touching it eg Nɛmɛ ɛ ley ŋu ? Which animal is this ? Nɛmɛ ɛ dit ŋu? Which bird is this? 2. Cut it from edge..

Nɛmnɛm The smallest or thinnest part that holds two items together.

Nɛmɔ That one. (while pointing). See Nomœ.

Nɛn 1. The sense of seeing or sight 2. Here, e.g. Jɛn nɛn: It is here.

Nɛɛn Plural of Neen being the spectator as explained above.

Nɛnɛ 1. This one. 2. Just see or look here.

Nɛŋ 1. Sorghum stalk that contains sweet juice which attracts chewing. 2. Slang for a gentleman as being very heavy, dignified and who can not be moved by simple issues. See Thiak. 3. State of becoming so thin due to either sickness or as part of wood, a tree when being cut or eroded..

Nɛŋnɛŋ State of being so narrow or about to get cut quickly.

Nɛp A style of drinking milk, beer etc.

Nɛt Very thin due to sickness or born thin. See Nɛtnɛt.

Nɛtnɛt State of being so thin to walk properly.

Nɛtnɛat Plural of Nɛtnɛt state of being thin as explained above.

Nɛth 1. Having taken enough food or drinks. As a meal. 2. Lower part of the body or the waist. 3. To become thin around the waist.

Nɛthnɛth State of being thin and tight in the middle part of the body.

Nɛy 1. When. eg, Bi jiɛɛn i̱ nɛy? When will you leave? 2. We, of first person plural eg Bi nɛy wä i̱ ruun: we are leaving tomorrow. 3. Plural of Naath eg Nɛy titi bäkɛ wic: These people are coming from the rural area.

Nɛɛy To pull your hand from someone hands as when fighting or wrestling.

Nɛynɛy State of being weak or thin.

Ni 1..Where eg. Tee ni? Where is it?. 2. A suffix for plural of regular countable nouns. e.g. – Biiyni = clothes Kɔamni = chairs, seats Jiöpni = axes Kɛtni = sticks etc.

Nia̱r To nod,to show support or acceptance half way. e.g. Cuɛ

nia̱r thin: Do not just accept.

Niààr Plural of Niàr being nodding or show of support as explained above.

Nie̱n Sleep. Nuer counts only the sleeping days not the working days. eg Ci nie̱n ni kä Makaal? *Where did you spend a night in Malakal?*

Ni̱eŋ To shake one body as when dancing or playing.

Ni̱eŋni̱eŋ State of shaking one body as explained above.

Niey To slow down the process, or being not fast in doing something.

Nieyniey A person who acts very slowly and not very fast or quick.

Niɛr 1. The appearance of water surface which indicates the fish movements. 2. The fatty parts on top of the soup or the stew.

Niɛt Dirt, see Nit.

N̲ik The dusty part of the grains or cow dung.

Nik 1. To ask a reporter or a speaker the confirmation question 2. To take care of oneself, someone or any other thing.

N̲ikn̲ik 1. State of being in powder form or state. 2. State of being shaky or trembling due to sickness, cold or when carrying heavy load,

Nim Style of eating very slowly.eg Pälæ la mithæ nim : Leave him/her, he/she eats very slowly.

Nimnim Having that behavior or style of eating.

N̲in Plural of Nièn being a day of sleeping as explained above.

Nin Before or at the time eg̣. Kɛn ni hä nɛn ɛn nin? You did not see me before or at the time?

N̲iin 1. To close eyes. 2. A person who sleeps a lot.

Niinniin A game which is played by young boys (children) where participants close up their eyes inside a cattle hut luak.

N̲iŋ To become thin due to long illness such as paralysis.

N̲iŋn̲iŋ 1. State of becoming so thin due to such diseases or illness. 2. The appearance of a thin or weak person who stands without any support.

Niip 1. Fainting. 2. A situation when clouds cover the sun rays .See Tik.

Nipnip Being quite soft, cool or having nice shadow.

Nir 1. To have aimed and hit something with a gun, spear, bow and arrow. 2. To point out or tell what is expected by all.

Nit Plural of Niɛt being the dirt as explained above.

Niit A name of a baby born thin. e.g. Niit (Male) and

Nyaniit (Female).

Nitnit State of being naturally thin, tiny or slim.

Nith Which one of many items put before you. See M̲ith.

Niw 1. State of being quite thin. 2. The movements of eyelids.

Niwniw 1. The frequent movements of eyelids. 2. State of becoming very thin to the point it can get cut very fast or quickly.

No That is. e.g. A täh no: let it be like that.Bi nien ino. Bia buut ino : You spend a night without food. You spend a day without food.

Nok 1. To raise one head as when angry or when feeling pains. 2. A way of sitting as when one is quite tired, sick or hungry. 3. A disease which throws its victim down unconscious.

No̱k A person whose front teeth are bending inward.

Noknok A way or frequent movements of things from place to another.

Nol 1. A newly born dead baby or that dies immediately after birth. The baby is called Nol simply because it is buried together with umbilical cord.

Nom 2. To collect and put together items in one place. State of being quite soft, calm without disturbances at all.

Nomnom Being quite soft comfortable and very smooth to lie on.

Noan 1. Difficult in pronouncing a word or whatever. see Nonnon. 2. To go zigzag instead of straight or short cut route.

No̱o̱ŋ To bring something or some one to a place. See Nööñ

Nop To accumulate soft pieces to make a seat or a mattress.

Nopnop State of being quite comfortable, smooth or soft to sit on or sleep in.

No̱r 1. A type of trees. 2. To deprive a baby or a calf from sucking mother.

Nor To scratch something to pieces or powder forms.

No̱o̱r 1. A person who deprives a baby or a calf from its mother milk.2. Plural of Nòr being a kind of trees as explained above.

Nornor State of being in form of small particles, debris, or dust particles.

No̱t 1. The noise of Hippopotamus when it appears in the midwater. 2. State of movements up and down eg. No̱t wum : Nose up and down movements 3. A style of cooking fish.

Not 1. A cooked fish without bones. See Dëakɛ. 2. Slang for mass killing of people in combatant. Eg Ciɛ ruœdh ! caa rœ not: It is not combatant but have Massed up themselves.

Nothnoth State of being mixed up such as fish or meat after it is cooked for long period.

Noway A food prepared of fish and sorghum flour mixed together in Nuer fashion. This mixture gives wonderful taste even the White people failed to name it, because it is quite delicious.

Nowɛɛ A mixture of fish or meat with fried flour made food. see Kop.

Noy To be quite weak to face difficulties such as wrestling,fighting Even walking or standing for long time.eg Caa ŋœc cuæ tææth Æ noy : When they run he/she fell due to sickness.

Noynoy Being weak to wrestle or run, due to sickness for quite a long time.

Nɔk 1. A sudden way of falling as a result of fainting due to injury. 2. A long feathers or bull tails as part of decoration which is put on the head as an ornament from ostrich feathers, cow or bull tail.

Nɔ̱k 1. To bend down something, usually trees, poles, stalks, sticks flags, leaves etc. 2. State of not knowing or ignorant of what is happing around you.

Nɔ̱ɔ̱k State of being unable to feel or know what is happening around you or taking place.

Nɔ̱knɔ̱k State of being not active in doing something or things.

Nɔl To make flour from grains by pounding it very soft.

Nɔn 1. To find difficulties in pronouncing a word or to go zigzag road. 2. That is, as in eg. Jɛn nɔn: that it is.

Nɔnnɔn To have difficulties in either pronouncing or walking.

Nɔɔr 1. State of having something scratched or destroyed completely in pieces, 2. The broken pieces of the completely scratched utensil, egg or pot.

Nɔat Having been malnourished, such as a baby or a calf.

Nɔatnɔaat State of being malnourished. Eg Kɛ ŋaani kɛn ti nɔatnɔaat ti? : Who are these malnourished?

Nɔt A kind of fish with long tiny mouth.

Nu A word which is used for the confirmation of a question or the availability of something eg Jɛn ɛ thin i̱ nu: Is he/she/ it there?

Nuak State of being completely powerless.

Nuan To take as much as possible without counting.

Nua̱n A state of being thin due to lack of good and regular diets.

Nua̱a̱n State of being quite weak due to lack of proper feedings see Nuän.

Nuannuan State of getting difficulties in carrying something. See Nuɛnnuɛn.

Nuaŋ General weakness or difficulties in doing something.

Nuaŋnuaŋ State of being so weak to move or do anything.

Nuar To mix or put together things which are not supposed to be Mixed or put together according to Nuer beliefs and customs such as utensils.

Nuat 1. To join two or more either with string, by welding or with gum.. 2. Dog mating union where a bitch joins up with male dog for some minutes. 3. A slang for troubles, problems etc.

Nuatnuat State of being sticky or with sticky conditions.

Nuay 1. Chronic disease or sickness which drags on for sometimes. 2. To take hold of something from someone hands. 3. A type of food which is a mixture of more than two ingredients.

Nuaynuay State of being always sick or suffering of illness.

Nuelnuel Being quite sticky or difficult to separate.

Nueŋ State of being paralyzed.

Nuer 1. To get evil or misfortune for having eaten or drunk before certain rituals are performed usually when one killed or murdered someone. 2. State of having been affected by such customs. 3. It is the colonial distorted name for Nuär people or Naath.

Nuet 1. To join two or more items or elements using gum or whatever sticky substance. 2. To be dirty due to lack of bathing.

Nuæa 3..Things which are already been joined or sticked together. A mixture of food ingredients such as fish and grain flour. See Nuay.

Nuɛk A sort of head movements as when nodding.

Nuɛknuɛk 1. A continuous movement of one head up and down when agreeing of something. 2. A movement where you come and go. Eg Raan butɛ ɛ nuɛknuɛk kœari hœœk: *A person in continuous movement after cattle.*

Nuɛn To mess up things, confuse up or complicate the problem.

Nuɛɛn Having a lot of confusion or messing. Eg Jɛn ciku nuɛɛn œ ? : It is what you have just confused ?.

Nuɛnnuɛn A person who confuses, complicates things or makes them difficult to follow.

Nuɛt Slang for troubles caused by confused person or by implicating others.

Nuɛɛt A calf or a baby which has been malnourished by depriving it to suck mother milk.

Nuɛtnuɛt 1. State of being sticky or tends to join things together. 2. State of becoming thin due to lack of good feeding.

Nuuk State of pain feeling or suffering.

Nuknuk Not feeling well, eg. Nɛnɛ tɛɛ nuknuk: See him/her is not feeling well.

Nuok 1. To be overcome by pain, usually fever. 2. To wait for indefinite thing. 3. Having a lot of fruits on top of a tree. 4. Having a lot of items being carried on the head top. 4. To add some decorations, ornamental tools or instruments on the horns of a bull.

Nuook 1. State of having a tree full with many fruits. 2. To stay without knowing what is happening around you.eg Tut cæ nuook ci yak Wagrial : Tut was not aware like Hyena of Wagrial.

Nuoy 1. State of becoming wet with water, fat, or oil. 2. State of falling down very fast as a result of no resistance when wrestling or fighting.

Nuoynuoy Slang for a short or little person who can not walk very fast..

Nuɔ̱r Tiny particles of sand, soil that remain at the bottom of water container.

Nup 1. The flour of any type. 2. The tiny particles that looks like flour.

Nuy Having been made wet by either water, fat or oil.

Nuynuy Slang for a person who does not express him/herself clearly in front of people.

Näc Plural of Nac being the heifer of cow as explained above.

Näk 1. Näkpiny state of having killed a lot of people or ishes.. 2. To kill, hurt, harm or wound etc. 3. To put the final touches when making a container see Dieny.

Nääk 1. The person who extracts the children or whoever teeth. 2. The one who makes the final touches of a container or a Utensil

Näl 1. To add wild area along the farm edges so as to expand it wide or large. 2. The edges of a farm or garden.

Nääm 1. Person who escorts guests or visitors. 2. State of escorting someone being guests, visitors etc.

Nämnäm A style of walking with long steps usually by a tall person when in a hurry or in muddy ground.

Nään To separate by making the distance wide between two points or persons.

När 1. To have some milk frozen or fermented. 2. To pretend to be sleeping.eg Cu rɔɔdu när jiɛc rɔ : Do not pretend to be sleeping, get up.

Näär 1. Uncle, the mother brother or maternal uncle. 2. A cow that is given to uncle in the marriage of his niece or sister daughter.

Närnär State of being not rough after series beating.

Näwnäw Very weak and thin membranc that connects two parts.

Nuäknuäk State of having difficultie in walking.

Nuääknuääk That situation when one is forced to carry a heavy load..

Nuän To become thin due to some problems connected with starvation, sickness, worries etc.

Nuännuän State of being very thin and slim.

Nuäŋ Paralyse due to sickness or long illness.

Nuääŋ Paralysis or whatever causes paralysis.

Nuäŋnuäŋ Having much to do with paralytic behavior.

Nuär A type of sorghum grains from which Nuär as a tribe derived its name and later on in history got distorted to Nuer.

Nuärthɛɛr A type of tall grass.

Nuät Style of pricking fresh part of the body when making decoration see Biir.

Nuätnuät State of being so soft or fleshy when being continuously pricked. see Biir.

Nuäy To add some water or soup to food in order to make it soft.

Nuääy A mixed ingredient food which is already prepared or made.

Nök A kind of disease which knocks down a person. It is both single and plural.

Nökni Plural of No̱k being who has his /her front teeth bending inward as explained above.

Nöŋ 1. State of bringing whatever to someone or to a place eg. Bä

nöŋ i̱? Shall I bring it to you? 2. A female person who is a member of the bride final celebration day.

Nööŋ Plural of Nöŋ being a female guest that in company of the bride to her home in the final celebration.

Nöp A verbal message common among illiterate people.

Nööp Plural of Nöp being the verbal message as explained above.

Nör To deprive a calf or whatever from its mother milk,food or rights.

Nööri Plural of Nor a type of tree just the same like coccanut family. eg Cukɛ nyuur thaar nööri.:. They sat under coconut trees

Nöt The whitish creams that is formed when milk ferments.

Näy 1. State of being very difficult to give up whatever one is doing.. 2. State of becoming weak as a result of long wrestling or sickness.

Näynäy 1. Having that behaviour where one does not give up. 2. State of being weak due to chronic disease which have exhausted one energy.

Nh

Nh The sixteenth letter in Thok Nath.

Nhiac 1. To press or squeeze very hard in order to extract juice, blood, milk, pus etc. 2. A meat of a cow or bull slaughtered for Kujur which iœ cooked in one place and served by pushing a piece of meat into one mouth. See Nyuɔk 3. To do something very slowly as a style of lazyiness

Nhiaac Plural of Nhiac being a piece of meat of sacrifice as explained above.

Nhiacnhiac A nik name for a person who does not do his /her work very fast.

Nhiacnhiaac State of being so very lazy to do some work very fast.

Nhial Sky, up, above or high of any thing

Nhiaal 1. Rain or rainfall. 2. Having much to do with up, sky, etc. eg. Ba naŋ röl nhiaal:Will be taken to Heavenly kingdom. 3. Name of a male child born on rainy day. See Nyanhial.

Nhiam 1. Front part of anything including the face. Eg Poc nhiam du : Clean your face. 2. A head or to be on the lead or to head the group.eg Wer nhiam cu luny jok : You go to the front do not come back.

Nhiamnhiam 1. To face something difficult or problem in order to over come it. To go forward. See Jɔakjɔak.

Nhian 1. A testicle with stress on (a). 2. Plural of Nhian being testicle as explained above.

Nhiany 1. To hit, blow or box someone thoroughly till he/she becomes powerless or weak. 2. A result of heavy load..

Nhianynhiany That load which could cause one much suffering due to it is being heavy.

Nhiat Having been pushed back with both hands or legs. Eg A caa nhiat jok :Let it not be pushed back.

Nhiel Plural of Nhiaal being the rain or rainfall as explained above. Be sure that there is no plural for up, high or sky Nhial

Nhiem 1. Plural of Nhiam being the front or the face as explained above. 2. Distorted pronunciation of Mim the hairs.

Nhieny To feed some one with food till he/she gets satisfied.

Nhier Plural of Nhieer being the turtle as explained below.

Nhieer Turtle.

Nhiet 1. Push back with both hands, and legs, poles, paddles etc. 2. To push a stick as when one can not move without such a supporting stick..

Nhieet An instrument that is used for pushing back something, or supporting in walking.

Nhɔk 1. Love, liking, accept, agree etc. 2. To answer a call by saying Yes or No.

Nhä The sound of this letter Nh.

Nhiäny That can cause great satisfaction.

Nhiääny Having been well satisfied and not ready to ask for more.eg Gat ɛmɛ cɛ bi nhiääny mi ba tɛɛ räpräp kɛ mieth: This child can not get satisfied if he/she acts very fast with food.

Nhiänynhiäny Having clumsy volume or bulky shape.

Nhök 1. Love, like, to accept, to agree. 2. To answer a call by saying "yes". Nuer have gender differences in answering a cal l where a male says Wec, while a female says Wiew.

Ny

Ny The seventeenth letter of Thok Nath.

Nya 1. A suffic which is used to indicate a female gender. It comes before a name of a person eg Nya Douth where Douth is a last twin for male baby and Both being the first twin for male where Nya Both is a female. 2. Means female girl. e.g. Ɛ nya ŋa? Whose girl ?. see Nyal.

Nyac 1. To smear wall, floor etc with mud. 2. Dirt on the eyes. 3. A fish in a pool or pond which could be fished for feeding. 4. To second spearing at someone or something as when fishing in a group.

Nya̱c A period when harvesting is carried out in Nuer land.

Nyaac 1. Plural of Nyac being the availability of fish in a pool (s) to be fished for feeding. Eg Yier tææ kæ nyaac :The pool has some fishes. 2. Being the dirts that appear on the eyes when one gets up from sleep in the morning or when the eye is sick.

Nyak State of having something not well cooked, prepared or smeared etc.

Nya̱a̱k A situation of hatred behavior between two or three wives where each one tries to own the husband and thus causes quarrel amongst them.

Nyal 1. Girl or a young female of human being not yet married. 2. A situation when something have changed to the opposite expectation. Eg Ruac ɛɛ lat nɛ cɛ rœ nyal: What we discussed has changed opposite.

Nya̱l 1. The movements of a fish outside water. 2. To remember or recall **someone** or something you know before usaully bad or good deeds.

Nyaal 1. The greenish colour that appears on top of stagnant water usually pond, pools etc. 2. Plural of Nyal being a girl as explained above. 3. An exclamation word for describing a great number of girls in one place.eg Ciæ nyaal cæ piny thieñ ! : A lot of girls they covered the ground !.

Nya̱a̱l Plural of Nyäl to remind about bad or good deeds done early.

Nyalnyal State of being changeable or fond of changing a topic as when discussing issues or various topics.

Nyalualɛdiŋ A kind of sorghum plants where its grains make good flour.

Nyam 1. A short form for eg Nyal kæl that is one girl, it is said e.g. Nyam kɛl: one girl instead of Nyal kæl. 2. The noise as that is heard when chewing or eating something.

Nyamnyam A tribe which had been in both Western Equatoria and Western Bahr-el-Ghazal long time ago which was alleged to have been eating human beings or cannibal.

Nyamaar 1. My sister or literally girl of my mother. 2. A name given to a female baby born when relationships are exceptionally very good.

Nyan 1. Failure to hold one person as when fighting or wrestling. 2. A green plant pest which feeds on geeen leaves. 3. To add some mud to the walls or floors already been mudded. 4. To clean something with tongue, or lick it. 5. That is difficult to be handled or stopped.

Nya̱n Difficult to be controlled or be handled.

Nyannyan That can be swallowd vey fast because it is delicious or sweet.

Nyaŋ 1. Crocodile. 2. A colour which combines different colours in dimensions. 3. To make or dirt with shits, blood etc.

Nya̱ŋ 1. High or thin cloud which gives shade in hot sunny day. 2. Plural of Nyaŋ being the crocodile as explained above.

Nya̱ŋni Plural of Nya̱ŋ being the cloud that shades in sunny day as explained above.

Nyaŋnyaŋ A type of amphibian, one of marine life. See Cöm.

Nyaŋkuacja̱ŋ One of the wild vegetable or greens.

Nyaŋle̱w A small coloured bird which surprises a passer-by by making a quick move of flying.

Nyaŋkät A kind of gum which is reddish in colour.

Nyany To pull away and leave a path to someone passing e.g. Nyany rɔ:.

leave the way.An old version. see Guæny ro, Nyelæ.

Nyar 1. A group of bushy or small trees. 2. A type of trees which is usually short and thick. 3. To reproduce milk by allowing baby or calf sucking once more.

Nya̱a̱r 1. A person who lost his/her front and upper teeth. See Kueeth. 2. The early growth of plants.

Nyariɛw A type of trees which grows in wetland areas.

Nyarnyar 1. State of being very light and not heavy flood. 2. State of showing little growth or appearance on the surface.

Nyatnyat State of being difficult to push back or overcome.

Nyath Failure to execute orders or lack of taking a decision in carrying out a request.

Nyathnyath A person who fails or who tends not to carry out the orders.

Nyaaw Cat or cat family.

Nyaawni Plural of Nyaaw being a cat as explained above.

Nyawnyaw Being very colourful usually black and white,

Nya̱y Oozing with either water or blood.

Nyek A woman who shares a husband with another.

Nyekni Plural of Nyek being a woman who shares a husband as explained above.

Nyielɛ A word which means let me pass or allow me pass (an old word).

Nyem 1. A single lower front teeth. 2. A fin of the fish which helps it to move in water.

Nyeeny To quarrel or fight.eg Cuarɛ nyeeny: Do not quarrel or fight.

Nyeŋ A small child or young one.

Nyeeŋ Plural of Nyeŋ being a small or young child as explained above.

Nyer Plural of Nyal being a girl as explained above.

Nye̱t Plural of Nyet being a rib bone as explained below.

Nyet A rib bone.

Nyeynyey The tasty and delicious part of bone marrow which is soft and breakable, rich with Calcium.

Nyɛth To imitate someone way of talking, walking or doing things.

Nyi A feminine suffic for his/her sister opposite of Dä. Eg Nyiman maar.: My mother sister.

Nyiam Sound or noise which is heard when chewing something.

Nyic To give very little when dividing something.

Nyicnyic State of being very little or small piece.

Nyie Plural of Nyi as in Nyiman: His/ her sister become Nyie kæ : His/ her daughters.

Nyiem Plural of Nyem being a single lower front teeth as explained above.

Nyieŋ Youngsters or small children.

Nyier To hate or dislike someone or something.

Nyieer A person who hates greatly.

Nyiernyier State of great hatred to someone.

Nyiemɔɔr Your sisters or daughters of your mother.

Nyieth 1. Stubborn, trouble some person. 2. Mosquito.

Nyiethni Plural of Nyieth being the mosquito as explained above.

Nyiethnyieth Problematic or troubleshooter.

Nyiew A game which is played on sand beach.

Nyiman His/her sister or his/her mother daughter.

Nyimaar My sister. My mother daughter

Nyimɔɔr Your sister.Your mother daughter.

Nyin 1. Plural of Waŋ being the eye as explained below. 2. Belonging, luggage, or properties.

Nyimnyim Very small or little in size for both human beings and things.

Nyiŋnyiŋ

Nyioat Very little, tiny or minute in size.A type of tree which is used for making spear woods.

Nyongol The vulture.

Nyongool Plural of Nyongol being the vulture as explained above.

Nyiot 1. To stir something such as food while getting cooked. 2. Plural of Nyioat being a type of tree as explained above.

Nyir Plural of Nyier to have great hatred or dislike as explained above.

Nyirnyir 1. State of being very small or tiny. 2. Great hatred to someone or something.

Nyith To cut from the bottom or lower part of a stem, stalk or a tree.

Nyithnyith State of being sharp as when it cuts at once.

Nyiwnyiw 1. Being quick. 2. State of being very fine, dusty as with the grains or sand particles.

Nyol To cut, pick or select before it/he/she reaches the maturity age.

Nyo̱c Plural of Nyɔac being fish fins as explained below.

Nyon 1. Old grass pulled out of a thatched roof. 2. To cause confusion or to confuse.

Nyoɔn Plural of Nyon a state of great confusion and difficult to put right.

Nyo̱o̱n A boy who milks a cow into his own mouth.

Nyonnyon A person or animal that causes confusion of anything.

Nyoŋ 1. To suck very slightly as when lacking interest or have got satisfied. 2. To tie up or twist something with string or rope etc.

Nyoŋɛ A bag made of cloth for filtering food or drink substances.

Nyooŋ 1. A disease that disturbs stomach or upsets it. 2. Slang for a person who hates people and does not cooperate.

Nyoŋnyoŋ The movement of insect, snake, worm or any movement as when in dancing.

Nyor 1. The nursery stage of growing tobacco plant. 2. Becoming much, in plenty or in great quantities.

Nyornyor Steady growth of tobacco in a nursery.

Nyot To rain with few drops for a long time. See Diŋdiŋ

Nyoot A continuous drizzling of rain for quite a long time.

Nyownyow State of being naked or walking naked.

Nyɔac 1. State of having much to do with flood, eg. Rɛy nyɔac: In the flood. 2. Fish fins or part of fish organ for breathing

Nyɔak State of having much to do with repetition in talking or chewing.

Nyɔakni Plural of Nyɔak being repetition of anything as explained above.

Nyɔc Flood, which is the rise of river water due to heavy rainfalls.

Nyɔk 1. To repeat once more or to repeat oneself. 2. A wild plants or weed. 3. To recall or reclaim whatever you have had given out, or said.

Nyɔknyɔk A behaviour where one reclaims whatever he/she has given out.

Nyɔl 1. To mark a very young person by cutting on his face six traditional marks. 2. A slang for young person or non -matured one. eg Nyœl ɛmɛ wœc rœ nhiamdä: You little one be away in front of me. 3. To cut maize bundles before proper ripening

Nyɔlnyɔl 1. State of being very small in size. 2. A type of plants which is collected before it gets ripened for making ropes. See Thie̱t.

Nyɔn To do the art of milking into one own mouth.

Nyɔny 1. To reach a person or an object you are chasing in a short distance. 2. Having the broth exhausted water before the food gets cooked.

Nyɔɔny A short legs person or animal eg ɛ wuor mi diit ci nyœœny ɛ bi luaŋ: It is a great racing where short legs can not make it.

Nyɔnynyɔny The way, the short legs person walks.eg Dɛŋ ja̱lɛ nyœnynyœny nhiam wutni: Deng being short legs is walking slowly before the men.

Nyɔp A person who does not do good,act very fast or clean things.

Nyɔɔp State of being not able to do something very fast or clean.

Nyɔpnyɔp State of laziness or not very fast in doing things.

Nyo̱a̱r To dry something by hanging it over fire flame.

Nyɔɔr A Nuer belief, that when an elder person defecates stool in the house, at home or garden,it causes much harm to the family members.

Nyɔrɔr State of being not well cleaned or being not cut smoothly.

Nyo̱t 1. To stir the food or whatever using a stiring tool. See Pic. 2. To cause confusion or a slang for trouble shooter.

Nyɔt To touch by hand or with something. eg Cuɛ nyœt bɛ mär:Do not touch it will explode.

Nyɔtnyɔt 1. Very little in regard to size (human) or rainfall. 2. State of feeling when something is moving on the head or body.

Nyuak To share something with someone or people.

Nyuaak The art of sharing things usually food, cow etc with others.

Nyuaknyuak State of having bright colours usually black and white for both decorated bull or painting.

Nyua̱n State of being helpless.

Nyua̱a̱n State of being quite helpless ẹg ɛŋu cia nyua̱a̱n inɛ mɛ? *Why did you become helpless like this?*.

Nyuany To cause bruises on a body with hard and sharp iron tool or wood.

Nyuanynyuany State of having the surface not smooth.

Nyuanyany State of being quite rough surface.

Nyuar To take or grab something in a bulky manner.

Nyuaar Plural of Nyuar being whatever is collected or taken in such away as explained above.

Nyuarnyuar A person who always takes anything in a bulky way or manner.

Nyua̱a̱th State of having muscle got dislocated see Nyuäth.

Nyua̱thnyua̱th That can get cut or harm very easily or simply.

Nyuek The actual sharing of things with other people eg Jin nyueki kɛ?:Are you sharing with them?.

Nyuel Lack of respect shown by a young person to an elderly one. See Dho̱l.

Nyuɛlnyuɛl State of being aggressive or lack of respect to elders.

Nyueny To forge sharp points on iron tool by a black smith.

Nyuey The actual chewing of food substance before swallowing it.

Nyueey The waste of a chewed stalk, sugar cane etc.

Nyueeyni Plural of Nyueey being the waste of chewed stalks as explained above.

Nyuɛa To chew food materials or whatever with teeth.

Nyuɛal Lack of respect shown to elders.

Nyuɛny A metallic device instrument for fighting among boys etc.

Nyuɛɛny Such a device instrument made with sharp points.

Nyuɛnyni Plural of Nyuɛny being such a device as explained above.

Nyuɛnynyuɛny State of having sharp points that scratch on a surface to scare people away.

Nyuɛr 1. Drop of rain water or any other liquid. 2. To forge sharp points or decoration on metallic tool.

Nyuɛɛr Plural of Nyuɛr being the rain water or drops of liquids as explained above.

Nyuɛri Plural of Nyuɛr being the device of sharp points or decorations as explained above.

Nyuɛrnyuɛr State of having a metallic tool made with teeth as that of sawing machine.

Nyuok The growth of new leaves in spring season.

Nyuol To cause bruise on the skin or surface

Nyuon Having been confused, or confusing.

Nyuornyuor The early stages of tobacco growth.

Nyuoth To point at, to show something or to make a thing known.

Nyuɔk To put a piece of cooked meat into the mouth of someone as part of ritual performance.

Nyuɔɔk Plural of Nyuœk being a piece of cooked meat which is put into people mouths as explained above.

Nyuɔlnyuɔl The early growth of plants particularly tobacco or whatever.

Nyuɔ̱m A sesam plant which is used for making oil or seed oil.

Nyuɔɔn Plural of Nyuon being state of confusion as explained below. eg Ti nyuɔɔn : You have much confusion.

Nyuɔ̱th To show or teach someone something.

Nyuur 1. Sitting or to sit down. 2. A meeting, conference etc.

Nyuuri 1. Plural of Nyuur being a sitting or a meeting as explained above. 2. You sit (second person singular).eg Jin nyuuri dueel : You sit in the hut(room).

Nyuuth 1. To teach.2. A teacher. 3. The teaching 4. A signal or whatever indicates that something is going to happen in future or in short period.

Nyuuthni Plural of Nyuuth being signal or an indicator as explained above.

Nyäk 1. To have spoiled, misused or mismanaged something or someone. 2. To share a husband.

Nyääk Having been spoiled or made useless. Eg Cuɛ gaŋ cɛ nyääk ni wal: Do not prevent,it has already been spoiled long ago.

Nyäl 1. Cow colour which is brownish with some whitish spots on various parts. 2. To point out or remind someone about bad or good things done early.

Nyääl 1. Python snake. 2. Plural of Nyäl being reminder of what had happened sometimes.

Nyälnyäl A style of fish movements outside water.

Nyämnyäm Being short and fat. See Ruethrueth.

Nyäŋ 1. Plural of Nyaŋ being both crocodile and a certain colour. 2. Sudden or unexpected actions as when dodging something.

Nyäŋnyäŋ Very minor thing that delays or prevents something to fall or to take place.

Nyäny 1. The bulky part of a thing or body.2. The outer part of something.

Nyänynyäny State of being so bulky or not sharp.

Nyär The gum or that part of the mouth which accommodates teeth.

Nyärnyär State of being not well grown on the surface such as nursery stage. See Nya̱a̱r.

Nyät Difficult to overcome or to push back. Failure to overcome something.

Nyäth To smooth cattle compound after a heavy rainfall.

Nyääth Light or scattered light clouds in the sky.

Nyäthnyäth 1. Being muddy due to rainfall or cow dung. 2. Not well cleaned or washed from dirts.

Nyäw A whitish colour type of beads.

Nyäwnyaŋ A nickname according to bull colours.

Nyäy An insect that attacks people during the harvest of surgheom.

Nyiöp To mix up something with hands and feet usually mud, soil, etc.

Nyiöt To touch by hand or whatever.

Nyuän 1. Helpless person. eg. Ɛŋu jin nyuän ɔ̱? Why are you helpless? 2. To pull out something without difficulties.

Nyuännyuän That could be easily pulled out or which can be pulled out very fast.

Nyuäŋ

Nyuär To attempt to chew or suck something and leave it half way.To be bulky, thick or huge.

Nyuärnyuär State of being very thick or huge, gaint or fat.

Nyuäth An accident w hich causes muscle dislocation.

Nyöc Plural of Nyɔc being the flood as explained above.

Nyök To repeat or to do something many times.

Nyöl State of being too little or very young as a case with human being.

Nyööl Plural of Nyöl being little in size like a child or kid as explained above.

Nyön To milk cow into one own mouth, usually by uninitiated boys in cattle camps.

Nyöön Plural of Nyo̱o̱n being one who milks a cow into his own mouth as explained above.

Nyöny State of having reached someone in a short distance of running or walking.

Nyöŋ Food or intestine movements in the stomach.

Nyöt The action of touching a person or anything around.

Ŋ

Ŋ The eighteenth letter of Thok Nath.

Ŋa Who, for all genders.eg ɛ ŋa bɛɛ œ kie ŋa wææ œ? Who iscoming and who is going?

Ŋaani 1. Who are they? 2. Plural of Ŋa..Eg kɛ yɛn ŋaani? Who are you?

Ŋac Plural of Ñaac a drop of human being sperms as explained below.

Ŋa̱c 1. To know or recognize something or someone. 2. The milking or to milk a cow, goat etc

Ŋa̱a̱c Plural of Ŋääc a person who milks cows or goats as explained below

Ŋaac A drop of sperms.

Ŋacŋac A fight provoking insult statement that refer to sperms.

Ŋak 1. Failure to get down from the top of a tree, building or whatever. 2. Difficulty,one faces to pull out his hands or legs from a hole,a branch etc. 3. To clear weed in a farm by making a circular shape around Grass or weeds. 4. To make a surprise attack on the front part of the enemies. 5. To argue out something in a dialogue. 6. To go ahead of the cattle in order to change the route of their movements.

Ŋaak The semi- greenish fluid which appears or oozes from an old wound.

Ŋa̱a̱k Plural of Ŋääk being a youngman of showing off in cattle camp as explained below.

Ŋakŋak State of finding difficulties in speaking due to cold,stammering or fear.

Ŋaknɔm Argument where each person tries to be telling the truth.

Ŋal To be quick in doing something. see Mal or Dap eg.Ñal kiæ mal kiæ dap ben : Come quickly, very fast, in short time.

Ŋalaŋ.1A knife like device which is worn around the wrist for self defence in a fight. 2. State of being very sharp such as knife, spear etc. that cuts very fast.

Ŋam 1. To stick to someone or many people when begging or implicating him/her or them into troubles. 2. To pretend biting something or someone. 3. A relative or person of connection in one way or the other, eg. Ɛ ŋamdu or ɛ ŋamdɛ? What is your relationship? or what is his/her relationship?. 4. A single grain of boiled surgheom.See Ŋaam.

Ŋa̲m 1. Yawning due to being so tired or exhausted. 2. To open one mouth as when eating,taking drugs or talking

Ŋaam 1. Plural of Ŋam being boiled grains as explained above. 2. The cracking of clay soil due to dryness. See Bak.

Ŋamŋam State of being cracking due to draught or dryness.

Ŋany To open very quickly without following the right and proper ways.

Ŋanyŋany State of being restless or suffering of stomach troubles.

Ŋaŋ 1. To pretend to hit or spear a person with a big stick, spear etc. 2. To take a big piece from a bulky or solid material such as food, soil etc. 3. To take or cut off some part from the main stem or body.

Ŋaŋŋaŋ A person who hesitates in beating, spearing, hitting someone or something.

Ŋap 1. Bat. It is known as Ŋaprɔ kɛ dhɔ̱t : Meaning which hangs itself by its bottom. 2. To hang either oneself, someone, or something. 3. Hanging up a piece of cloth or whatever.

Ŋapŋap The bird Bat that hangs itself by its bottom.

Ŋar Play, game etc. to amuse or learn by practicing.

Ŋarŋar 1. State of tears falling when in a deep sadness or great laughter. 2. To misuse something or wrong usage of someone or something.

Ŋat 1. To sharpen the horns of a young bull, or to show one bull horns in a dance.The shaping of the horns. 2. To sharpen a stick in order to fit or fix a metallic tool such as spear or anyother device.

Ŋa̲a̲t A person who shapes or sharpens the horns or sticks. see Ŋät.

Ŋa̲th Belief or faith.

Ŋaw 1. A small wild animal of cat family. 2. To tell untrue stories or reports.

Ŋawŋaw Being fat meat,which gets chewed very fast.

Ŋa̲y A condition of clay made utensil which gets destroyed very fast.

Ŋa̲yŋa̲y State of being soft or very loose and difficult to be kept or held.

Ŋayŋay Full of fats such as meat or fish.

Ŋep 1. Being at the verge or point of weeping due to deep sadness or sorrow. 2. To make marks or decorate by making marks on wood. See Ŋuɛk.

Ŋer 1. To cut grain bundles as when harvesting. 2. A type of smell which releases by a certain type of plants.

Ŋe̱e̱r 1. The person who cuts bundles or harvests the field. 2. Plural of Ŋe̱e̱r being he/she who cuts or harvests as explained above. 3. That type of plant which produces smell when burned.

Ŋet To wish death to someone by wearing mourning clothes.

Ŋeet Plural of Ŋɛt being a piece of a broken clay utensil as explained below.

Ŋetet State of being in series confrontation with someone ready to fight.

Ŋɛc A bird that feeds on sawn seeds from Guinea bird family

Ŋɛcni Plural of Ŋɛc being that bird which feeds on sawn seeds as explained above.

Ŋɛak A person whose Ŋɛk tip of back bone has petruded further.

Ŋɛk 1. To make a minor surgical operation where one opens a bruise or swollen part with a knife to release fluids. 2. The last bottom part of the backbone particularly when it pretrudes. 3. To extract grains from the newly ripened surgheom or bundle.

Ŋɛɛk The person who performs surgical operation on bruise or fracture.

Ŋɛɛkŋɛɛk An insult to such a person whose Ŋɛk is pertruded.

Ŋɛl A word which is used to express anger. See Ŋɛm.

Ŋɛlŋɛl An insulting word to a person who makes silly, bad actions or mistakes.

Ŋɛm 1. A word which expresses anger or insult. 2. To bite parts of something and leave the other part as that is made by a rat, mouse on gourd utensil. 3. A long knife like device which is used for cutting grass or grain bundles in harvest.

Ŋɛmŋɛm An insult to someone who keeps on talking to angry person due to a mistake made to him/her.

Ŋɛany State of anger that provokes fighting.

Ŋɛny 1. To open widely the mouth, door etc. 2. Plural of Ŋɛany being the way of opening as explained above. 3. To put something down usually food, container,body etc.eg Ŋɛ̈ny ni jɛ piny: Put it down.

Ŋɛnyŋɛny 1. State of being restless or suffering from pains or sickness. Ñæñ 2. Bravery and ready to face danger. Being courageous person or animal. The head or top of human being penis.

Ŋɛŋŋɛŋ That device which has edges or scales like penis top.

Ŋɛp 1. State of being sad. 2. A style of drinking, sleeping etc. 3. To select or choose what you want from things that are to be divided later.

Ŋɛpŋɛp That have bright colour such as black and white or white and red.

Ŋɛar 1. To get surprised or shocked of unexpected scenery. 2. To become or get tired due to having walked or run long distance.

Ŋɛr To backbite. someone, people or to talk ill of them.

Ŋɛɛr 1. Having much to do with harvesting or cutting of grass.eg Nyadak cɛ wä ŋɛɛr: Nyadak has gone harvesting. 2. A small animal game such as Tiang, Dìæl, Kæaw etc.

Ŋɛrŋɛr 1. A condition which causes a person not to be active. 2. That can get cut or broken very fast.

Ŋɛt A piece of broken earthern or gourd utensil.

Ŋɛtŋɛt A half broken utensil which is still in use or service.

Ŋɛth Plural of Ŋëth being the aches as explained below.

Ŋɛw 1. A broken utensil such as gourd or hearthen utensil. 2. Having stopped flowing or oozing either water, blood etc. 3. Difficult or hard to be handled. 4. To break a part of a gourd or earthen utensil.

Ŋɛwŋɛw State of utensil having parts broken away.

Ŋɛy 1. A well prepared kind of Surgheom food in Nuer land. 2. To make noise with faint sound as when unhappy, or by mosquito wings noise. 3. Clearly visible to the sight or which is completely in full sight

Ŋɛyni Plural of Ŋɛy being a type of food as explained above.

Ŋic 1. To recognize someone,or something.2. To identify someone or something. 3. Tiny insect of ant family which is usually brownish in colour. 4. Piece(s) of food which remains between teeth. 5. Slang for being brownish in colour.

Ŋiic Plural of Ŋic being the tiny pieces of food as explained above.

Ŋi̱i̱c 1. Teacher. 2. Ṭhe art or action of cautioning a person.

Ŋiec Plural of Ŋi̱i̱c being the teacher or the teaching work. as explained above.

Ŋiew 1. A stomach disease such as gardiais that causes troubles. 2. A type of grass with sharp leaf blends.

Ŋiey 1. State of being well soaked in fats or butter. 2. Continuous faint noise which disturbs the ears.

Ŋieyŋiey That kind of continuous low voice as that is made by mosquito wings when flying.

Ŋik 1. To persuade someone to tell or disclose the secrets with threats of beating or punishment. 2. To behave in a way of threatening where one shows to spear at someone.

Ŋi̱l 1. The precipitated part of butter where pure and liquid parts are collected. 2. The metaphour or slang of being the nice part of a talk or discussion.

Ŋin 1. The preparation of traditional food Kuän using many devices with flour. 2. To put down someone or something. See Ŋinpiny.eg Kuän baa ñin piny nhiam nath :The food is put down in front of the people. Eg Bia kæ ñin piny : You just put them down. 3. To cause delay by slowing the collection of things at departure time.

Ŋinŋin A person who causes delay or have the habit of delaying.

Ŋiny To break, or to cut the last part.

Ŋinyŋiny State of being very short or small after breakage or cutting. See Ŋuɔ̱ny.

Ŋi̱ŋ Not quick in doing, talking or taking a decision.

Ŋiŋŋiŋ A person who hesitates in taking a decision.

Ŋir A smell of flowers or plants.

Ŋi̱i̱r A type of plants that excretes very powerful smell.

Ŋi̱rŋi̱r Having that powerful smell.

Ŋirŋir The appearance of the smeared skin with fat, oil or butter.

Ñirñiir Plural of Ñirñir being a state of having this type of smell frequently as explained above.

Ŋit 1. Full or filled to the brim. 2. Slang for having got a problem. eg. Cɛ wä ŋit. : It has become very difficult or no way out.

Ŋi̱tŋi̱t Having become full of water, beer or whatever liquid.

Ŋiw 1. A feeling when someone chews something you hate or do not like. 2. To cut at once with a sharp spear, razorblade etc.

Ŋi̱wŋi̱w 1. That feeling when someone chews what you hates. 2. It is a sound.

Ŋiwŋiw State of being so sharp and fast in cutting.

Ŋoac Running, racing or jogging

Ŋoak A person from Dinka of Baleet County.

Ŋoa̱ny A type of trees with large green leaves.

Ŋoa̱ŋ To become too tire to continue doing something.

Ŋok To cut, see gi̱m, yäp, tɛm etc.

Ŋo̱k A kind of birds that lives along the river or water ways. Ị̣t is Grayish or grayish in colour.

Ŋol A slang for ugly face of human being.eg Woc rœ ñol nyìn : Get away ugly eye.

Ŋoɔl A piece of compact thing as that of tobacco, soil, clay etc.

Ŋo̱lŋo̱l State of having that type of not smooth appearance which is not straight.

Ŋon State of having some reservation or doubts to some one opinion.

Ŋonyŋony State of being not handsome or bulky in shape.

Ŋoŋ Plural of Ŋoaŋ being quite tired as explained before.

Ŋop To sip or to take a mouthful of some liquid, see Yöp.

Ŋo̱r Smell of giraff meat or fat. See Ŋi̱r.

Ŋor Stomach pains.

Ŋo̱rŋo̱r The smell of giraff meat fat.

Ŋorŋor The beginning of stomach troubles or pains.

Ŋot 1. To cut the goat or whatever throat or slaughtering for sacrifice. 2. Not yet completed or ready eg Wä rɛɛk ŋotɛ: Going to town is not yet. 3. To eat as that of goat, cows etc. 4. A slang for eating.

Ŋo̱tŋo̱t A maize bundle that has not yet ripened properly which is chewed only from the bundle.

Ŋo̱tŋo̱tni Plural of Ŋo̱tŋo̱t being the chewing of not well ripened maize as explained above.

Ŋothŋoth An insult word just like Fucken or fucked up.

Ŋo̱w 1. To eat something which is not yet ripened. 2. To tell unverified news or coined stories which are baseless.

Ŋɔak Property, luggage or personal things.

Ŋɔal Having much to do with lame person. eg. Ɛ gat ŋɔal: A son of lame person.

Ŋɔan A type of rope that is made by twisting materials to make a rope. see Ŋo̱n.

Ŋɔaani Plural of Ŋɔak which is a plural by itself which means things as explained above.eg Titi ŋœaani ti baa nañ : These are things to be taken.

Ŋɔa̱p Having much to do with Ŋɔp being a tree. eg. Thar ŋɔa̱p: Under this ŋœàp tree.

Ŋɔa̱a̱r Plural of Ŋɔa̱r being a centain type of beans as explained below.

Ŋɔɔk Plural of Ñœak being a person from Dinka section who lives between Shilluk and Eastern Jikany Nuer.

Ŋɔl A lame animal or human being. See Ŋöt.

Ŋɔlŋɔl State of being not straight or forward due to some bending and curves.

Ŋɔm Knife or whatever is used for cutting.

Ŋɔa̱mni Plural of Ŋɔm being a knife as explained above.

Ŋɔa̱ny A type of trees with large conical green leaves.

Ŋɔɔm An insult answering to a call which means fucken.

Ŋɔmŋɔm An insult which is said to someone who behaves badly.

Ŋɔ̱ny Plural of Ŋɔa̱ny being a type of trees as explained above.

Ŋɔɔny Stomach troubles or pain when food eaten being digested.

Ŋɔnyŋɔny 1. State of being not straight or smooth as that of surface. 2. A bad style of walking or running.

Ŋɔ̱p 1. A type of trees which grows along the river banks.2. The taking of mouthful of milk,soup, water or beer. see Buny

Ŋɔ̱ɔ̱p State of having something to do with Ŋåp tree.eg Wia thaar ñååp : You go under this tree.

Ŋɔ̱a̱r 1. A type of beans which has several colours. 2. To take as much as possible from free heap or bundles.

Ŋɔ̱rŋëac A type of wild beans eg. Coŋoŋ eg Nɛmɛ ɛ ŋɔrŋëac :This is a wild bean.

Ŋɔth An insult where it is said while pointing a finger at person.

Ŋu What. Eg Tä kæ ñu ? What do I have?

Ŋuac A kind of insect which provides delicious high protein food.

Ŋua̱c To smell or the smelling see Ñua̱ny.

Ŋuak A newly cleared ground for cultivation or farming purposes. See Kuac.

Ŋuak Plural of Ŋuäk being the neck as explained below.

Ŋuaak 1. Having much to do with Ŋuäk.eg ɛn duɔɔr bɛcɛ ŋuaakdɛ The thing is paining on his/her neck 2. Having a fat or long neck.

Ŋual Debt, loan or borrowed item such as cows, money etc.

Ŋuan Great in number or quantity.eg Görkɛ nɛy ti ŋuan : Many people are wanted.

Ŋuaan Figure or number (4,four).

Ŋuanŋuan A series of fours or by four.

Ŋuany Not smooth but with a lot of stones or debris.

Ŋuanyŋuany State of being not smooth.

Ŋuaŋ 1. A practical invitation for a show off in a dance in marriage ceremony. Eg Wer ŋuaŋ gat way du : Invite youraunt son for show off dance. 2. To threaten someone as if you want to beat or spear him.

Ŋuaŋŋuaŋ 1. State of being shy due to respect or hesitation in doing or saying something. 2. A person who does not take quick action

Ŋuat Plural of Ŋuäät a parasitic worm which lives in human stomach. As explained below.

Ŋuaw To pick not yet properly ripened grain bundles.

Ŋuawŋuaw State of feeling shy or afraid to do a thing in front of many people.

Ŋuek 1. To clear a wild land for a farm or field in wet or rainy season. 2. To cut or curve a wood in a certain style of decoration.

Ŋuen A situation where one thinks to ask or avenge on someone who did something bad.

Ŋueny 1. State of picking mud for modeling. 2. To take hold of someone body part while fighting or wrestling.

Ŋueŋ 1. A practical move to inform people particularly relatives and friends about marriage settlement celebrations.It is an ancient way of notifying people about marriage celebration and settlement. 2. To select a person usually a friend, cousin etc in a dance in order to show off before ladies and peers.

Ŋueeŋ Plural of Ŋueeŋ a person who selects for dance show off as explained below.

Ŋueeŋ A person who selects a person for a dance show off.

Ŋuer 1. To extract out or pluck out grains before ripening well. 2. Plural of Ŋue̱e̱r being a type of trees as explained below.

Ŋue̱e̱r A type of trees which produces gum and thick carved thorns.

Ŋuetni Plural of Ñuet a state of scratching the skin with fingers nails or tools.

Ŋuɛan Plural of Ŋuɛn a state of feeling angery to the point of revenging when someone has done bad to you as explained below.

Ŋuɛk To prepare a peg out of a piece of wood. See Ŋɛp.

Ŋuɛkŋuɛk State of having scales as a result of decoration or carving..

Ŋuɛl A slang for a circumcised person.see Thöny.

Ŋuɛlŋuɛl State of having a circumcised penis.

Ŋuɛm Being with very small size.

Ŋuɛmŋuɛm State of having small buttocks which is an insult.

Ŋuɛn An angery thinking for revenging for bad done to one Sometime back.

Ŋuɛny 1. To pick up mud, etc or take hold of someone while fighting or wrestling. 2. A dried soil which becomes so hard and sharp. 3. Slang for running a series race eg Ci kɛ ŋuɛny ni jɛ kɛ wuor ni kɛ tukdɛ :They started running a series race.as from the beginning.

Ŋuɛnyŋuɛny 1. That can allow chances for holding something.

Ŋuær 2. State of being rough surface. To collect unripened grains from a bundle.

Ŋuɛrŋuɛr Grain bundle that has not yet ripened.

Ŋuɛt 1. Youth or young man. 2. To cause injuries with finger, nails or tools. 3. The art of magical power that plucks out gravels, pieces of bones out of human being by a witchdoctor.

Ŋuɛtni Plural of Ŋuɛt being a young man as explained above.

Ŋuɛɛt State of youthful or being youth and having ornamental requirements and decoration fashions.

Ŋuɛth State of being not smooth or clean.

Ŋuɛthŋuɛth Being not clean,, smooth, dirty with sands or grains particles.

Ŋuɛyŋuɛy Not well shaped or framed body.

Ŋuil 1. To have something got broken at once as glass, steel iron device, etc. 2. Take a sharp decision when very angry or to get cut easily.

Ŋuilŋuil Being breakable or easy to get broken.

Ŋuim Very little or small as when giving very little quantity to someone.

Ŋuimŋuim Very tiny or little such as buttocks or anything.

Ŋuin To give very little or small to someone.

Ŋuiny State of being very small or little.

Ŋuinyŋuiny Very short or small piece of something. See Ŋuɔ̱ny.

Ŋuit State of being bitter,sour as with food taste.

Ŋuith To cut off completely or to have severed relationship.

Ŋuithŋuith That can get cut very easily as with glass,steel, iron etc.

Ŋul To close hand palm.

Ŋuul 1. A kind of plant which grows in deserted compound. 2. The back part of a human being foot.

Ŋulŋul

Ŋuny Closed hand palm or any round shape. To cut something short such as a tree or whatever.

Ŋunyŋuny Short piece of any thing,or state of being short See Ŋuɔ̱ny.

Ŋuok 1. A piece cut of something eg Wer baa ji wä käm ŋuok: You go,you will be given a piece. 2. A decision taken in a court or a ruling statement.

Ŋuook 1. Plural of Ñuok being the decisions in a court as explained above. 2. Pieces cut from a log or a rope.

Ŋuol 1. A piece of a solid matter or substance such as tobacco or soil. 2. To spit, send or drive out liquids as that with saliva or water. 3. To close the hand fingers when boxing or giving a blow.

Ŋuolŋuol A state of being round, put together or having a round shape as that of a ball.

Ñuolol Being in round state or position.

Ŋuon To have or live on hopes that something good or bad is there.

Ŋuonŋuon A person who thinks that good or bad thing may still be there.

Ŋuony 1. A piece of wood or whatever which is short. 2. A slang for a short, little person or thing.

Ŋuoŋ As a whole, not in pieces or parts.eg Käm ni jɛ kɛ ŋuoŋdɛ : Give it to him/her as a whole.

Ñuoot Stage when a female of human being stops reproduction due to aging.

Ŋuɔk 1. To cut something. 2. To take a decision as in a court of law.

Ŋuɔ̱ɔ̱k 1. Plural of Ñuuk a person who has power to take a decision in a court as explained above. 2. Plural of Ŋuok a piece or a case which was settled by a court as explained above.

Ŋuɔɔn Plural of Ŋuon state of living with good or bad hopes as explained above.

Ŋuɔnyŋuɔɔny Plural of Ŋunyŋuny being quite short or a piece as explained below.

Ŋuɔ̱t 1. Plural of Ñ ut being a decision, custom, tradition and methods of doing things as explained below. 2. To slaughter by cutting throat. 3. To decide or take a decision.

Ŋuɔ̱ɔ̱t Female of anything animals, human beings,birds, plants etc.

Ŋuɔ̱th A decayed, decomposed, rottened piece or body of organic matter, which releases nasty, awful or filthy smell.

Ŋuɔ̱ɔ̱th 1.Plural of Ŋuɔ̱th being decayed or decomposed thing as explained above.

Ŋut 2. A statement which is pronounced when someone is speared or hit in a traditional combatting. Being a decision, custom or traditional way of doing things.

Ŋuthɛ A plant which releases nasty smell which provoked being named like that, long time ago.

Ŋuthŋuth Having nasty, awful and decaying smell.

Ŋuy 1. To put something or someone to its end,or to annihilate, destroy etc. 2. Hyena in Dinka language,but Nuer took away (A) from Aŋuy.

Ŋäm To open one or to have mouth opened as when yawning or having a container being not well shut.

Ñääk 1. A youngman who goes for show off with his bull around the cattle camp. 2. A person who goes and changes the direction of grazing cattle.

Ŋääm Plural of Ŋäm a state of yawning as explained above.

Ŋämŋääm State of being half opened or not well shut. eg. Tɛ ŋämŋäämä: It is not well shut.

Ŋän 1. To open the legs apart. 2. Informal pronunciation of first person speaking eg I : Hän.

Ŋännän A situation when one opens his/her legs apart as when restless.

Ŋäny Being fragile due to series decomposition such as organic matter.

Ŋänyŋäny State of being restless due to troubles or as when suffering of severe pain.

Ŋäŋ 1. To pretend to be giving someone something while you do not mean it. It is common amongst the children. 2. A big piece from a bulky material or solid matter.

Ŋääŋŋääŋ State of pretending to give something while you do not mean it.

Ŋääp 1. Whatever is used for hanging criminals or things.eg Ti kæ ñääp Kuakni ?: Do you have luggage hanger? Næmæ æ jæn ñääp nath :This is human being hanger. 2. Slang for a bull with horns standing up and looking like a hanger.

Ŋääpni Plural of Ŋääp being whatever is used for hanging as explained above.

Ŋäpŋäp Light blinkings and winkings in a stormy night. See Biɛr.

Ŋäär 1. The noise or sound which is made by an angrey lion. 2. Some sudden movements of the eyelids or any part of the body which is considered to be a sign of weeping or seeing someone, such as a new comer or a stranger. Eg ɛŋu camɛ tet dä ŋäär œ?Why my hand is affected by sudden movements?

Ŋärŋär The sudden body or flesh movements.

Ŋät 1. Dark yellowish fats on top of the meat soup.2. To shape a bull horns.

Ŋäät 1. The person who shapes the bull horns. 2. The one who sharpens sticks in order to fit or fix metallic tools.

Ŋäth 1.A belief, respect or faith to God, father or brother etc. 2.Means what is wrong with the other: Ñäthi or ŋäthæ : Meaning what Iœ wrong with you (i) or him (æ). This word has been interpreted by Eastern Nuer to be an insult.ɛ gu ŋäth? *What is wrong with you?*

Ŋäwŋäw Which gets cut very easily or gets chewed very quick,

Ŋɛäh A female ram that does not produce and which always looks fat.

Ŋëŋ The tip or top part of the male genital organ or Penis.

Ŋëap The edge, brink, brim or further end of something.

Ŋëp Plural of Ŋëap being the brink or edge of something as explained above.

Ŋëth The ashes or dust powder that result of burning woods. charcoals or cow dung.

Ŋuäc The smell. See Ŋuäny

Ŋuäcŋuäc Style of smelling anything as that with dog/, he goat or oxen etc.

Ŋuäk Neck of any kind.or type of human being or creature

Ŋuäkŋuäk State of having very clumsy shape.

Ŋuäl Plural of Ŋua̱l being the debt or loan as explained above.

Ŋuän Better or become a little better or having subsided.

Ŋuäny A smell of anything or type.

Ŋuänyŋuäny Smellful type as that of perfume or tobacco. Having nice and good smell.

Ŋuänyyiŋ A kind of tall grass which grows in swamps or waterways.

Ŋuäŋŋuäŋ 1. State of being ready to take something or carry it. 2. State of moving with something and ready to do anyhing with it.

Ŋuär State of being feverish due to lack of proper sleeping or sickness.

Ŋuärŋuär Feeling of sickness or feverish due to lack of proper sleeping.

Ŋuäärŋuäär The appearance of the ripening sorghum grains in early stage.

Ŋuät 1. A state of fermented milk in a gourd container. 2. A slang for having some food, wood, etc in plenty or in abundance.

Ŋuäät A parasitic worm which lives in the human stomach or intestines.

Ŋuätŋuät A way of talking when one has nasal or a flu case.

Ŋuäth 1. To eat very fast as an animal such as lion, hyena, dog etc. 2. State of being rough or ready to get angry very fast or quick.

Ŋuäthŋuäth Clumsy way of talking, speaking or angry way of answering.

Ŋuɛɛt The person or witchdoctor who extracts out worms from human body. See Tìt

Ŋuëët Plural of Ŋueet being the witchdoctor as explained above.

Ŋuöl.A slang for a penis being a literal or poetry word.

Ŋöc 1. A big cow as being referred to in marriage or dowry settlement. 2. To run a race. 3. To say something bad or good in series discussion or talk.

Ŋök To vomit or to discharge food from the stomach through the mouth. eg Pal payæ ñök : Pal has just vomited. Æ ña täh ñök wan æmæ œ? Who has vomited in this place?

Ŋöl Lip of a hook or a harpoon.

Ŋöm 1. The action of pushing the male organ into female part when playing sex. 2. An insult to someone who asks insulting question meaning he will push his penis into that person anus.

Ŋön 1. To raise one leg high. 2. To prepare a rope for tying goats or cows.

Ŋönŋön State of bad behavior way where one raises leg very high.

Ŋöŋ 1. The out lip of the hook or harpoon. 2. It is part of penis.

Ŋöŋŋöŋ State of having such a shape or appearance.

Ŋöt 1. Plural of Ŋɔl being the lame person as explained above. 2. To eat something using only teeth such as fruits, maize etc.

Ŋöth Fucking action, the art of playing sex or intercourse.

O

P

Pac 1. A piece of cloth which is worn around a woman waist. 2. To seal or cover the area usually with people,cattle or wild life. 3. A word that is said when tasting something once more after adding some ingredients. 4. To walk abouts or linger aimlessly.

Pacni Plural of Pac being a piece of cloth as explained above.

Pacpac A word of tasting food after some ingredients were added.see Pac.

Pajiey A nickname which is given for a colourful bull.

Pak Lineage system in Nuer for example Gatkiir, Nyayow etc.

Paak Plural of Pak being the lineage system as explained above.

Pa̱a̱k 1. State of breaking a piece of wood into small pieces, with axe. 2. Plural of Pàk being a collection of wooden made devices that are tied around Human being or Bull necks in cattle camp as ornaments.

Pal 1. To pray, prayer, services or to call the Almighty or ancestral gods to open for you or relief you from difficulties, sickness or to support or forgive. 2. Having gone deep in side or a long distance. 3. A kind of colour which is used for painting walls, faces and clay Utensils but with light stress on (á).

Pa̠a̠l 1. State of telling something secret which may cause troubles. 2. To have something appeared from to the surface of water. 3. A place where a midwife prepare hot water for newly given birth woman.

Palac A container for collecting urines at night when there is general fear of murderers or wild animals.

Pam 1. To close, seal or cover something completely, see Pac. 2. A sound of clapping hands or hitting two sticks.

Pa̠m A leaf of a tree but not grass. See Jith.

Paam State of such noise of clapping or hitting as explained above.eg æ ŋu ci wä paam ɔ? What makes such hard noise?

Pa̠a̠m Plural of Päm being the stone or mountain as explained below.

Pa̠mni Plural of Pa̠m being the leaf of a tree as explained above.

Pampam 1. State of such continuous noise of clapping or hitting sticks. 2. An insult for someone with flat buttocks.

Pan 1. Yesterday. 2. A large open area without trees. see Toc. 3. To keep oneself away from the scene.

Pankä jɛ The day before yesterday.

Panpan State of being aloof and not ready to participate in anything.

Pa̠n 1. A goat skin which was used for covering woman genital organ in ancient days. 2. The second growth of sorghum in winter or cold months. 3. To make threads or strings out of cotton fibres 4. To enlarge something by adding another.

Pa̠npa̠n 1. The noise of bird wings when about to take off. 2. Slang for doing something in a hurry.

Panɔm A plot, home stead or compound.

Pany A partial broken pot, or any clay made utensils.

Pa̠ny 1. To build a wall. 2. A wall.Eg Reath cæ wä pàny kæ duel :Reath has gone to build a house wall.

Pa̠nyni Plural of Pa̠ny being a wall as explained above.

Paŋ Lack of appetite due to sickness.eg Dhööl æmœ cæ lœc dæ pañ :That boy lacks appetite.

Paŋpaŋ A series lack of appetite as explained above.

Pap 1. A person or animal that joins any group on the way. 2. To prepare a bed or sleeping furniture.

Pappap A state of being simple and ready to be dragged away by any person or group to stay with.

Par To hide near something or someone so that you are not seen when one is expecting an attack or about to attack.

Pa̱r 1. To mourn, wail or weep due to a lost of dear person. 2. Sudden noise by a sleeping person in a dream.

Paar 1. A type of weed plants which covers the field or garden. 2. A cow,bull or anyother animal fat meat. eg Riŋ thààk æmæ æ paar: This bull meat is fat.

Pa̱a̱r Being equal or to equalize or similarize.eg Cia pààr yæn gat moœrlen :You become equal with your aunt son.

Parpar State of being in hiding so that to make sudden attack or to escape.

Pat 1. A hand made simple food of flour which is served to children ortobacco when mixed with water. 2. To slap with opened hand or blow with opened fingers. 3. A game of young ladies where they sing while clapping their hands.

Pa̱t 1. The outer scales of grains when pounded. 2. To miss something or someone narrowly by touching the body slightly. 3. Having increased in size or volume such as boiled grains. 4. To sharpen the knife, spear etc.

Pa̱a̱t Plural of Pàt being the outer scale of grains as explained above.

Patpat 1. A piece of fermented flour pressed flat before it is given to a child to go and have it roasted. 2. State of being thin and flat.

Pa̱tpa̱t 1. State of being so fat and thick. 2. A kind of whitish flat large fish.

Path State of having much to do with moon Pay e.g. Ṉin path kɛ di? Moon days are how many?

Paw 1. A flow of fresh liquid such as blood or water.2. To walk or move aimlessly.

Pa̱a̱w 1. State of sudden flowing of water or blood. 2. A slang for plenty of food in geat quantities. Rec cɛ wa̱h pa̱a̱w:The fish becomes in plenty.

Pawpaw State of being fresh blood not clotting or thick.

Pay 1. Moon or month. Eg ɛ pay ɛ mith ɛn nɛmɛ ? Which month is this?. Ci pay tææth pan : The moon appeared yesterday. 2. Just recent or most recent event. 3. To clear water surface when one wants to drink. 4. To widen a hole or a wound to allow pus or blood oozes or gets removed.

Paypay Wider or large such as water surface, opened wound or a hole.

Pec 1. To raid and collect the property or to loot by force. 2. A distorted English word for a page.

Pecpec State of being quite hard and tight.

Pek 1. A group of camps, one section or clan. 2. The end of measurement. eg 1——————1 3. Share or each person amount in division of something. 4. To remain or stop where you are e.g. Cɛ pek jɔɔr: He/she never come back. Cɛ pek piny: He/she never got up from sleep or as a result of a terrible blow or stick hit.

Pen Not to allow something or someone to do or go.

Pep To pretend to be fat by filling one stomach with air to look huge.

Peppep 1. A kind of shapes which looks large and short such as tool, spear or utensils. 2. Having filled one stomach with air so as to look fat.

Perer Being apart as that of ears, fingers,fence, not well thatched roof etc.

Perper To do somethings in a hurry or quickly where it looks not proper.

Perpeer State of being not systematic or bad style in doing things.

Pet 1. A shoulder or part of the upper chest. 2. A kind of plants which produces fruits which are eaten by young boys in the bushes, See Petcibony. 3. State of being tight when wearing a piece of cloth or a bell which is not properly fit. 4. A condition when one have eaten good meal or delicious food.

Petcibony A kind of plants which yields sweet fruits.

Petpet Style of doing something very fast.

Petpeet Situation where one shows strength while doing something.

Pɛɛac Plural of Pɛc being the loots or whatever have been collected as a result of raiding, be it property or people.

Pɛɛc Anything to do with raiding Pɛc e.g. Wă pɛɛc: I am going to raid.

Pɛl Cleverness, deceiptful or being witty or cunny.

Pɛɛl To draw someone with cunny words to a place in order to get caught.

Pɛlpɛl 1. Clever or cunny person. State of readiness to answer any question. 2. A small game of rabbit family.

Pɛlpua̱ny State of being active and ready to do something at once.

Pɛn 1. Plural of Pëan being falling down from above. 2. State of having a piece of skin or cloth torn apart

Pɛnpɛn State of being in such a bad shape of being torn apart, or worn out.

Pɛny To open with hands in order to check e.g. Dhɔɔl titi pɛny kɛ mactapni: These boys are opening maize bundles.

Pɛnyɛny Being quite opened beyond any doubt.

Pɛnypɛny State of checking anything with hands.

Pɛp Having round shape as that of a head.

Pɛppɛp State of being round shape.

Pɛr 1. A colour of cow which involves brown and dominant white colour. 2. To put thin layers or grass when thatching or mudding a hut.

Pɛɛr A kind of birds Nuer believes to have evil eyes.

Pɛrɛny State of large ears (leaves) being a type of plants, Pɛrɛny jith.

Pɛrpɛr State of rough way of building with few quantities available.

Pɛt 1. Burning or fire flame burning. 2. The second month of Nuer Calendar. The name was derived because in that period the weather, becomes very hot and burning. 3. A kind of fish with black and smooth skin. 4. An old container for carrying babies and other things, see Dieny. 5. A born dead calf.

Pɛɛt Plural of Pɛt being a black or dark fish as explained above.

Pɛtni Plural of Pɛt being a born dead calf as explained above..

Pɛth 1. It is an evil eye. 2. A person with evil eyes. 3. To do or act very fast or quickly e.g. Ku rɔdu pɛth: Just hurry up, be quick or fast. 4. Plural of Pɛth being a person with evil eyes but with stress on (æ) as explained above..

Pɛthpɛth Being always very fast in taking action.

Pɛw Having better taste.eg Cɛ thokdɛ wäh pɛw: He/she hasbetter taste

Pɛɛw State of having something widely opened.

Pɛwpɛw 1. Being largely openend that allows much air or wind in. 2. Having good and acceptable taste such as food or whatever.

Pi 1. Water. It is also slang for beer or drinks. 2. A slang for sperms when already in the womb.

Pibor White Water being one of Sobat river tributaries between Akobo and Burɛbei.

Pic 1. A device made of wood for stiring food or broth when cooking. 2. Being straight without bending eg Duop mi cuñ æ pic :This is a straight road. 3. State of being quite true not lie at all. 4. Plural of Piec being the art of making fire from wood in the forest as explained below ẹg Tä pic mäcni ræy ruoop: I was forging fire in the forest.

Picni Plural of Pic being such device for stiring broth as explained above. Eg Bia wäh kok kæ picni ti ñuan :You go and buy many stiring sticks.

Piec 1. To forge fire by making friction on two pieces of wood. 2. To prepare a light food for children with Pic. 3. To pass and twist the leaves of certain plant in order to show the others when the leaves turn to the direction.

P̠i̠e̠c A cow that has little milk for human and calf consumption.

Pieh Plural of Pi being water in river or rainfall water as explained above..

Pik 1. To pay back or refund what you have got from someone. 2. To put goats, cows or animals into the hut -byre in rainy season.

Pi̠k 1. A diseae which affects the nose to stop the sense of smelling for sometimes. 2. To take one cow to a neightbour or relative hut when you do not have cow hut.

Piel A grinding stone or a man-made clay for grinding grains.

Pil To go through where there is no door or to let go through when sewing with needle.

Pi̠l 1. To make much effort to complete a difficult task e.g. Cɛ rɔ pi̠l thin: He has made much effort to do it.2. A grinding stone.

Pilpil A state of moving anyhow entering without permission or respect.

Pieel Having so many holes as a result of unnecessary piercing.

Pieeli Plural of Pi̠l being the grinding stone as explained above.

Pilual A name of a village that is characterized with red or brown water.

Pileer A domestic plant which provides shade.

Pim 1. To give a blow or to box someone. 2. To add some mud on the walls of a hut when renovating it.

Pi̠m State of being so strong due to fatness.

Piim Plural of Pim being the boxing as when in a fight with hands.

Pi̱im Plural of Pim being additional mudding on hut walls.

Pimni Plural of Pim to make several blows to someone as explained above.

Pi̱mpi̱m Well built youth, bull or ox.

Pi̱mpiny An angery action where one hits the ground when one he/she hates says something to him /her.

Pin To aim at, when shooting with a gun or a bow and arrow.

Pi̱n Plural of Piɛn being a type of insects as explained below.

Pien A kind of snake which is very thin and black.

Piɛn A type of insect which gives very painfull sting.

Pie̱ny To add some soft mud to the walls or hut floors.

Piny Earth, ground or floor.

Pinydiiŋ The earth.

Pinypiny State of being rather fat or healthy.

Pi̱nypi̱ny Slang for health and clean person.

Piŋŋiŋ State of being in a puzzling stage where one does not know what to do.

Pir To run for life due to imminent danger.

Pi̱r 1. A tall thin grass or wood put across water ways to alert the fisherman about the fishes movements in order to attack. 2. A tiny hole on any container which leaks out liquids.

Piir State of being in panicking or terribly scared.

Pieeri Plural of Pi̱r being a tall thin grass or wood as explained above.

Pirpir State of being in panicking state of running anyhow.

Pi̱rpi̱r Noise of wind when blowing on leaves or grass in winter.

Pirjoor Having panicked and run to unkown destination.

Pit To throw a spear or whatever very far by force.

Pi̱t 1. State of being well closed without airlet or ventilation. 2. A sound of gas as that is released through anus.

Piet 1. To fish thoroughly in grass water. 2. To exhaust, defeat or overpower someone.

Pi̱tpi̱t State of having no ventilation in a room full with people.

Piitpiit Little fish such as Ril and Luth.eg Cɛ kap kɛ piitpiit: *He has a little fish.*

Pith 1. Growth for both human being and plants. 2. To add a piece of string, rope, thread in order to complete the required length. 3. To add something to let a person reaches a high object.

P̲ith 1. The cental part of back bone which is known as Pithjɔak. 2. Out growth in the nose which causes chronic flu. 3. To go further than the distance you are to cover, or make additional statement than what is needed.

Pieth 1. To have something sharp pierced through the flesh or body such as thorn or needle. 2. To saw seeds in a field or a farm.

Pithpith A child ways of movements in a crowd or mob.

Piw A sound of gun shot or arrow shot.

P̲iw A fast running style.

Piew 1. A type of beads that has water colour,hence being named as a result of similarities in colour. 2. Fresh milk.

Piwpiw 1. The sound of very fast blowing object such as gun shot, arrow, etc. 2. State of being very fast in running.

Poa To bathe being a short form for Poak.

Poak 1. Bathing or washing oneself. 2. The lineage system of any family. 3. To call a baby or a child with his grand lineage, see Monyyow, Gatgong, Gatkiir etc.

Poal 1. State of being light weight not heavy. 2. A piece of meat which is cut by butcher when skinning and gives it to a small boy to roast.

Poaŋ Plural of Poŋ to call someone according to his/her ancentral lineages.

Poar 1. The thick substance that remains on top of boiled fresh milk. 2. State of having milk, water, food cool down after boiling.

Poat To beat properly the marriage drum after settlement.

Poath 1. Being quite clean or cleanliness. 2. A middle age bull. 3. To have peeled the maize,banana etc.

Poathni Plural of Poath being the middle age bull as explained above.

Poc 1. To clean the face or whatever using hands or fingers. 2. To squeeze out the nut from its shelf see Kuoc.

Pocpoc Whatever is squeezeable or slippery.

Pok 1. Ashes of cow dung, see N̈ɛth. 2. To wash oneself with water or bathing. See Poak. 3. To scater the seeds on the ground to grow.

Pon To pick something dangling or hanging fruits, leaves, etc.

Ponɛ A room inhabitant mosquitoes, see Tirit kiɛ manɛtɔm.

Ponpon 1. A tool or device which is used for pulling out a thorn or foreign body from a wound or an injury. 2. A slang for young energetic fat child or baby.

Pony To praise someone with songs.

Ponypony 1. State of being energetic,strong and ready to act violently. 2. State of being very slippery when being handled.

Pop To hold something with two hands from the bottom.

Poppop That has such a shape which could be held or carried by hands on both sides.

Por 1. To clean by weeding the grass from the farm or field. 2. Cloud, the whitish one that is seen in the sky in rainy climate. 3. To scatter powder or flour on boiling milk or to scatter tobacco seeds for nursery. 4. To perform rituals for a dead baby. 5. To perform some rituals for an injuy or wound inflicted on someone,in order to have it healed very fast.

Pori 1. Plural of Poar being the cloud as explained above. 2. Plural of Puur being a device tool for cleaning or weeding wild grass in a farm, field or garden.

Poor 1. A dead baby who dies before its teeth could grow. 2. Plural of Poar being a kind of animals Water buck as explained above.. 3. A type of trees where its stem is used for making sticks or handles.

Porpor 1. A fast tasty food which is made of fresh milk and flour by young boys. 2. Early stage of grass appearance.

Pot 1. To run away or escape the troubles, disaster or imminent danger. 2. To have got cut such as rope, string etc. 3. To pluck off the leaves from the plant or bush. 4. To get swelling due to injury or damage. The noise that comes out when anus releases gas see, Thö̈t, Rat, Kuik Pit, Kuok, Thɛt etc.

Poot A wooden hammer for hitting or driving down wood pegs.

Potpot 1. State of having a rope or whatever does not hold on properly on the neck, on the peg or whatever. 2. A type of small animals that attack the eyes of its victim (human being). 3. State of being fat huge in volume such as youths, calves or fishes.

Poth Blessing. To ask Almighty God to bless the gift or whatever is wanted.

Pow One of human or cow veins on the body or neck.

Powpow The part which oozes blood such as the veins or the nerves.

Pɔɔc Cow dung which is dried to be relaid in luak for cows to sleep or lie on.

Pɔk 1. To scatter the seeds of tobacco on soil. 2. To honour a child by calling him/her according to lineage. 3. To bathe or wash a child or sick person.

Pɔl 1. State of being very light in weight or no fear on the way. 2. Plural of Poal being the white piece of meat which is given to a child.

Pɔlpɔl 1. State of being very light in weight. 2. State of being save and no fear. 3. Slang for a person who lost his respect,dignity etc.

Pɔhal State of being not sharp or dull such as spear, axe etc.

Pɔhl 1. A stage where one looks fool,dull,stupid or ignorant before people. 2. A knife like tool for cutting pieces of leather for ornament or clothing

Pɔhlpɔhl Being not sharp or dull as a knife, spear, axe etc.

Pɔ̱t To hammer or hit continuously to drive in the nails or pegs.

Pɔth 1. Lung or the natural oxygen supporting organ. 2. Food materials for supporting the inlaws. 3. Very clean or to make it clean by sweeping or wiping with hands. Also a bad smell.

Pɔ̱th To ask Almighty God, elders or parents to bless the family in their difficulties or whatever.

Pɔɔth Plural of Pɔth or Poth both lungs or food items to inlaws as explained above.

Pɔ̱ɔ̱thni 1. Plural of Pɔ̱th being the blessing. 2. Food materials for in-laws.

Puc 1. Musical strings that make tones of musical instruments. 2. Being true, not a lie. It comes after (ɛ) or (a) in speech.Eg

Ruac ɛmɔ ɛ thuɔk ɛ (a) puc?: That talk is it true.? 3. To have nothing left after marriage, raiding or theft incidents.

Puk 1. To empty the sour milk from the gourd container when butter is formed already. 2. A name of a person borne and blessing by powering cow dung ashes on him/ her.

Puok 3. Plural of Puok being the cow dung ashes as explained below. The cow dung ashes.

Puuk Plural of Puok being the cow dung ashes as explained above e.g. Ŋul puuk : Pieces of solid cow dung ashes.

Pukpuk A state of being in powder form.

Puny To cut a piece or break a part from a solid substance.

Puony The ideal, the example of good or the best e.g. Wut puony: The best or ideal man.

Puɔny 1. Plural of Puny being a piece broken from the main body or the substance. 2. To carry out the breaking substance by hands. 3. Body of anything be it human, animal, plant or object.

Punypuny State of being breakable by hands.

Puŋ A kind of fish with big head known as Puŋ nyapanɛ.

Pup A quick way the big fish catches small fish.

Puppup Having a round head see Pɛppɛp.

Pur 1. To take hold of something by force and quickly. 2. Having much to do with the weeding, e.g. Ta̱a̱ pur: I was weeding.

Puur A device tool made of metal for weeding grass in a farm or garden.

Purpur.State of being of medium size not small or large.

Put To cut by pulling any thing such as a rope, a string etc.

Puth 1. The rituals that are performed for the twins birthday see Puth Cuëëkni. 2. The handling of food materials support to in-laws. e.g. Gac cɛ puth: Gac has sent food materials to in-laws.

Puthputh The awful or nasty smell of birds.

Puypuy 1. State of being not solid, but breakable. 2. A sound which is heard when walking,crossing or running in water.

Pä The sound of the letter (P) the twenty first letter of Thok Nath.

Päc To groan or moan due to severe pains or grievances.

Päk 1. A type of bush trees which is green and short, with air bag like fruits. 2. To postpone, adjourn or cancel a meeting,a journey etc. 3. To divide something by changing it to its small components. Borrowed from Arabic language, exchange.

Päl 1. To leave or let something or someone goes free. 2. Allow to pass. 3. A place where a woman bathes after delivery where she gets massage with warm water. 4. To say what people consider to be top secret.

Päläŋ State of being in complete peace and harmony.

Pälikä To forgive, to let someone goes freely after captivity.

Päm A stone, hill or a mountain.

Pääm Plural of Päm being a stone or a hill as explained above.

Päämni Plural of Pääm being stones as when among stones, hills and mountains.eg : Täh wii päämni: I am on top of the stones.

Pämpäm State of being thick or bulky such as a hill, a mountain etc.

Pänpän State of being flat and large.

Päny Wall of both mud or bricks.

Pänyni Plural of Päny being a wall as explained above..

Päp The sound of a falling light object.

Pähr Similar, equal or the same height or size.

Pärpär A small flying insect which flies in the evening.

Pät 1. A locally made utensil for filtering flour particles. 2. To miss the person with spear, gun shot, an arrow etc. 3. The opened palm or foot.eg ŋuɛt mi cɛ tet dɛ pät: A young man who has opened palm.

Päth 1. To stop someone or animal in order to tell something or to kill when hunting. 2. A slang for having encountered a problem by stopping someone on the way where you fall victim. 3. A type of marine plant (Papyrus),

Päthpäth Slang for a person who looks for troubles eg.ɛ ŋu la ti

päthpäth ɔ? Why do you look for troubles?

Päw A sudden sensing of a danger when walking in the forest or in darkness.

Päwpäw State of such fearful feeling of danger.

Pääy 1. The noise or sound that is heard when one jumps into water or liquid. 2. Slang for plenty particularly food materials.

Päypäy The sound of birds in water or human being in water when fishing or bathing.

Päyäy A sound or noise of falling body into the water.

Pɛ̈ɛ̈n The falling of anything from high place.

Pöc The feeling of shame or shy due to mistake committed.

Pöcpöc 1. State of feeling shame or being shy for having done wrong. 2. A person who is always very shy before people or who feels shame.

Pök To make a big cut out of something e.g. Meat, wood, stone etc.

Pökpök That can be cut into large pieces or big ones.

Pöl A short period rain which is a result of a wandering cloud.

Pööl A large stagnant water surface which looks like small lake.

Pöm Plural of Pöm which is a bank of a river with little differences in stressing (ö).

Pööm A severe noise or sound as that is made when someone is blown or hit with a big stick.

Pömpöm That noise or sound which is a result of wood works or hitting logs.

Pön Having what to do with Pöön as explained below.

Pöön 1. Aquatic type of grass which is used for thatching hut roofs in temporary housing in cattle camps. 2. A slang for stool or the slid waste from the body. e.g. Bia doanyɛ ni pöön: That you only step on soft matter (shit).

Pöŋ To call someone by his/her good deeds or by his/her ancestral heritage, e.g. Gatkiir or Lua(k)diit or Nyamoŋ etc.

Pör 1. Plural of Pöör being.a sign of footprints as explained below. 2. To cut as big as you can such as meat or gourd container when being opened. 3. Slang for the style of bad behaviour in talking or eating.

Pörpör 1. A person who does things without the consent of others. 2 State of a large hole.

Pöör The meaning of this word depends on how you pronounce it in a sentence. It has the following meanings: skull, trace, foot paths or shell. Eg Nɛmɛ pöör thɔal –Kä nɛmɛ pöör nhier- Kä mɔ ɛ pöör ran: This is a snake path- this is a turtle shell- that is a human skull.

Pöt A part of spear, axe, rake etc, that joins it with wood handle or wooden part

Pööt Plural of Pöt being the part that joins the wooden handle with the spear,axe etc as explained above.

Pöth 1. A piece of skin which joins two pieces of traditional pipe components or which covers a rough part of device for handling.eg Næmæ pöth tööny kä mæ æ pöth juoth tööny : This is a pipe joining piece and the other is a pipe filter joining piece. 2. To peel by pulling away the outer cover of maize bundle.

Pöthpöth 1. That can change its skin due to aging or being old. 2. Cleaning by sweeping or wipping with hands. 3. Being bad smell.

Pöy To open a utensil or a container widely than necessary.

Pöypöy Being widely opened such as a barrel, gourd, utensil etc.

Pöyöy State of being quite widely opened.

R

Ra The sound of letter (R) the twenty second letter of Thok Nath..

Rak 1. The locust pest which attacks fields. 2. A slang for a thin or slim person. Eg Gat ɛ rak ɛmɔ tit rɔ: You thin child take care of yourself.

R̲a̲akni Plural of Rak being the locust, as explained above. see Kɔryɔm.

Rakrak 1. State of being thin or with little flesh on the bones. 2. A slang for a good runner in a race.

Ral A part of Female.Genitol.Organs.

R̲a̲al A nerve or vien through which the blood flows.

R̲a̲ali A slang for a thin person who does not get tired easily.

Ram A word which is used to indicates one person, e.g. Ram kɛl: One person.

Ramraam The behaviour of a greedy person who tries to collect much in a short period of time in fishing, eating or harvesting.

Raan Human being eg Ram mi raan: The real man or the ideal human being.

Ran Having much to do with Raan as in human being eg ɛ gat ran: A human child or baby.

Ranh To come nearer to the speaker.See Ràth the opposite.

Rany Failure to do something due to many tasks or duties at ago.

Ranyrany State of being in a very difficullt position to manage a task When one has much to do.

Raŋ 1. Ability to shoot without missing the target. 2. The hard covers of the sugar cane, surgheom stalk etc, which is peeled away before chewing. 3. Part of the face.eg Cua pat ni raŋdɛ :He/she was slapped on his/her face. 4. Slang for a woman who has got coneived or expecting.

Rap To miss something by causing injuries or bruises on the body.

Raprap A sound of broth when getting cooked. The beginning of the rain.

Rar 1. Outside the room, the building or the water. 2. An area far from the river like Bimbim, Koatlaak etc. 3. Slang for not being part of troubles,quarrels or fighting. 4. A slang for long call in the bushes or in opened ground away from home.

Raar 1. State of being out or against e.g. Cɛ kac raar: He/she has rebelled, defected. 2. Being away from home.

Rat To do something before its right time such as eating or attacking.

Ra̱t Noise of gas when being release or pass through anus.

Ratrat Noise of engine or thurnderstorm.

Rathɛ A kind of fish.

Raw A part of human female.genital organ see Ral.

Rawni Plural of Raw being part of human female G.O as explained above.

Ray To level down the heap or whatever looks high. Eg Ku mun ɛ Mi, ray piny: You ljust level down, that soil.

Rayray State of being leveled or smoothed.

Raypiny To level down the heap of soil or whatever.

Rɛath Draught, dryness, lack of rainfalls.

Rɛɛth A kind of plant which is used as one of the traditional drugs for herpes.

Rec Fish of all types in rivers, lakes or oceans.

Re̱e̱c A person who separates people quarreling or fighting.

Reec Plural of Re̱e̱c being he/she who separates people fighting or quarreling

Rɛk 1. To deliver twins. 2. Having two persons say Or do something at ago.

Rekrek State of being stubbornly difficult to allow anything to pass or be taken.

Rel Bruises or signs of bruises on the viens or the body.

Reel 1. Being the appearance of bruises. e.g. Ɛŋu cikɛ reel inɛ? Why did they appear like this? 2. A person who likes to eat alone or who does not share food or meals with others. See Hææl. 3. A kind of plants which grows along the river or water ways.

Reemreem A series way or hungry way of looking for either food or an Enemy eg Cɛ pay guic ɛ reemreem ɛn wanɛmɛ: He/she has just been looking seriesly in this place.

Reny To reject the advice or to act alone.

Reŋ A person who does not share things with his/her immediate people.

Rew Most of, greater part or the majority of people, things or animals.

Rewey State of forgetfulness. eg John la widɛ ɛ rewey : John used to forget.

Reweec State of forgetfulness e.g. Wic reweec: forgetfulness.

Rewɛy Spitow or spit.

Rewɛɛni Plural of Rewæy being the spit aœ explained above. e.g. Cu nyuur wii rewɛɛni: Do not sit on spitows.

Rɛam Plural of Rɛm being a membrance in the nose as explained below. eg Guickæ ci wumkien thiäñ kæ ræam : Look at them their noses are full of membrances.

Rɛc 1. Plural of Rec being a fish as explained above. 2. A slang for being coward where one dodges like a fish.

Rɛk 1. A town, a city, a district or whatever of that nature. 2. A fence made out of wood and thorns to keep away the animals from the field,farm or garden. 3. Involvement into someone affairs.

Rɛɛk Having much to do with either fence of thorns, town or city.eg Bä wä rɛɛk i yœœ : I will go to the town later on.

Rɛkɛk State of being thin due to starvation or sickness.eg Nænæ cuñæ Æ rækæk : Look he/she stands in such a state.

Rɛl 1. Ant or ant hill. 2. To refuse sharing something with others particularly food cows or whatever.

Rɛm 1. A group of people in a line or queue, ready to perform some dance fashion or styles. 2. To spear someone, animal or anything which causes a wound which can kills.3. A membrance inside the nose cavity which helps in sound vibration.

Rɛmrɛm A very thin part or membrance. see Nɛmnɛm.

Rɛŋ 1. A colour of cow where the lower parts are whitish while the other part can be any colour. 2. A means person or he/she who does not give out anything of his/her belongings.

Rɛɛŋ 1. Having much to do with such colour. eg Nœmœ æ yañ mi rææñ : That is the combination of this colour cow as explained above. 2. State of being means or selfish.

Rɛp State of being very thin,weak or a slang for a person who has no defence or support.

Rɛɛp 1. A feeling of burning on the skin in hot climate. 2. A kind of plants which is used in traditional drugs making.

Rɛprɛp 1. Being very thin such as a piece of cloth, paper etc. 2. Slang for a thin person or also a person who belongs to small family, section or clan.

Rɛr Very sharp noise as that of plane engine.eg Eŋu ci wäh rɛr inɛ œ? : *What a sharp noise like this?*

Rɛrrɛr State of such sharp noise which causes headache and disturbances.

Rɛt 1. A torn piece of paper, cloth etc. 2. Plural of Rɛl being an ant hill as explained above. 3. To tear a piece of paper, cloth etc. 4. To continue one way without stopping at all.eg Bia rɛt piny cia bi looŋ : You will continue without resting!.

Rɛɛt 1. State of having something got torn.eg Biiy mi ci rææt jiäkæ A torn cloth is bad. 2. A name for a baby who lost his/her father or mother just after birth.

Rætrætni Plural of Rætræt being the torn piece of cloth or skin as explained above.

Rɛtni Plural of Rɛɛt being a baby who lost his/her mother or father just after birth as explained above.

Rɛtrɛt State of being in pieces due to being torn or worn out.

Rɛtpiny To continue the journey, walking or running without stopping or resting.

Rɛth Having much to do with Ræath belongings e.g. Tiiluak Rɛth : You were in Rɛath byre or cattle hut.

Rɛɛthä Being much to do with Rɛath as the draught e.g. Ca dap rɛy rɛɛthä: She was born during the draught.

Rɛaw State of series or much thirst or lack of water. e.g. Tä rɛy rɛaw: I was in thirsty area.

Rɛw 1. Figure (2) or number two. 2. Thirst or lack of drinking water.

Rɛwrɛaw In twos, not in one or three but in twos.

Rɛwrɛawni Plural of Rɛwrɛaw being whatever in twos as explained above.

Rɛy In or inside or within.eg Jin tii ræy ñukä? :You were in what?

Rɛyrɛy A sort of feeling as that is felt in sexual intercourse.

Ri A suffix as in sit e.g. Nyuuri̱ : You sit. Plural eg Ruori : Babies

Riac 1. Those dirts that appear on the eyes when one gets up from a deep sleep or when one has eye problem. 2. To break by crashing.

Riak 1. To shout in order to confuse up the issues in question. 2. That noise of a falling object to the ground. 3. A tall black and whitish bird with a cluster of yellowish feathers on its head.

Riakkuac A kind of birds with black and white spot colours.

Riakni Plural of Riak being tall black bird as explained above.

Riakriak State of continuous sharp noise as explained above.

Rial 1. A mixed of black and white colours e.g. – Rial ca̱r. White and black.--Rial thiaaŋ.White and brown.--Jio̱k rial, kerial, Bilrial kiæ Cotrial. White and black. 2. To push someone down when fighting or wrestling.

Rialpiny To push down someone after being first thrown in wrestling or fighting.

Rialikä To prepare or to put something right.

Rialbɛɛk A large black and white bird with yellowish legs and beak.

Rialrial State of movements when one is suffering of severe pains.

Riam State of being overcome by fever or sickness.

Riaam One of the standard traditional combatting where sticks being the only tools for fighting, are used properly.

Riamriam State of being always sick without quick recovery eg Tut täh pœnydɛ riamriam ni waljœm: Tut body has been sick since last winter.

Riany To widen a tight metallic tool by pushing or driving in another solid metal known as Tatiey.

Rianyriany Widely opened to accommodate the stick or whatever.

Riäŋ 1. To be satisfied or state of satisfaction. 2. Ṣlang for richness of food, cattle etc.

Riaaŋ 1. An opened high ground without trees, and also with less grass that does not keep rain water.2. State of being shining or glittering.

Riaŋriaŋ 1. Reflection by shining or glittering against light or sunrays. 2. The appearance of someone who smears himself/herself with oil or butter.

Riap 1. State of being not ready to go further or move ahead due to fatigue or sickness. 2. A shape of a gourd container or a clay made utensil.

Riapriap State of having that shape which is large at the bottom.

Riar 1. To have sharp noise as when breaking hard wood. 2. The period between the sun set and seven o'clock in the evening. 3. To roast grains by keeping it on hot fire. see Tuktuk. 4. The light of whatever, be it sun rays, burning fire or moon rays. Eg Riar caŋ, riar mac kɛ riar path:Sun rays, fire flame, and moon light.

Riarriar State of having sharp noise such as jet engine or hard wood.

Ria̱th 1. Plural of Riey being a canoe, plane, boat, cars etc as explained below. 2. A style of walking or staggering with difficulties due to sickness or drunkenness.

Riaw 1. The sunset light or the glowing of the fire or moon light rays. 2. A confused situation or dubious manner. 3. To confuse things in a talk or in court. 4. Slang for death or disappearing of something.

Riawriaw State of being in flashing or glittering situation as with lightning, electric lamps etc.

Riay 1. Having much to do with Riey the canoe, car, plane boat etc.eg Tä rɛy riay : I was in a canoe, boat, plane,or a car. 2. To level a heap of sand, soil,ashes etc.

Riayriay State of becoming leveled such as the heap.

Ric 1. Age group or age mate. I̱t is for both single and plural.eg Ric mi Cœali Tuytuy kæ Ric ti ñuan Lieethni, Daañni,Cayatni inœ : Age Mate called Tuytuy and many age mates of Lieethni,Daañni, Cayatni etc.2. To straight a bending thing.

Ricric 1. State of having no bending but stiff or straight forward. 2. A continuous denial of anything. 3. To dodge or having ability to dodge.

Riek 1. A pole of wood which is dug down in the court yard of a home for keeping spears, guns or sticks., 2. A special wooden pole being the shrine which is placed in the middle of home stead, as a family traditional logo.

Rieel 1. State of being tight or difficulties one faces when entering into tight entrance or when one forces shoes or whatever into tight space. 2. Plural of Ril being a kind of fish as explained below.

Riem Blood or a stage when a cow gets heated for mating.

Riemni Plural of Riem being the stage of cow heating for mating.

Rieny 1. To be straight or to straighten something. 2. A disease that makes someone becomes stiff or difficult to bend or look down. 3. Straight path, road or line.

Rienyni Plural of Rieny to make straight line as explained above.

Rienyrieny State of becoming straight, stiff or rigid.

Rieŋɛ A reported speech about he/she who is satisfied with food or richness.

Riep A sharp metallic tool for fishing in shallow water by young boys.

Rieepni Plural of Riep being a metallic tool as explained above.

Rier State of being sexy as a case with male or female of human being

Riernyaŋ A kind of plants which is used in making containers or baby cots.

Riet 1. A word, a statement or a sentence. 2. To turn to any direction.eg Riet rœ wer caŋ : You return and go home. 3. State of being in a critical situation where one is pressed to go for long or short call.4. To pull out something from its right place, hole etc as a case with nail, nut etc. 5. To turn to any direction when walking or running.

Rieet Plural of Riet being a statement as explained above.

Rieth 1. To roll something such as a string, rope etc. around a piece of wood or metal. 2. A stage when sugheom stalk is about to produce grain bundle. 3. Having awful smell such as grass or tree leaves.

Rieeth 1. Green, not yet ripen such as fruits 2. State of having tall grass in the forest and not yet passable because the routes are still covered up with creeping plants.

Riethrieth The awful smell which is released by tree leaves.

Riew 1. A dance show in front of the expectators in drum dance. 2. To put a stick or any object across road or path to prevent movements.

Rieew 1. Whatever is put across road or path to stop peoples from passing.2. A pole or a log of which is used for making a roof.

Riewriew He/she who has the ability to confuse by giving wrong statements.

Riey 1. Canoe, car, boat ship, plane etc. 2. To roll something be it tobacco, or carpet etc.

Riɛk 1. A kind of tree which grows along the river bank. 2. To put someone in hard time. 3. A problem, danger, difficulty etc.

Riɛl Become difficulties in passing through a door, or a hole due to size or space.

Riɛr A kind of plant which is used for making baby cot. see Dieny.

Riɛɛr 1. Plural of Riɛr being that plant as explained above. 2. A kind of poisonous snake.

Riɛt The growing part of the plants which appears between the leaves of the apex.

Riɛth A rolled bundle of dried grass which is alighted for searching anything in darkness.

Riɛthni Plural of Riæth being a rolled bundle of dried grass as explained above.

Riɛɛw State of being naturally very thin or slim.

Riɛɛwni Plural of Riɛɛw being that is naturally thin as explained above.

R̲ik Plural of Riɛk a problem or difficulty as explained above.

Rik State of being upright as the hairs, plants, trees etc..

Rikrik State of being tightened or difficult to pass through.

Ril 1. A kind of fish that looks greyish with long head and tail. 2. State of becoming very rigid or stiff when sick 3. Being not well cooked as a case with meat or fish.

Rilril Not well cooked as a case with meat or fish.

R̲ilr̲il Being difficult to put on or pass through as a case with clothes, shoes etc. see Riɛl.

R̲im Plural of Riem being the blood of any type as explained above.

Rìŋ To run or running or racing, jogging etc.

Riŋ 1. Meat, flesh or meat in general. 2. Plural of Riŋ with stress on (i) being meat in general as explained above.

Riiŋ 1. Running towards the speaker.eg Mɛɛ cä cœl cuɛ riiŋ : When I called him/her,he/she ran to me. 2. Having much to do with meat Riŋ eg Tä kɛ mith riiŋ : They Were in meat eating.

Riok Plural of Riök being one of the teeth that chew the food as explained below.

Riop 1. Plural of Riöp being a hand finger or foot nail as explained below. 2. To beat or lash continuously without stopping.

Rioop Having much to do with Riop being the continuous bad beating. Eg æña ku dhöli rioop œ? : Who is continuously beating children ?

Riopriop The noise of a continuous beating or lashing.

Rior To lose something completely.To have lost something.

Riow 1. Hard dead piece of log, wood or tree. 2. The big particles of grains after it has been pounded.

Rip 1. A sharp point metal rod which is used for fishing or playing by young boys. 2. A quick movement when in great danger.eg Cikɛ wä rip kɛ **wour** mɛɛ ca lony nɛn: They made panicking running when they saw a lion. 3. To urge someone to do something quickly or faster e.g. Rip bow: the goat action when in mating mode.

Riipni Plural of Rip the iron or metallic device or rod as explained above.

Riprip State of being strong or energetic as young man or restless cow.

Ri̱pri̱p State of being narrow or not widely opened.

Rir 1. A kind of tree, which is, useful for making or carving tools. 2. To become mad or nervous specially when angery.

Riir Having much to do with Rir a kind of tree.eg Juuth riir : Smoking pipe filter.

Rirrir State of being quite nervous due to anger or sickness.

Rirriir State of being nevous due to madness, anger or sickness when looking for troubles.

Ri̱rri̱r He/she who is fond in causing troubles.

Riit 1. Whatever is used for turning something in order to go or get opened. 2. The noise of engine when turned on.

Ri̱w 1. A sudden flash light appearance. 2. A sudden sharp pain.

Riwriw The state of when one always takes the opposite direction in a dialogue. A behavior where a person goes contrary to others.

Ri̱wri̱w The feeling of sharp pain.

Riɔk To confuse or cause a problem. To disturb tranquility.

Riɔkriɔk State of being troublesome or a confusing agent.

Rokrok 1. The noise of moving or hanging things such as utensils. 2. A state of having many things in disorder or not organized.

Ro̱l 1. World or globe. 2. Throat. 3. A person from a different race, tribe, section or clan.

Ro̱o̱l Having much to do with the world or throat e.g. Bɛæ ro̱o̱la:He/she came from our country (Continent).Ŋäcɛ ni mi wä ro̱o̱lɛ: He/she knows what goes into His/her throat.

Ro̱o̱m A container that is used for carrying things.

Romrom A semi rectangular shape.

Ron 1. A stage when a plant or tree makes new leaves after dryness see Nyok. 2. State of becoming thin due to hunger or malnutrition.

Ro̱ŋ Fit, enough, complete.eg Nɛmɛ bɛ ji ro̱ŋ? This one will fit or be enough or complete your need?

Roŋ To mistreat or cheat.eg ɛŋu mi roñi dämour?: Why do you cheat your brother?

Roŋroŋ Being thin or bony which is a lack of flesh on the bones.

Ror To scatter, spilt over something some powder, fine drops, dust particles, grains or seeds in order to give good colour etc.

Roor A kind of lizards that raises its head up and down as when looking or gazing.

Roori

Roth Plural of Roor being a lizard that gazes as explained above. 1. An arm pit or the part or area below a shoulder. 2. To cause harm to someone intentionally.

Róth 1. With stress on (ó) being clotted blood after oozing or flowing. 2. With stress on (ó) a quick swift running as when in race. See yuɔ̱th. eg Dak kænæ Tañ cukæ yuth kæ róth kœœñkæ : Dak and Tang they quickly or swiftly started running in a race. Eg Næy tææ Caa käp jälkæ róth róth kæ lathkææri : The people got caught were walking quickly with police. Lathker is a borrowed word from Arabic language.

Róthróth With stress on (ó) is a fast, swift or very quick action of running or follow up.

Ro̱w Plural of Rɔw being the Hippopotamus see Röth.

Ro̱wro̱w A kind of brownish insects from the ant family.

Ro̱wro̱wni Plural of Ro̱wro̱w being that type of insect as explained above.

Rɔa Having much to do with Ro̱w e.g. Ɛ gɔ̱p rɔa: A skin of hippo.

Rɔac Having much to do with Rɔɔc e.g. Ɛ taŋ rɔac: A stick of rɔɔc (a fishing device in Nuer land only).

Rɔacni Plural of Rɔɔc being a metallic device as explained below.

Rɔak 1. State of having much to do with tying down an animal with a long rope so that it can be able to graze a round. 2. Whatever is tied up to be carried along in a journey.

Rɔkrɔak Plural of Rɔkrœk being whatever is carried along as explained above.

Rɔal Noise, to make noise or disturbances.

Rɔlrɔl Being noisy or whatever causes disturbances.

Rɔam 1. A ram or sheep. 2. Whatever is being taken care of or being carried along, such as a child or whatever.

Rɔamdoar Wild ram or sheep.

Rɔany Sugar cane or sorghum stalks.

Rɔath 1. Plural of Roth being the arm pit as explained above. 2. State of becoming seriese, wild or fierce. Eg. Nænæ rœathkien :See their arm pits.

Rɔc 1. Failure to come back from where one has gone to. 2. To delay something by not carrying out or executing the order. 3. A state where one is pressed down by force in wrestling or fighting.

Rɔɔc A metallic device for fishing in Nuer lands only.

Rɔcrɔc A slang for a person who delays and who does not carry out any assignmentat once given to him/her.

Rɔ̱crɔ̱ɔ̱c A habit of delaying due to laziness or intentional disobedience.

Rɔk 1. A rope that is used for thatching huts. 2. Sort of noise which is heard when hanging objects are disturbed or moved.

Rɔkrɔk 1. Slang for a person who disturbs,causes troubles or looks for problems. 2. A style of movements when climbing from branch to branch of a tree.

Rɔhk 1. A type of trees where its trunk is used for carving canoes. 2. Sort of noise which involves leather materials, or broken tools.

Rɔ̱l 1. A mixture of colours where whitish dominates the lower parts of a cow. 2. A Nuer fashion or habit of all cattle owners' way of resting while rearing cattle. It is always one leg rests on the other eg Cuŋni kɛ rœl: Stand or rest on one leg. 3. To give a bad look at someone you hate to stop him/her from going further. 4. A slang for a police badge which is an authority or government. 5. To clear wools or hairs on the skinny meat by exposing it to fire. 6. Style of standing or dancing during drum dance.

Rɔɔm Plural of Rɔam being the sheep as explained above..

Rɔmɛ 1. A very important village near Yomding station Wec Wocel Dit. 2. With stress on (ɛ) is a piece of ornament made out of elephant tusk and it is worn on the right hand wrist 3. Take hold of it.

Rɔmrɔ A complete sentence in Thok Nath meaning : Hold yourself or do not give up. Ịt is said to someone in danger of an attack.

Rɔnrɔn Mistreated or underfed child or calf see Nör

Rɔnrɔan Plural of Rɔnrɔn being underfed young one as explained above.

Rɔny Plural of Rɔany sugar cane or sorghum stalks as explained above.

Rɔŋrɔŋ Stage of being thin or twisting,not straight e.g. Ɛ taŋ mi rɔŋrɔŋ: Not a straight stick.

Rɔt State of being thin due to sickness or starvation.

Rɔtrɔt Being terribly thin due to illness or starvatiom.

Rɔɔtrɔɔt Having much to do with being terribly thin e.g. Ja̱lɛ rɔɔtrɔɔt:He/she is walking while staggering due to being terribly sick or weak.

Rɔ̱th A person who allows things go bad or get destroyed intentionally.

Rɔth The whirl wind which moves very swift and moves objects round and round.

Rɔw The Hippopotamus. See Rödh.

Ru Is a suffix for all those words that ends with (R) when addressing the second person singular, e.g. Näru, Maaru, Bäru etc. Uncle, relationship and height.

Rua A short for Ruadh being the male calf of a cow, goat or ram.

Ruac Talk, speech, speaking, dialogue discussion,statement etc.

Rua̱a̱c Plural of Ruäc the missing or to miss narrowly with touching as explained below.

Ruaac State of much talk as when someone misbehaved. Eg Ruaac kɛ ji ni ciaŋ : You are talked to daily.

Ruacruac He/she who talks a lot or a talkative

Ruadh 1. A male calf of a cow, goat or ram. 2. A slang for a male born child or baby.

Ruaadh The initiation celebration of the first born male boy to manhood.

Ruadhruadh Slang for song or talk which is continuous without repetition or stopping.

Ruak To cause troubles, create problems or difficulties to people.

Rua̱k 1. To mishandle a cooked fish in the soup. 2. An old piece of material such as cloth, skin etc. 3. A sound or noise of a falling object or cooking broth. See Ruàkruàk 4. Plural of Rua̱a̱k being the in-law as explained below.

Ruàkruàk 1. The sound or noise of broth when getting cooked. eg Liŋæ mœ Täh ruàkruàk œ : *Listen to what makes such sounds or noise*.2. The noise or sound of food when getting cooked.

Ruaak Plural of Ruak that is troublesome or troubles shooter as explained above.

Rua̱a̱k 1. Plural of Ruäk that is an old piece of material. Eg Titi kɛ rua̱a̱k biiyni Tut:These are old pieces of Tut clothes as explained above. 2. An in-law from both side of bride or bridegroom parents.eg. Ban wäh dhœr ruààkädan : We go to our in-laws' home or house.

Ruakruak A noise or sound as that is heard when tied up things make such sounds when people are on the move.

Rual 1. A glowing piece of charcoal. See Ruɛl. 2. To prepare charcoal. eg Wer rual mim ti bi nœŋ moœrdœœŋ: You go and prepare charcoals for your grandmother. 3. Plural of Ruaal being a ritual which causes death as a result of sharing sex with blood relative as explained below. 4. A group of animals or herds grazing or moving together.

Ruaal 1. The ritual belief that causes death when one has sex with a relative or blood relating person by mistake. 2. State of having charcoal fire goes off. e.g. Ci jɛn ruaal: The state of having wood fire got off.

Ruan 1. Plural of Ruán being nose faculty or chamber as explained below. 2. A piece of dried grass under bushes.

Ruán With stress (á) is a nose faculty or chamber.

Ruanruan Such dry grass beneath the bushes or shrubs.

Ruaŋ A style of wrestling amongst aged people.

Ruaŋruaŋ A person who plays at any time or fond of playing.

Rua̱ŋrua̱ŋ State of being weak due to aging or sickness.

Ruany To feel or fetch for something by hand in darkness.

Ruanyruany A bad manner where one searches by touching,or disturbing people who come near him/her.

Ruanyruaany Plural of Ruanyruany being the bad habit or behaviour as explained above.

Ruar To fetch or search something by hands in darkness. See Ruany kiɛ ruer.

Ruarruar State of being possible to fetch by hands in darkness.

Ruat State of being thin due to sickness or starvation

Rua̱t Snoring or to snore while sleeping.

Ruatruat 1. State of being thin due to illness. 2. Dry grass under bushes or small trees.

Ruaay State of being very sick for quite a long period.

Ruayruay Being always sick and thin due to illness.

Ruudh To make two or more animals or human beings to share one thing be it a peg or a dish.

Ruec 1. Authority, powers, responsibility or control. 2. A way of climbing a tree or a pole that has no climbing devices or branches.

Rueec 1. Plural of Ru̲iic being a leader, president, ruler etc as explained below. 2. State of forgetfulness in memory.eg Tɛɛ läti hä pan cikɛ rueec: What you told me yesterday got forgotten.

Ruedh To take milk or.drink milk only.

Rueedh 1. Having much to do with drinking of milk or the action of taking milk only. e.g. Bia rueedh: You have to drink milk. 2. Plural of Ruadh being the male calf of both cow or goat.

Ruel 1. To prepare charcoal by burning pieces of wood. 2. A season of the year that starts as from May,June to July, which marks the beginning of rainy season.

Rueny 1. To search by feeling with hands at night or in darkness. 2. To cheat someone as when dividing something.

Ruenyrueny A person who does not give people their rights, when dividing things.

Rueŋ To cheat someone when dividing or distributing something.

Rueŋrueŋ State of being thin or having bad shape or being physically thin in formation or appearance.

Ruet 1. To get conceived or a state of being pregnant. 2. A pregnant woman. 3. A sound which is heard when an animal or human being is speared at.

Ruetruet The sound which is heard when someone or animal is being speared at continuously and very fast.

Rueth 1. A kind of fish which lives in river water.2. To drink milk only.3. To have something to do with adding mud on the walls.

Rueeth 1. Plural of Rueth being that type of fish as explained above. 2. To have drunk or taken milk only. see Rueth.3. Plural of Rueth being act of drinking milk only as explained above.

Ruey Having been lost in memory.

Ruɛa State of having anything to do with Ruɛy being saliva of an elder person spits on the head of a child, a young person etc as greeting or blessing.

Ruɛc To have climbed up the tree that has no climbing branches or devices.

Ruææc Plural of Rueec being who climbs the trees as explained above.

Ruɛcruɛc Slang for a hard food that is eaten without stew,milk or soup to **push** it down the throat.

Ruɛdh To add some mud clay or soil to the hut wooden walls.

Ruɛk The noise which is heard when a broken metallic tool is thrown **down.**

Ruɛkruɛk 1. State of having such noise of metallic tools being thrown down here and there. 2. A slang for a poor speech that has such tones where listeners get difficulties to understand or follow.

Ruɛl Plural of Ruɛ̈l without stress on (ɛ̈)meaning a glowing piece of charcoal as explained below.

Ruɣ̈l The glowing piece of charcoal.

Ruɛm To destroy by cratching or breaking something into pieces using **a** stick or hammer. See Kuɛm.

Ruɛmruɛm A small piece of a cratched of a tobacco bundle. e.g. Cäŋɛ mi ruɛmruɛm: Even a small piece.

Ruɛny Having eyes bulge out of the face. Eg Wöc rɔ ruɛny nyin :Get away bulging eyes.

Ruɛnyruɛny State of having bulging eyes

Ruɛŋruɛŋ State of being very thin in body or appearance.

Ruɛr To fetch something by hands in darkness. See Ruar, Rueny.

Ruɛt 1. To be ready to fight, quarrel, wrestle or to attack. Be in a terrible anger. 2..Slang for danger or troubles. 3. To open a rope so that you tie it on a peg or whatever.

Ruɛth Slang for being fat to the point of loosing shape.

Ruɛthruɛth State of unnecessary fatness that makes a person looses features of his/her shape. See Juäk juäk.

Ruɛy Saliva, spitow, spit, or the liquid that is produced by the mouth.

Ruk 1. To have tied the rope etc. or knot of anything. 2. The payment of cows for adultery or a child whose mother is divorced. 3. Slang for ganging up to do something bad or good.

Rukruk Those small pieces, particles or solid bodies in fresh milk or soft drinks.

Rul To hide a crime or mistake committed.

Ruul The appearance of the bruises or scars on the face or body as ornaments. Eg Ci biirkæ ruul a gœa:His/her ornament scars appeared good.

Rum 1. To overcome or over power someone or whatever.2. A nice taste of food items.

Rumjio̱k 1. A kind of birds.2. A type of beads.Both with black and whitish colour.

Rumciduaar A small animal that has black and whitish defensive feather with sharp points.

Rumputh A kind of bird with black colour on the head and tail with the rest of its body whitish.

Rumrum Having nice smell or acceptable smell.

Run Plural of Ruɔn being a year as explained below.

Ruun Tomorrow. It is always comes after the future suffix (i) eg I ruun.

Runyruny State of being very slippery, or having some slippering points.

Runwaŋ The morning or the early morning or dawn.

Ruoc To swallow, also see Ba̱t. eg Ruocɛ mi ciɛ nyuɛy :Swallow it if you have chewed it.

Ruodh 1. To be in the front line in fighting. 2. A combating fight where men come too close to each other. 3. Whirl winds that blow very fast. 4. To make two or more human beings to share one spoon,dish or one peg in regard to animals. 5. Slang for fast runninge.g. Tɛɛkɛ ruodh: He has the ability to run very fast.

Ruok 1. Plural of Ruɔk that is kidney as explained below. 2. The shape of cow horns as when the two ends come together 3. A knot or having been tied in a way. See Ruk. 4. Whatever you pay for either adultery committed or a divorced mother child usually in kind of cows.

Ruook Plural of Ruok being the knots,ropes or whatever is paid as explained above.

Ruokruok 1. To find difficulties in pronouncing a word due to a nasal or linguistic problem.eg Ruacɛ ruokruok: Talking with difficulties. 2. Being quite narrow or very tight as with a place. Such noise which is heard when a bell rang or a fish is caught etc.

Ruol 1. To collect, put together things or parts when in disarray. 2. Slang for wound being well, or closing up. 3. Barren or inferfile female of any thing.The land that does not produce or yield fruits or grains.

Ruom 1. To consume or burn up very fast. e.g. Mac cɛ juac ruom: The fire has consumed grass. 2. To distroy something by beating it to pieces.

Ruon 1. To form, make leaves or fruits after series dry weather, or climatic changes. 2. A year or the total of twelve months.

Ruony 1. Being whatever is worn on the body such as the cloths, skins, **shoes** etc. 2. State of land overflooding. Eg Wic kier cɛ ruony kɛliew: River bank is overflooded. 3. To hand over or pass something to someone. 4. Slang for eating without chewing the food.

Ruoŋ 1. To surprise someone who is not ready for a task. 2. An accepted way of sitting for a young lady. See Ruol. 3. Plural of Ruɔŋ being the hard parts of a fruit. 4. To make something looks like a ball shape.

Ruoŋruoŋ Having the very shape of circle or round.

Ruop 1. To put or assemble beads on a string. 2. A sudden noise of a movement as when in a danger. See Ruprup. 3. Plural of Rup being a forest. 4. A state of being in a hurry.

Ruoop 1. State of panicking as when in a great danger. 2. A rope that is used for carrying fish while fishing in a pool or pond.

Ruor 1. To scatter some tobacco seeds. 2. To colour by adding different colours.

Ruoor A kind of lizard familywhich gazes by raising its head up and down.

Ruot 1. To endure the pain or difficulties. 2. To tie up things tightly in a container. 3. To put people or animals caught up in a close place where it becomes impossible to escape. 4. To mix sour milk with fresh one to give a good taste. 5. State of shrinkage due to sickness which usually affects the chest.

Ruotruot Having a shrunken chest.

Ruɔk Kidney.

Ruɔɔk Plural of Ruɔk being a cow which is paid or given for either adultery or a child whose mother is divorced.

Ruɔl 1. Scar appearance particularly when it is bulging. See Ruur. 2. To put many scattered things together. 3. State of being unproductive such as a femle animal or human being.

Ruɔɔl Plural of Ruɔl being an unproductive animal or human being as explained above.

Ruɔlruɔl State of being closed or put together.

Ruɔ̱m 1. A big fly that attacks human, animals and other dometic animals. See Rum. 2. State of having nice smell.

Ruɔ̱n One year or twelve months. See Run.

Ruɔŋ The hard part of certain fruits which is thrown away.

Ruɔp One of the four teeth that grow first on baby gum. See Rup.

Ruɔɔp Few pieces of beads which complete a string.

Ruɔ̱ɔr 1. A type of plants which is used for making fences. 2. The heavy sound as that is made by a lion, Hipo. etc. 3. A baby or child in the mother eyes or consideration.

Ruɔɔri 1. Plural of Ruɔɔr being a child as explained above. 2. Plural of Ruoor being the lizard type as explained above.

Ruɔɔt Plural of Ruot being a bundle of tied luggage or things as explained above.

Rup Plural of Ruɔp one of the front teeth which grows first on the mouth gum as explained above.

Ruprup State of being in panicking stage or in a hurry. See Ruop.

Rur 1. State of being not ready to tell or disclose the secret. 2. Foggy weather.

Rut 1. Having got swollen due to an injury or wound. 2. To endure the pain or difficulty.

Rutrut State of having some swelling on the skin. See Rut.

Rutot A stage when one become tight and in round shape.

Rutut State of being very fat or round as a result of swelling.

Ruiy That is got lost in memory

Räc To clean or clear the baby or child's stool when it defecates out the solid waste.

Rääc 1. The person who carries out the cleaning of waste. 2. Being what is used for cleaning the stool when defecated.

Räk 1. To tie up several ropes so that an animal is to be tied down while grazing in the vicinity. 2. To make a network like a spider.

Räkräk The network which is made by spider in bushes, roofs, walls etc.

Räkpiny A slang of a greedy person who plans to collect as much as he/she could get by putting all his/her resources in many places.

Räl Plural of Ra̱a̱l being a nerve in the body as explained above.

Rääl Having much to do with nerves or viens.eg Næmæ tææ ræy rääl : This is in the nerves or veins.

Rämrääm The behaviour of a greedy person who tries to get much in a short period of time usually in fishing, eating or gathering.

Räny Improper way of sitting or doing something.eg Cuæ räny thin lätni jæ gœa: Do not be rough but do it well.

Rääny Rough way of falling on slippery surface.

Ränyräny A quick way of carrying out duty, while not willing to do so.

Räŋ 1. One of the popular dancing styles in Eastern Jikany in Gaat jiook Section Region. 2. Reflection of light or glittering against the mirror surface.

Rääŋ A person who does not miss in shooting, spearing etc.

Räŋräŋ State of being glitting or showing reflexive light.

Räp 1. A sudden way of sitting. 2. A sudden feeling of fear.

Rääp 1. State of being very fast as that of lightning. 2. A marriage ceremony or dance appearance. 3. The movements of flag orwhatever against the winds.

Räpräp 1. State of fear or frightening due to a danger. A behavior of a greedy child to get food. 2. The noise as that is made by a flying flag or a piece of cloth against the wind.

Rär The opening of the apex as when maize or, sorghum grows before the appearance of grains, see Här

Rärräk A noise or sound which is heard when pouring water out.

Rät Plural of Ral being a part of Female Genital Organ as explained above.

Räträt The noise of a heavy rain fall.

Räth State of having gone far as stated by the speaker.eg Jɛn cɛ räth: He/she has gone far.

Räw Style of dancing where both male and female jumps up and make jerks.

Räwräw The appearance of flash light when lightning or raining.

Rëëc The person who separates people fighting or querraling.

Riäm The sound of falling old and huge object (Tree, luak) as a result of wind.

Riämriäm A situation when one becomes weak and easily falls due to aging.

Riän To bend or get bended.

Riänriän State of being in bending or moving in dancing. That can easily gets bended.

Riär 1. State of becoming sexy or heated. 2. Plural of Rier being common or prostitute as explained above. 3. To have lost a thing completely.

Riäth 1. A way of walking due to weakness or sickness. 2. Plural of Riey Being a canoe, boat, car,plane etc as explained above.

Riäthriäth A way of walking with difficultes due to weakness or sickness.

Riök 1. Half burned food at the bottom of cooking utensil. 2. One of the big teeth that chews the food before swallowing.

Riöny A bad way of sitting amongst young ladies.

Riönyriöny Ackward way of walking, moving even sitting.

Riönyriööny An ugly behavior of moving or walking.

Riöp 1. A finger or toe nail of human being or hoof of an animal. 2. Slang for a thief or a person who steals.

Ruäc To miss with slight injuries or bruises.

Ruääc Plural of Ruäc being the narrow missing with bruises as explained above.

Ruädhruädh Ugly or bad tones which is heard when singing or talking.

Ruääl State of being slow or hesitant in doing something.

Ruälruäl A very slow way of doing or handling things.

Ruäŋ To chew with difficulties when the teeth have a problem.

Ruäŋruäŋ State of being weak due to aging or sickness.

Ruäny To cause a bruise on someone. See Ruäc

Ruät To snore or to make noise when in deep sleep.

Ruäät 1. State of being in heavy snoring situation. 2. Slang for heavy loud noise of series shooting.

Ruätät Face to face confrontation in drum dance.

Ruël A glowing charcoal or wooden fire.

Ruöt Heavy noise of breathing as a result of chest problem or when in deep sleeping.

Röc To carry out massage on the body of a sick person.

Rööc 1. A woman that carries out the arts of massaging 2. Has two meanings as following :Cɛkɛ rööc piny: He/she has masscared.them Cɛkɛ rööc piny: They have been overcome or bogged down by disease or epidemic.

Rök 1. The noise of utensils as when disturbed in the kitchen. 2. Another pronunciation of Riök the chewing teeth (Molars). 3. To tie, join or connect things together.

Röl 1. State of weeping,crying etc see Röt. 2. To make noise, disturb or shout.

Röm 1. To meet, confluence of water ways, meeting.eg Wä kœ mäi kä röm yieri :We are going to summer at rivers confluence. 2. To take care of something or someone. 3. To bring up a child, a family or anyother persons. 4. The meeting point, spot or place agreed upon. 5. Connection or relationship. 6. To tie together poles when building hut roof. See Muk.

Rööm 1. The baby seater or any person who looks after someone or people. 2. Whatever one uses for bringing up a child or a family.

Röt 1. Weeping, crying or making noise such as the animal e.g. Cuo röt: Do not cry or weep. see wie or lul etc. 2. To claim something by weeping from someone else.

Rööt Having much to do with noise making or weeping as a case with human beings or animals.eg Nomœ æ thäk mi rööt: That is a good sound bull.

Rötni Plural of Rööt being a good sound bull or a great singer for both human or animal as explained above.

Röth 1. Plural of Rɔw being the hippopotamus as explained above. See Row. 2. To smear the floor of a room with soft mud or clay.

Rööth The person or the area. Being he/she who carries out the smearing or the area smeared with clay mud.

T

Taa Condition or situation where someone enjoys or suffers.

Tabäw 1. Such noise that is heard when something falls into large water surface. 2. Slang for plenty food or availability, particularly grains and fish.

Tac 1. A field plant that acts as weed. 2. To spread out or to go to so many directions.

Tactac State of being spreaded and covered a large area.

Tak 1. A standard way of sitting for a young Nuer man where both legs are crossed on one another. 2. A disease which causes deformity, particularly on back or joints .eg Ca töl ɛ tak : He/she was deformed by such a disease. 3. An unorganized way of talking or walking. Eg Cua rɛ jal kɛ tak : Do not walk any how. 4. A way of making ropes and plaiting hairs. To prepare tobacco leaves for later consumption.5. Spleen or that part of internal organs of both animals and human being.6. A taste or smell of food.

Ták With (á) stressed is when a baby released some food in vomiting.

Taak A type of tortoise which is the smallest one.

Taktak State of having such taste or smell.

Tal 1. A style of cutting fish so that it gets dried. 2. To expand the fish side ways in order to have it dried faster. See Liac.

Talaŋ A person who does not care of him/herself or his/her personal belongings or property.

Talaaŋ Plural of Talaŋ being a person who does not care of him/herself as explained above.

Tam 1. A sound or noise of a broken wooden tool. 2. Slang for telling lies or untrue statements known as Tambööri.

Tamtam 1. That noise or sound which is heard when breaking wooden logs continuously. 2. A sweet taste such as sugar components.

Tany 1. To clean carefully the hands, the body etc. 2. To push down or aside by force to open way or path. 3. To force grass, dura stalk to fall or bend down.

Tanytany State of having difficulties to push back or to make it straight.

Taŋ 1. A long stick which is fitted to spear, pipe, harpoon etc. It can be solid or hollow stick. 2. Slang for a specific thing or person intended by speaker.eg Ruacä kɛ taŋdu: I am talking to you personaly.

Taŋnyaŋ A decorated stick for a special spear.

Taŋtaŋ State of being whitish in colour or clear from dirts.

Taŋrial A large flat white fish with red fins.

Taŋraw A type of sorghum grains which was popular in ancient days.

Tap Tobacco in general. Tobacco might had originated from Africa where most nations in Africa called it (Tap, Thap, Thapa etc).

Tapɛ A large clay made utensil or a large native pot.

Ta̱p Plural of Täp being the low land or depression as explained below.

Taap Plural of Tap being Tobacco in general as explained above.

Taptap State of being very wide,vast, large or extensive water surface,forest etc.

Tar Upside down or state of having the back part down.

Taar State of having bull horns bending backwards eg. Tuŋ taar, Kal mi taar etc. Opened horn and an opened fence.

Tartar State of being opened or lying on the back.

Taraw Period of starvation, famine or food gap.

Taraaw Having much to do with that period of hunger, starvation or famine eg. Ruɔn taraaw:The year of starvation or hunger.

Tat A type of stalks that has no sweet juice when being chewed.

Taw A sound of gun shot or whatever sound.

Tawtaw 1. State of being opened or transparent and who tells or expresses whatever one knows of anything. 2. Series noise of gun shots.

Tay Plural of Taay being the symptoms of starvation which appears on the buttock in forms of wrinkles as explained below.

Taay A wrinkle which appears on human buttock during starvation as explained above.

Taytay Very large or vast extensive area of water or treeless area.

Tec To clean by polishing the surface.

Tectec A fancy legend which makes any problem or difficulty not so harsh.

Tek A disease that affects fingers, joints, known as leprosy, see Dhop.

Tem One of the Female Genital Organ of human being.

Teem What is used for cutting eg. Razor blade, spear, knife etc.

Tep 1. A word that is used for rejecting any question or idea. 2. Being difficult to handle or manipulate.

Ter A situation when a wound gets swollen.

Terter State of being badly swollen due to decaying.

Tet 1. State of being hard,strong or difficult to handle. 2. Plural and single for Tet being a hand or hands ẹg. Tetdu :Your hand, Tetku :Your hands.

Tettet State of being difficult to release or give out something.

Teth Slang for death or passing away of an elderly person. It means falling in general.

Tey To remain or to stay.eg Kua tey banɛ lɛ jek : You remain we meet.

Tɛɛ A complete sentence Tææ : He/she/it, has.

Tɛac A kind of wormlike insect that lives in dusty room floor.

Tɛah A piece of a dried wood which is used as fire wood for cooking. See Tɛy.

Tɛäh A food which is hidden to be given to the beloved one, a guest,A husband or a son.

Tɛakni Plural of Tɛɛk being an Aluminum metal ring as explained below.

Tɛal Lower part of the leg below the kneel.

Tɛc Plural of Tɛac being wormlike type of insect as explained above.

Tɛk 1. A noise of whatever thing moved or pulled by night. 2. A share or quota of whatever divided such as food.

Tɛɛk 1. Having much to do with life or living eg. Tee tɛɛkä: He is living or still alive.2. An Aluminum metal.

Tɛkɛ A piece of wood fixed on the wall for hanging things on.

Tɛkɛni Plural of Tɛkɛ being a piece of wood as explained above.

Tɛl 1. Plural of Tɛal the lower part of a leg from knee as explained above. 2. To shake something, leg, finger, grass etc. 3. A fishing method which depends on fish movement in grass water.

Tɛltɛl A style of walking among girls or young ladies.

Tɛm Art of cutting something with razor, knife, spear etc. eg Bia tɛm kɛ rɛɛt : You cut it with razor.

Tɛn To do something on individual basis.eg Gony cæ tæn kæ tændæ: Gony Acted on his own way.

Tɛnh State of falling or bending towads the speaker.

Tɛnhpiny Starting a journey towards the speaker.

Tɛny 1. To be bright or being opened without cover or clouds. 2. To open widely as that with teeth. 3. The native belief to be the master of heaven including rainfalls.

Tɛɛny A Kujur belief to have power that causes thunderstorms.

Tɛnydɛr An opened space without cover or roof. State of being clear under sun rays.

Tɛnylɛc A Nuer legend story for frightening children at night.

Tɛnynyɛny State of being apparently clear or opened to everybody sight.

Tɛnytɛny 1. Being so sunny dry morning. State of being of pure background or clean of crime. 2. The noise of rain fall on hard roof or the melting of fats on frying fan.

Tɛŋ 1. A plant that is used for making mats or fences. 2. To stir away dust, dirts, insects or whatever is not wanted. 3. A small quantity of food, the cook gives to a child to sustain him/her from hunger. 4. To finish whatever you were doing be it eating, weeding cutting wood etc.

Tɛŋpiny To get rid of something by pushing it away, aside or down.

Tɛŋtɛŋ To be free from troubles, not committed or state of being innocent.

Tɛp A cry or noise a baby makes when his/her playing tool is tempered with by an elderly person. see Tɛpbɛɛw.

Tɛptɛp State of being very small or little in size.

Tɛptɛap Plural of Tɛptɛp being very little in size as explained above.

Tɛr Conflict, quarrel, dispute see Gɛam.

Tɛɛr 1. The Ninth month of the year in Nuer Calendar. 2. To have much desire or zeal to do something.

Tɛrɛk A sound or noise of a falling wooden object, metallic equipments or utensils. see Torok.

Tɛrɛɛm A noise or sound which is heard when a rat or whatever is **eating** or breaking things in the store.

Tætl. A device or part of a stem which is used for climbing a tree, a wall or whatever. 2. A person from Shullok tribe Chollo. 3. With stress on ('æ') is a plural of Tæt as explained above.

Tɛɛt 1. The claim which happens when relationships get severed, where each person demands his/her gifts or whatever from the friends or so.2. Plural of Tæt being one person from Shullok tribe as explained above.

Tɛttɛt State of being very small or little in size. Eg Guäthæ mœ tææ kæ mi tætæt: That place has small out growth.

Tɛth 1. The falling down. 2. The appearance of the new moon. 3. Those fallen sorghum stalks or bundles due to heavy rain or winds. 4. A state of happiness e.g. Tɛth lɔaac.: Heart felt happiness.

Tɛɛth Having fallen or appreared. A state of becoming so happy e.g. Ci jiath tɛɛth?: A tree has fallen?. Ci pay tɛɛth?: The new moon appeared?. Ci lɔcdu tɛɛth?: Your heart is happy?

Tɛw Being very small or little in size or volume.

Tɛwtɛw Being very small in size such as human being or whatever.

Tɛɛw A fast style of slaughtering rams or chickens.

Tɛwɛw Being difficult or being alone. see T̲ir̲ir.

Tɛy Plural of Tɛah being the dried piece of wood for firewood as explained above.

Ti 1. Is a suffix for both single and plural questions at the end of a word with (T) e.g. Gati bia: youth come. Kɛn titi? These ones?. 2. Is a short form for word Titi These. see Tɔtɔ.

Tiac Whatever food items cut to small pieces to be dried for later time consumption such as domestic meat or wild meat.

Tiaac An aimless style of walking. see, Läw Luay, Loar, Laath.

Tiak 1. To cut beyond the expected parts or shares. 2. To insult someone very badly where you abuse his/her father or mother See Tiɛk.

Tiam To overcome someone in a fight or wrestling.

Tiaam State of being overcome by sadness or bad news.

Tiany To open or search in the cow dung fire or whatever.

Tiap 1. A large fire. 2. A largely developed ugly wound.

Tiaptiap State of being large or extensive fire or wound.

Tiaap Being quite large as the fire or wound.

Tiar 1. To break hard thing such as grains or stone etc. 2. To cause menustration before the usual period. 3. Having much to do with Tiɛr being an insult to such a person.

Tiaar A distorted Arabic language word for Air-port or Air-trip etc.

Tiath 1. Breakage, fracture or cracking on the skull, gourd, or clay utensils. see Tööl 2. The pain which affects old wound or scar. see Kuuk e.g. Tiathɛ piäär: The scar is itching. 3. An insult to someone eg. Tiathɛ ji? Are you being itched by naughtiness ?

Tiathtiath A noise which is heard as a result of hitting two iron rods, bars or stones.

Tiaytiay State of being very large or vast such as water surface, lakes, pools, seas etc.

T̲ic 1. A building Luak, Duel etc. 2. With stress on (i) is a farm or field weed plant which has a network of roots which cause difficulties in weeding to cultivators and farmers.

T̲iec 1. Plural of T̲ic with stress on (i) is being the weed plants as explained above. 2. To pull something either from place to another or from the soil or ground. 3. To pull away or give a space or move to another spot.

Tieec The state of pulling something or oneself towards the speaker .eg Tieec ni rœ wanɛ : Pull yourself here or come here.

Tiec kɔn Pull us a part or give a space.

Tiek 1. Cloudy day where sunrays do not reach a certain spot on the earth surface. 2. State of having hairs, grass or tress grown in great quantities in the forest or on the head.eg ɛŋu ci juaac tiek inœ ? : Why the grass become thick like that?

Tieek State of having hairs,trees or grass grown up greatly.

Tieel 1. State of comfortable or rich way of life eg Gaat Ruac cikɛ tieel :Ruac children are rich. 2. A kind of fish with hard scales.

Tiem 1. To think, recall good or bad deeds, events, names or people. 2. Having that awful smell of fish. See Cieŋ.

Tiemtiem Young leaves or buds of twigs of certain type of trees.

Tiemtiemni Plural of Tiemtiem being the young leaves as explained above.

Tien To widen a tight object or opening. See Tian.

Tientien State of being widened as that of shoes etc.

Tieny 1. To wipe out something from eye. 2. To take something as a whole. 3. Slang for sudden running or jumping.

Tiep The shade or shadow.

Tieepni Plural of Tiep being the shadow as explained above.

Tiet The witchdoctor who makes magics by extracting stones,bones or whatever from human body.

Tieth A small child or baby.

Tieeth Plural of Tieth being a small child as explained above.

Tiewtiew State of being in early stage of ripening. See Tiäw.

Tiey 1. The soul. 2. The eye retina.

Tigiliŋ Only one eg. Nya tigiliŋ: The only one.

Tik 1. Bead grains of different colours. 2. Chin, the tip of the beard area or organ.

Tìk Being the grain particle after pounding.

Til 1. Comfort, richness or better living conditions. 2. Transparent as that of water, fat, oil etc.

T̲il 1. To discriminate when dividing something, being a lack of transparency. 2. A ring shape brass metal which is worn on wrist as an ornament. 3. Keep silence when one says: Bit ni ɛtìl: You be silence. eg. ɛŋu ci wää tìl inɔ? why did keep silence like that?

Tiil Anxiety or state of worries as when one loses a dear person.

Tiltil A rich man or a rich woman.

T̲itlt̲il A kind of plants which grows in water, or in marshes.

Tiltieel Plural of Tiltil being a rich person as explained above.

Tiliŋ The noise or sound of a small bell such as what is rang in the school.

Tiɛk 1. Plural of T̲ik being the small pounded grain particle as explained above. Eg Titi kæ tiæk bææl tææ thaar : These are last year grain particles.

Tiɛɛk Puzzling statement of Tiɛk being pounded grain particles become extraordinary very great eg.Ciæ tiææk caa piny thiàn̈ : What a great quantity of grain particles which have covered the floor.

Tiɛɛl Being means or greedy when dividing something where one gives very little to people and takes the greater part.

Tiɛr Being clitoris or part of female genital organ.

Tim Great desire to meet or see the one you love or like very much.

Timtim A smell of not well cooked fish.

Tin A word which refers to things known well by the speaker eg. Nọọni tin kɔn: bring those before.

Tindi̱i̱r 1. A sound of sudden movement of fish, wild life. 2. A sudden fire outbreak burning particularly in the forest.

Tinytiny State of being clean or neat in body condition.

Ti̱ŋ 1. To shake in order to know the quantity at the bottom of a container. 2. To make regular sound as that with a bell. 3. To defecate some liquid waste when suffering of severe diarrhea.

Tiiŋ A person or a bull that is good in shaking a bell to give regular sounds.

Tiŋtiŋ 1. Sound of a bell. 2. The state of being in a shaking position.

Ti̱ŋi̱ŋ Long waiting while standing in one place.

Tip 1. A kind of feeling when having taken oily food or sugary materials. 2. A word which is used for describing whatever is soaked in water, fat, oil, urine or any liquid. eg. Cɛ wä tip kɛ lieth: It is well filled with butter. 3. The second or third release of milk by a cow after every sucking by its calf.

Tìptìp State of being properly filled or soaked with butter, water etc.

Tiptip 1. State of being in a shaking position as with flag or a piece of cloth in a windy day. 2. Style of dancing by good dancer.

Tiọp 1. The mixture of cow dung and urine in side a cattle hut -Luak. 2. A bulky light plant which is used for making protection devices. 3. Slang for confusion where one mixes up different topics or issues during discussion.

Tiot A food that becomes bad for having been mixed up with other ingredients for quite a long time.

Tiottiot State of food being in a bad shape or appearance.

Tiɔ̱k To mess up food when eating.

Tiɔ̱t To mess up food or something or part of it.

Tir 1. To raise the other end of a stick or a pole by pressing the near end of it. 2. To make certain sounds in water to stimulate fish to move in order to spear them.

T̲ir Plural of Tiɛr being Clitoris or part of Female Genital Organ.

Tirir Not well covered or closed up such as a tooth or a wood in thatched roof.

Tirtir State of being not well fitted or smooth.

Tiriew Being very strong, hard to bend, break, straight or quite rigid.

Tiriw Being difficult, or thin. Ạ slang for a legend known to be the far spot in the history.

T̲irit A device which makes heavy noise or sounds when turn round several times.

T̲irr̲it A type of mosquitoes that stays in the room.

Tit 1. Plural of Tiet being the witchdoctor as explained above. 2. To clean or extract all the grains particles on sorghum bundles.

Tiit 1. A string or thread which is tied to a hook or a snare for catching fishes. 2. Having the ability to recall whatever one has had seen or heard in the past. 3. A guide, a pole or a sign that helps the travelers to follow the right path.

Titi 1. These.see Tœtœ and Tìtì.eg Titi kæ nyinku, kä tœtœ kæ kuak Gac,Kä tìtì kæ nyin wec : These are mine and those are Gac luggage and those far belong to the village,town, country or nation. Here Nuer have three steps in pointing things in three different locations such as Titi, Tœtœ and Tìtì.The other example also can give the same point. Nɛmɛ = this. Nɔmɔ = that. Nimi = that far.

Tith State of being red or pink. Eg. Biiy mi tith : A red or pink cloth.

Tiith The first milk of a cow which appears yellowish.eg Cak ti tiith jiäkæ :The first milk is bad.

Tithtith Reddish or pink in colour.eg æ läh ñu æn tithtith æmœ ? : What is this reddish or pink ?

Tiw 1. Peak or top part of a thing. Eg Wer tiw thoa : You go the top of Acacia Nilotica tree. 2. The last part of the tail. Eg Käp tiw juälæ : Take hold of its tail.

T̲iwt̲iw The last point, height or peak of anything.to A word which complete a statement. Eg. Kɛ nyin ŋa kɛn to? *Whose things are those?*

Toak Being nonsense or meaningless things or talks. See Tok.

Toani Plural of Tot being very small or little as explained below.

Toany Having much to do with criticism. See Töny ẹg æñu toany naath œ? Why are you criticising people?

Toap Having much to do with skin desease Top eg Næmæ æ duñ toap:This one belong to skin disease.

Toar 1. A kind of plants that has long spherical green leaves. 2. Plural of Tor being all those stories or talks meant for passing, amusing etc.

Toac A nut of Acacia Nilotica tree fruits.

Tooc Plural of Toac being the nut of Acacia Nilotica as expained above.

To̱o̱c To lie down either to rest or to sleep.

Toor Plural of Toar being a kind of plant as explained above.eg Guicɛ rɛy toor: See it in these plants.

Toc An opened grass land with swamps.

Tòc Plural of Toc being the opened grass land,where the stress on (ó) Makes the difference of the two words.

To̱glo̱ŋ 1. A noise of a falling huge local bell. 2. A lame person way of walking.

Tok.Laughter or to laugh to express happiness.

Tœk 1. A dominantly black bird which is one of the rare species. 2. Being awful or nasty smell which attracts such as tobacco.

To̱k A slang for making someone to believe what is not true.

To̱l To break a piece of wood, ivory,metal tool, a bone etc.

Tol 1. A smoke,or carbon monnoxoide (Co). 2. A small bird with black and gray cotour with front part blue.

Toltol A sound which is heard when pouring water out of a container.

Tom A noise or sound of breaking wooden tool or log. See To̱m.

To̱m Noise or sound of breaking tree or gun shot.

Toom To make two ends meet.eg Kartoom :The meeting of two tributaries Such as White and Blue Niles.

Tomtom Slang for troubles, being actual fighting or stomach disease.

Ton A word which is used to complete a statement as eg : Kɛn ton: Here they are.

To̱ny A long native pipe with so many parts eg. Juuth, taŋ, pöth, **töny,** kuat, kuum.

Tony To criticize or to say something is not admiring or bad.

Tonytony State of being quite critical of whatever done by different persons or people.

To̱ŋ Plural of Taŋ being a piece of wood which is fitted to a metallic tool eg. Spear or whatever as explained above.

Top 1. To roast something in front of fire. 2. To have a wound escalated such as ulcer.eg Top dhœn riñ æmæ : Roast this piece of meat. Eg Böt ciokä dæ cæ top : His/her leg wound escalated.

To̱r 1. Having fallen short in what one is targeting. see Yet. 2. A sound of a falling object.

Tor 1. The formation of fungi on object. 2. A sound or noise of a falling object.

To̱o̱r 1. A stick the blind person uses to feel his/her ways when walking. It is used by any person in darkness to scare whatever on the path. 2. Having fallen short when playing such game as explained above. 3. A rod like device that moves and makes noise or sound in a bell. 4. A male human or animal that is born with one testicle instead of normal two.

To̱ro̱k A sound or noise of a falling object.

To̱rto̱r 1. A sound which is heard when pulling a hollow object or dried skin. 2. State of being hard to break easily.

Torom 1. Sound of gourd breaking or beating a wooden tool. 2. A sound of chewing bone meat or when a mouse breaks or chews things in dark corners.

Toromtorom Being such noise of shewing continuously hard objects in either darkness or by daytime.

To̱t 1. A name of a child that follows twins. 2. To raise up the tail as a dog, goat, scorpion etc does.

Tot State of having weeded the farm properly.

Toth Plural of Tɔth being a bundle of thatching grass as explained below.

Touth 1. To clean the mouth or teeth with tooth paste, cow dung ashes. 2. To polish a spear or any tool. 3. A piece of wood which is put at the end of a spear to protect it from touching any thing.

Toa̱w To keep or store something.eg Man Nyaañ toàw titi : Nyang mother keeps these.

Tow A sound of gun shot. Eg æñu ci wàh tow œ ? What made such sound?

To̱y A sound which is heard when beating a hollow object such as barrel.

To̱yto̱y The noise of frequent beating of barrel.

Tɔac The nut of Thow tree being Acacia Nilotica.

Tɔaŋ 1. A piece of dried grass or wood for cooking in rural area. See Tɔɔŋ. 2. To heap some dried cow dung for making smoke to scare insects. 3. To make shrine by heaping cow dung in front of cattle hut.

Tɔat State of being fluent in speaking or talking a language.

Tɔc Green colour.

Tɔ̱ɔ̱c To sleep or lie down, to lie a baby or a sick person in bed.

Tɔɔc Plural of Tɔac being the nut, of Acacia Nilotica as explained above.

Tɔk 1. To divide food to the consumers when cooked. 2. State of being over flown by water as a result of flood or breakage of a large container. Eg Piw cikæ tœk piny : The water has overflown the ground. 3. To knock or the style of knocking sound.

Tɔktɔk State of series knocking sound, noise or warning sound of a falling object.

Tɔl A type of plants or grass.eg Wia ñaræ ræy tœlä : You go and play in that grass.

Tɔɔl Plural of Tɔl being a type of plants or grass as explained above.

Tɔalɔar A type of plants which produces fruits whose colour turns yellowish when ripened.

Tɔ̱m To inject or prick with sharp point eg. Thorn, needle etc.

Tɔ̱ɔ̱m Plural of Tuum the person who gives injection as explained above.

Tɔŋ State of heaping cow dung to make smoke or building a shrine.

Tɔ̱ŋ 1. To stir bee hive or whatever eg. Tɔ̱ŋ tuar.2. Slang of when looking for trouble.

Tɔɔŋ 1. Slang for what has become nusiane or troublesome 2. What is used for clearing the pipe Juuth or pushing outwards Any bending on luak roof. 3. A bundle of dried pieces of grass or firewood for cooking in rural areas.

Tɔp A disease that affects young people with symptoms that appear like rings on sensitive organs.

Tɔ̱p A noise or sound of a falling gourd or clay utensil.

Tɔɔp A fermented flour which is dried for a long journey needs.

Tɔptɔp Very small groups or cattle camps.

Tɔr To go around as from place to another.

Tɔɔr Having become rusted or grown with fungi.

Tɔ̱ɔ̱r Swamps, marshes or plain grassland.

Tɔ̱a̱ri Plural of Tåår being the marshes as explained above.

Tɔrɔk The same noise or sound of a falling object.

Tɔrtɔr A sound which is heard when pulling a light wooden or gourd tool.

Tɔt Very small or little as in eg. Mi tɔt.

Tɔ̱t The wet season or Autumn,being the most floody and wet period **of** the year.

Tɔrɔt The niging or noise which is made by a frog.

Tɔth A bundle of grass tied up as a measurement for building or thatching purpose.

Tɔ̱ɔ̱w Whatever is used for keeping or storing things.

Tɔy Being not smooth,not flat and very rough.

Tɔɔy A noise of a buring fat or oil.

Tɔytɔy 1. That noise of burning fats or oil. 2. State of being not smooth.

Tɔyɔy A state of such sound of a burning fat, oil or forest.

Tuac 1. Leopard skin mainly but could be any fur eg. – Tuac Kuac: leopard skin. – Tuac Thɔ̱ɔ̱nä: A small game skin.– Tuac Gön: A cat family game fur or skin. 2. Is a wearing fur in court of law to end the dispute.

Tuak 1. Having got cooked already. 2. A word which is used for threatening a person by hitting or beating.

Tua̱k Plural of Tuäk being the muddy soil as explained below.

Tua̱a̱k State of having what to do with mud soil eg. Cu jäl rɛy tua̱a̱k: Do not move or walk in mud soil.

Tual 1. A kind of marine plant which has nice flowers around ponds or stagnant water. 2. Oozing or flowing of blood, water or any liquid.

Tuan State of being weak.

Tuantuan State of being tall and physically weak.

Tuany 1. To feel the hardness or softness of a thing with finger. 2. A word which means sick or feverish in Dinka language. 3. One of the early guns model which is shot by pressing a finger button.

Tuanytuany Continuous touching or pressing on something.

Tuaŋ To mix things with hands or fingers.

Tuaŋtuaŋ 1. That is mixable item. 2. Being tall and thin due to growth.

Tuar 1. Traditional song which is composed by either men or women. 2. Having much to do with bee or honey eg. Thiik tuar: Bee hive. 3. A slang for a thin fish where Nuer believe that it has had sung a lot.

Tuaar Bee or bee honey.

Tuari Plural of Tuaar being bee hive or bee honey as explained above.

Tuaari Plural of Tuar being the song as explained above.

Tuat A name of a cattle camp along Sobat river tributaries.eg Cä ñak kä Tuat :I had made a show up excercise at Tuat.

Tuat A type of grass which is used for making thatching ropes.

Tuel To dissuade, disway or tell someone not to do something. See Luɛk.

Tueel Plural of Tuel being he/she who tells others not to do things as explained above.

Tueltuel A style of walking such as a baby or a heavy loaded person.

Tuet Degeneration or state of becoming little slowly.

Tuetuet Having or being very little in both shape or height.

Tueth Cooking process where water mixes with food materials.

Tueth To perform certain rituals in order to forecast or foretell someone problem good or bad.

Tueeth 1. State of having much to do with Tueth being the art of performing such rituals to those who belief in it.eg Panom cæ wä tueeth dhœr Gatbææl :Panom has gone to perform such rituals in Gatbeel home. 2. A wooden component of weeding tool, device or axe eg. Tueeth Jiöp and Tueeth Puɔr.

Tuɛk A sound of axe as when cutting wood or trees.

Tuɛktuɛk The continuous noise of axe when cutting woods or trees.

Tuɛl A substance that is used for making smoke to scare flies away.

Tuɛm 1. To hit gently on something as a signal. Eg Kuæ tuæm æ jæn bæ rœ bar :Just hit him/her that will make him/her to run away.

Tuæmtuæm 2. A small group or a bundle of things. Being a small group or heap.

Tuɛmtuɛam Plural of Tuæmtuæm being such a small group as explained above.

Tuɛny Whatever has got some defects on.

Tuɛŋ The hollow part below the chin or the lower part of a neck.

Tuɛŋ ca̱r A kind of birds with a black spot below its beak.

Tuɛr

Tuæar To remove the hard remanents of food by either using fingers, spoons, snail shell spoons in cleaning. Plural of Tuær being the outcome of cleaning using those device as explained above.

Tuɛt To become short due to anger or when ready to fight. See Tuɛtpiny.

Tuɛttuɛt A style of walking by short or a deformed person.

Tuɛth Having grown up by heaping on top or having built up on top eg. Anthills, Gum, etc.

Tuɛthtuɛth State of being building up or heaping up things.

Tuɛy Nasty smell connected with goats or sheep places in the byre (Hut).

Tuɛytuɛy Having that sort of smell in such a place.

Tuil Retarding in growth or state of little improvement in growth.eg DengÆ gat mi tuil : Deng is not a growing child.

Tuiny.1. Calf diarrhea. Eg Dæy hœœk cæ kæ tuiny: The cow calves havegot diarrhea. 2. To grab someone with finger nails as punishment or looking for troubles.

Tuinyni Plural of Tuiny being grabbing as explained above.

Tuittuit Being quite short and small.

Tuoc 1. To bend or curve something such as wood or an iron rod. 2. To state the total number of cows as dowry in marriage settlement.

Tuocjœœr The total number of dowry cows agreed to be paid when available.

Tuocjœœri Plural of Tuocjœœr being the dowry cows to be paid as explained above.

Tuok 1. A sound of a falling or breaking object.2. A gourd container utensil. 3. To begin something or whatever.eg Tuok ruac bi naath ŋal jiææn : Start talk so that people could leave.

Tuook 1. Plural of Tuok being gourd container as explained above. 2. Plural of Tuok being whatever cause problems as explained above.

Tuoktuok 1. The continuous noise of breaking or falling trees. 2. The action of termite on a wooden object or whatever.

Tuol 1. The smoke or Carbon. 2. To make smoke to scare flies from cattle.

Tuoltuol 1. A sound which is heard when pouring water or any liquid out. 2. A state of being quite small and short.

Tuoŋ 1. Plural of To̱o̱ŋ being an egg, of any type as explained below. 2. To press or massage the paining or itching part. 3. To scatter the wet cowdung in order to get dried. See Toŋ wäär. 4. A game which is played by pressing knee joints gently while chorusing. Toŋ-toŋda lɛɛk kä nyagaak….

Tuoŋoŋ State of sitting without knowing what is happening around you.

Tuor To clean by removing whatever of no values be it on wood, garden, fingers, hands and even feet after some muddy soil work.

Tuot 1. To bend down one back as when entering a low height door.2. To bend a stick or an iron rod. 3. To go mating as with animals.

Tuɔɔc Plural of Tuoc being the cows stated in the marriage settlement on which the two groups bargain on till settlement or failure. See Tuocjœœr.

Tuɔk 1. To start something eg. Games, talks, plays etc. 2. An opened utensil bowl like made from gourd. 3. To look or stir up problems or troubles.

Tuɔl 1. A brown colour. 2. The boiled newly ripened grains.

Tuœɔl 1. The cowdungs that is kept for making smoke to scare insects. 2. The boiled newly ripened grains. 3. Anything to do with smoke or boiled grains.

Tuo̱m 1. To inject someone or animal. 2. Prick someone or animal or whatever with sharp point.

Tuɔɔm Plural of Tuum being he/she who gives injection as explained above.

Tuɔmtuɔɔm A state of walking anyhow without knowing the immanent danger is closed.

Tuo̱ny 1. To make smoke in order to chaste away mosquitoes or flies. 2. The appearance of anything in darkness or in distance. 3. The appearance of bruises See Tuuny.

Tuo̱ŋ 1. Plural of Tuŋ being the horn or handle of any thing or branches, as explained below. 2. Plural of Tuŋ being a wing in wars or battle field column as explained below.

Tuɔɔŋ An egg, of any type.

Tuɔr A small child. See Tuor nyuot being an old version word.

Tuɔ̱r 1. The dust which is a result of termite in a wood or whatever. 2. The dried fish cut in a way and stored for future uses.

Tuɔɔr. 1. Plural of Tuɔr being a child or little one as explained above. See Nyieŋ. 2. The signs of fish movement or motion in water.

Tuɔ̱ɔ̱r 1. Anything to do with termite made dust. 2. Plural of Tuår being the dried fish stored for later uses.

Tuɔt 1. Mating process by animals- cattle 2. Curve or turn as with road, water way etc.

Tuɔ̱t A kind of birds Goose.

Tuɔ̱tni Plural of Tuɔ̱t being the goose as explained above.

Tuɔttuɔt Having a curved back such as a person or a bow.

Tuɔttuɔɔt State of being in a bending position for quite along time.

Tuɔy Being very small and with a round belly. Eg Tuœy jìc :Round belly.

Tuc A sound or noise which is heard when a rope being pulled got cut.

Tuk 1. The beginning of anything eg. Tuk hɔa. Tuk ruac, Tuk ja̱l: Beginning of the world, Beginning of talk, Beginning of journey. 2. The starting of dusty weather. 3. To dismiss someone from your own territory or home. 4. To roast maize grains on cowdung fire. 5. Noise or sound of gun shot, or roasting maize grains.

Tuktuk A roasted maize grains.

Tul 1. The flames of fire. 2. The falling of something when placed badly.

Tultul 1. State of being not properly seated or placed be it a container or a bab. 2. That cannot stand without support. 3. A lame person style of walking.

Tum A sound of sudden meeting of two or more objects.

Tuum 1. To make two or more ends join or meet at one point. 2. A person who gives injections to human beings or animals.

Tumtum 1. A local drum which is played by tribeless factions in the town. 2. State of having bulging out part of main body.

Tumɛtum A nice smell of a frying fish with oil and onion.

Tunduur 1. The noise of fish movement. 2. The wild fire burning noise.

Tunh The appearance of the new plants from the soil.

Tuuny Being bulging out as a sign of fatness or bruise.The appearance of whatever about to jump out of the soil or ground in a distance.

Tunytuny 1. Having that appearance of bulging out as explained above. 2. Lack of being smooth or flat.

Tuŋ 1. Horn, horn shape or branch. See Tuɔ̱ŋ. 2. To pour out some liquids from a gourd utensil such as milk after fermentation.

Tuŋtuŋ A kind of fish which looks like a Helicopter that makes noise when caught. See Yiɛw.

Tup 1. Dusty soil which provokes dust storm. 2. To prepare white stuff beer by mixing the components (Thop, ko̱wac, Nup). 3. A sound of a heavy falling object.

Tuptup 1. State of being in dusty or in powder state such as soil, tobacco etc. 2. A village between Tɔ̱årbaar and Dhɔrɛdiŋ.

Tur 1. Dust which is caused by wind, moving animals,birds or whatever. 2. Dusty particles caused by blowing winds, someone or something. 3. The period when moon moves to stage of full moon.

Tuur 1. Having much to do with period of full moon. 2. A period where court cases are settled in Eastern Nuer land. 3. Whatever is used for scaring bird pests from the field.

Turuk 1. A Nuer name for both whites and Arab races. It is derived from Turks the first foreign race that arrived Nuer land in the history. 2. Slang for any one who adopts the urban, town or modern ways of life.

Turuok Eyelid defect where a whitish spot appears as a result.

Turuɔ̱kni Plural of Turuk being either a white, an Arab or an urban person as explained above.

Turtur State of being noisy or causing much disturbances when people are resting.

Tut 1. Plural of Tuut being an oxen as explained below.. 2. Whatever to do with cow mating period.

Tuut Ox – male cow that mates and produces calves.

Tut dueel A raised soil at the door entrance to stop water or whatever tries to get into the room.

Tuttut The noise of engine, bugle or pump.

Tuth 1. A noise of a falling object.eg Wœcæ rœ bæ pææn æ tuth : Get away it is falling with that noise. 2. To plait or stitch to the final form or shape of string or thread.

Tuthtuth The continuous noise of series shooting of guns or falling of heavy objects from above.

Tuy A sound of a heavy falling object.

Tuytuy 1. The noise of falling objects or continuous beating. 2. A kind of plants which floats along the river, water Hyacinth.

Tä The sound of (T) the twenty third letter of Thok Nath.

Tää I have or have been, eg. Tää kɛ dɛl, I have a goat. Tää möŋä: I have been chatting with friends.

Täc 1. To clean by polishing the surface. 2. To smooth something.

Täctäc A Kujur that cleans or clears away people problems.

Tämtääm Situation when a person knows few words of foreign language.

Tändäär 1. Being a sudden busting into laughting or laughter due to amusing statement. 2. A sudden availability of food materials in plenty such as fish or grains.

Täny To shake by hitting the milk container in order to make butter. see Jäk.

Tääny The fermented milk which has not yet become sour in a gourd.

Täŋtääŋ Rough ways of playing among young boys.

Täp 1. A depression or low-land where rain water gets collected. 2. A noise of a falling clay pot or gourd when full of water or whatever.

Täptäp Sudden and frequent noise of gun shots or falling utensils.

Täpiny 1. To tell or disclose whatever considered to be secret in front of people not wanted to know. 2. To have something broken or to have it fallen.

Tärtär State of being opened not covered or closed.

Tät 1. To search or fetch for remaining maize bundles in a farm. 2. To erect or being a male gets stimulated or feels sexy.

Täätät A word, the boys use when each wants to get erected in wilderness.

Täth 1. To forge clay, metal etc. To make a useful or usable tools or utensils. 2. A large forged spear. 3. To build a brick or clay walls.

Tääth Plural of Täth being a forged spear as explained above.

Täthpiny To consolidate one position, not to give up when in difficulties. eg Täth Ni rœ piny mi waa ji mak : Consolidate yourself if they attack you.

Täwtäw The sound of gun shots or whatever that makes such noise.

Tääytääy State of being unprepared or failure to prepare oneself before the right time.

Tëk 1. Life or living. 2. To deny rights or excess to something..

Tëëk Aluminum metal which is whitish in colour.

Tëkni Plural of Tëëk being the Aluminium metal as explained above.

Tëktëk 1. Having much to do with denial when dividing something. 2. A wooden device for torturing prisoners in early days of colonial civilizations.

Tëny To fry or melt fats or butter by fire.

Tër 1. Having got swollen due to decaying or decomposing. 2. Having what to do with Tëër being the hen. e.g Tut Tër or Juat Tër which is a cock, or hen feather.

Tëër Another name for a hen see Manpalëëk.

Tët 1. A Nuer name for Shilluk male or female. 2. To take back or to claim whatever one has given to someone. 3. A climbing step on the tree which help the climber to go up. 4. Plural of Tët being a climbing step as explained above.

Tëët Plural of Tët being a Shilluk man or woman as explained above.

Tiäk 1. The way one endures pains or sorrow in regards to death or insult. 2. The clouds that appear after a heavy rainfall.

Tiäktiäk The noise that drives away the coward people before the actual combathing.

Tiäl To shake something or oneself by moving slowly.

Tiäm 1. To have overcome or over powered someone or something. 2. The state of being overpowered or overcome by sadness or problems.

Tiän To widen the opening by pushing a piece of iron Tatiey through it.

Tiäp 1. To prepare a hard compact soil to be simple and ready be shaped for sawing seeds. 2. Slang for sudden saying or uttering of something secret.

Tiäptiäp 1. State of being soft such as potatoes or whatever. 2. Any soft surface to rest on.

Tiär To turn up the hard soil to soft and powder before sawing seeds.

Tiäär The foot prints or traces on the soil or ground.

Tiäw 1. Whatever is not yet properly ripened such as sugar cane or stalk. 2. Not fully grown up person.

Tiäwtiäw State of being not sweet, strong enough or not well ripened.

Tiöör The sign of fatness which appear on the stomach of a fat person.

Tiööri Plural of Tiöör being a sign of fatness as explained above,

Tuäk 1. A taste of not well cooked food made of grain flour.2. A muddy soil.

Tuääk State of having much to do with mud or muddy soil eg. Cɛ pɛn tuäak: It has fallen into muddy soil.

Tuäl A wound escalation as a result of burning.

Tuältuäl State of being well nourished or fattened.

Tuär To refresh oneself either with smoke puff or a cup of hot drink.

Tuät Plural of Tuàt being a kind of grass as explained above.

Tuäth To mobilize, organize or persuade people to act in any way.

Tuäy 1. To tell something secret. 2. A noise or sound of a broken container. 3. A sound of hitting something soft.

Tuäytuäy 1. Spinal cord of an animal or human being. 2. A continuous sound of hitting soft object.

Tuöktuök The maize grains noise as when being roasted.

Tuöy A sound of a falling heavy object.

Toäc 1. The lying or putting something in bed. 2. The green colour.

Toäw To store or to keep things. See Tow.

Töc 1. Colour powder which is used for painting, colouring faces or bodies on drum dance days. 3. Slang for a mixture of orange and whitish colours of cow. See Matöc.

Tööc Plural of Töc being powder colours as explained above.

Tök 1. The other name for Male Genital Organ. See Cul. 2. To divide food according to consumers. 3. To cut very far from expected part. 4. To clear a wild piece of land to make a farm. See Kuec.5. To laugh when one is happy or excited.

Töök Plural of Tök laughter or happy as explained above.eg Biel doolæ Ni töök thäri jææn : Biel is just laughing under trees.

Tööl A fracture, a breakage etc.

Tömtöm 1. The throat. 2. A kind of marine plants which grows along the river banks.

Töndör A state of failure to get sleep the whole night. 2. Being the failure to achieve whatever one wants to get or enjoy.

Töŋ A poisonous plant with red flowers.

Tönyni Plural of To̱ny being a native pipe as explained above.

Tööny Having much to do with that pipe as explained above.eg Taŋ tööny,

Juuth Tööny, Kuat tööny inœ.:Pipe stick, pipe smoking piece, pipe chain etc.

Tönytööny A bad and unadmirable style of walking.

Töör A one testical animal or human being.

Tööt 1. State of having the tail raised up. 2. An insult for a person whose buttocks are raised up a little.

Töttöt State of having a raised up part.

Th

Tha The sound of the twinty fourth letter of Thok Nath.

Thabalak A word which is used to express defiance.

Thac 1. A grass made stand for carrying things on the heads or for standing things properly on the ground or surface. 2. To roll around with string, thread or rope. See Rieth 3. To form a block or unite against a clan or a section.

Tha̱c 1. The waste part the mouth sends out after chewing a cane or stalk. 2. Being the dews eg. Rɛy tha̱c: In the dews.

Thak 1. An opened clay made utensil. 2. To carry something with open palm.

Thaak Having much to do with Thak eg. Rɛy thaak: In that opened container.

Tha̱a̱c Whatever is used for supporting something from falling or reaching down.

Thakthak State of being opened or flat as a container.

Thal Is whatever to do with cooking. See Tha̱t.

Thaal State of having to do with cooking eg. Cɛ wä thaal : He/she went cooking.

Tham To tell meaningless or nonsense statements. See Thap.

Thamtham A person who keeps on asking or telling nonsense. See Thapthap.

Thààn Part of something eg. Cam tha̱a̱n dæ : Eat part of it.

Thany 1. To push or hold back something or someone. To push down or up. 2. Opened or spreaded horns. 3. A slang for a naturally born circumcised person. See Thöny.

Thanypiny A stick that is used for supporting oneself while walking by aged or sick people.

Thanythany Anything that is huge or gaint where nobody can face it.

Thanythin State of clear failure to do something which is too difficult or heavy to handle.

Thaŋ Lack of appetite due to sickness or the type of food.

Thaŋthaŋ A behavior where one is rather deaf or foolish.

Thap 1. A sound of a falling object into water. 2. Fill up to the brim. 3. To tell nonsense to someone or disturb him/her.

Thapthap A person who keeps on disturbing or telling nonsense.

Thar The bottom, the buttocks, under or the end of anything.

Thaar 1. Whatever to do with the bottom. (2) Last year. (3) Next year But (ni) (i) respectively is put before it. Eg Båkæ ni thaar kiæ ithaar ber : They came last year or you come next year.

Tharaar A fishing style where one stands out side the water or river while the fishing tool is in the river or water.

Tharbap A big whitish colour bead which is put in a string and tie around

The neck as an ornament.

Tharbop A native white stuff drink which is drunk for period of five or several days.

That 1. To suck or milk to the last drop of milk.2. To do the cooking duty.

Tha̱a̱t Plural of Thäät being the cook as explained below.

Thaatha A word which is said when pulling a baby in order to move on two legs to avoid crawling.

Thay 1. To make a baby to move by pulling its hands along. 2. Slang for support or help rendered to someone as above.

Thec 1. Dews or drops of water which come as a result of cool weather. 2. A severe weeping when one is beaten, insulted or when mourning. 3. The removal of water from a container with hands or whatever. 4. To hit or beat with a special stick as that with 'Hockey' Games. See Dieer.

Theem A person who carries out the weighing or measuring.

Theen The word meaning evening and it is used by Lou Nuer.

Theŋtheŋ A person who hears very little or who is rather deaf.

Thep 1. A type of trees which produces whitish long thorns. 2. To add something by increasing the length or height.

Theep Having something to do with Thep tree eg. Pi wɔlä theep:.The water of thep tree pond.

Ther To make art of thatching style.

Theer 1. A disease or a believe that a pregnant woman causes sickness or bad fortune to a nearby wound. 2. A person or a woman who knows the art of thatching style. see Thɛɛr.

Therther State of having some parts still resist water.

Thew To defy something by saying it is not true or a lie.

Theew State of defying behavior word.eg Theew ruacæ æmœ ciæ thuœk: Ah that statement is not true.

They State of being fragile ready to get disintergrated very easily.

Theythey 1. Which can get disintergrated very easily such as clay, soil,

hairs etc. 2. Having much to do with flash light brightness by night.

Thɛc 1. To change direction of a person or an animal for a purpose eg. Thɛc raar.

Thɛc 2. To eat food mixed either with milk or soups, or butter with local spoon. 3. To collect liquids or fats from soup. 4. The removal of water from canoe bed.

Thɛcthɛc A person or an animal (cow) that does not follow one route or path.

Thɛk 1. Respect to inlaws where one abstains from anything like eating, drinking etc before them. 2. Nuer believe that when a girl or a women period comes she should not eat anything with cow milk and should not cross or jump cow rope.

Thɛɛk State of what to do with girl maturity as the first appearance of menstruation.

Thɛlɛk An expression for defying any word or statement made or said.It is preceded by (A).eg A thælæk ruac æmœ ciæ thuòk : Ah this statement is not true.

Thɛlɛm An expression for defying any talk. It is preceded by (A). eg A thælæm cäh dæ liñ : Ah I can not listen to.

Thɛlɛny State of being very small or little in body.

Thɛm 1. To weigh, examine, measure or estimate. 2. An area measured for someone to work on. 3. A sound of a moving small fish in the water.

Thɛɛm 1. Measurement or weighing device that is used for knowing quantity,height or length. 2. Plural of Theem being the person who carries out Measurements as explained above.

Thɛɛmni Plural of Thææm being whatever is used for measuring as explained above.

Thɛmthɛm 1. State of jumping here and there as a small fishes. 2. Little value.

Thɛn Being well eaten and satisfied with food or drinks.

Thææn A small river fish that attack very fast the snare.

Thɛŋ Sense of hearing or ability to hear.

Thææŋ State of having heard something eg. Bia l̲ikdɛ thɛɛŋ: You will hear its heavy sound..

Thɛp A borrowed Arabic language word for a sword.

Thɛr 1. To sharpen something by hammering the edges. 2. To walk parallel to the road or path usually in hunting. 3. To untie the luggage or whatever tied up. 4. To explain the realities of cows concluded in marriage settlemet discussions. 5. To check by putting each item separately in marriage settlement.

Thɛɛr 1. A hut thatched in a certain fashion or style. 2. The edge of anything such as spears etc.

Thɛri Plural of Thɛɛr being the hut thatched as explained above.

Thɛrthɛr Manner of walking parallel or talking contrary to someone.

Thɛrɛmpiny To have cut down relationship, rope or end up whatever.

Thɛt A kind of gas noise when releases through anus.

Thɛtthɛt Slang for troubles or problems.eg Wer ci täh thætthæt : Go, you have a problem.

Thɛthɛ A sound which comes out very fast to express disappointment.

Thɛɛw Slang for have crossed the river at once by swimming.

Thɛwthɛw Not regular in jumping, talking, singing etc.

Thɛy 1. Very cold or cool. It is always come after (ɛ). 2. Very weak, tired or exhausted.

Thiak 1. Decent, Dignity respect, politeness. 2. Heavy in weight.

Thiakthiaak Plural of Thiekthiek being a heavy object or weight as explained below.

Thiaal Having much to do with Thiɔl the fat meat.

Thiam 1. To sneeze when suffering of flu. 2. Slang for starting a long journey.

Thian 1. To delay a work or a task. 2. State of being not ready to do something due to laziness.

Thiaan A name of a person whose parents did not do their assignment very fast.

Thianthian A person who does not do whatever he/she is asked to do.

Thiany To break or push apart a glowing fire of charcoal or fire wood.

Thiaŋ Evening time as from 4:00 to 6:00 Pm.

Thiaaŋ Having much to do with evening time of today or the day before.

Thia̱a̱ŋ 1. A disease which is caused by a pregnant woman who allows a baby to suck after conception.2. Full of water, grains, clothes etc.

Thiaŋ kä jɛ The evening before yesterday evening.

Thiap To touch or to feel the condition.

Thia̱t 1. Not very powerefull as a piece of tobacco. 2. Not very strong or not brave person.

Thiààt Plural of Thiàt being a less powerful tobacco or less brave person as explained above.

Thiaw The rings of red or yellow copper metals which is worn on the left hand as decoration long ago by Nuer youth.

Thiay To kill, murder someone or animal in a group or herd.

Thiaythiay The appearance of burning flash light.

Thic 1. A sound which is heard when one sneezes. 2. Having much to do with second or third name of Thieec Enquiry eg. Tut Thic.or Jok Both Thic.

Thiec To ask, to inquire or to try to know something or someone.

Thieec A name for a person derived from Thiec enquiry. eg Thieec Gac

Thic æ ňuæt mi gœa: Thieec Gac Thic is a good youngman.

Thieek Neighbourhood or state of being neighbors.eg Tìt ciaňdu kæ ji

Thieekdu :Take care your way of life with those neighbouring you.

Thiekthiek Being heavy such as a leader, decent or dignified person.

Thiel 1. Plural of Thiɛl being a kind of grass as explained below. 2. A small game with back black and bottom whitish. See Thi̱l. 3. To milk the very little remaining milk.

Thielthiel State of having very little milk to be milked.

Thiem 1. To cut meat or whatevery into small or mouthful pieces. 2. A fried meat food. 3. To knock down someone or something by mistake. 4. To find or get someone you are looking for by chance or suddenly. It is followed by Piny.

Thiemthiem Tiny drops of rainfall water.

Thi̱en State of being full of meat or fat such as bull or whatever.

Thi̱enthi̱en State of being fat or full of meat and very strong.

Thieŋ 1. To endure or to pay a little attention to something. 2. A game or Tiang animal which is originated from Thok Nath and got borrowed and distorted by English language.

Thiep 1. A large stagnant water frog. 2. To touch in orde to feel something or find out.

Thiepthiep 1. Having something or substance not solid and ready to be dismantle.2. Little rainfall drops.

Thiepni Plural of Thiep being a series of touching or examining or exploring as explained above. Their 1. A pain, or a very sharp and hard pain in the bone. 2. A slang for whatever one eats to sustain hunger.

Thieer 1. A type of plants which is used for building or thatching huts. 2. Having much to do with Their a pole that raises hut roof. Eg Camæ thuœk ni mi thieer jìc :You eat it, the only thing is what raises up the stomach.

Thie̱e̱r A plant that is used for making utensils or mats. see Pät.

Thiet A type of plants which is used for making ropes by peeling the outer cover of the stems.

Thietthiet Well compact such as cotton pillow or mattress.

Thietpiny A plant which stem is peeled for making ropes for building.

Thiewthiew Having much slit of light.

Thiey 1. To liquidate or to collect the last drops of a liquid.2. To economize something by taking the quantity that can sustain living.

Thieey What is used for filtering liquids or whatever.

Thieythiey Being very slow in dropping liquids.

Thiɛɛk A bundle of wood fire, building wood, charcoal, stalk or grass being transported by water current to towns or markets.

Thiɛt 1. A male disease which affects testical area which causes bulky swelling. 2. Slang for a problem or difficulty.

Thiɛw To be straight physically as in Thiɛw lou. See Loulou.

Thiɛy The way liquid flows when remains very little.

Thiik 1. What is used for covering or closing the room or office door. 2. A slang for a person who protects or defends others.

Thil 1. State of being not available or not there. Eg Kua pal ɛmi thil : Leave it is nothing. 2. To milk the last drops from cow udder.

Thim The few drops of rain water.

Thi̱lthi̱l State of having little drops of milk from cow or goat.

Thimthim State of being the last few tiny drops of rainfall.

Thin 1. In, there, available or present 2. A breast of a woman or an animal or udder.

Thi̱n Plural of Thin being the breast or udder as explained above.

Thi̱nthi̱n Being physically well built.

Thiŋ 1. A corner inside the hut where rituals or spiritual are being performed by Kujur man. 2. Not to react or retaliate for a bad done to oneself.

Thiiŋ Having ability to endure, tolerate difficulties or resist pains.

Thiŋni Plural of Thiŋ being a corner inside a hut as explained above.

Thiŋthiŋ State of being not fast to retaliate in simple issues caused by opponents or friends.

Thiony To push away or do something roughly.

Thionythiɔny That has ugly, unadmirable or clumsy shape.

Thiɔl Fat of flesh be it a fish or cow or animal meat.

Thiɔljɔɔr To curse evils that about to be falling to people.

Thiɔɔr An expression which explains surprise when a good thing got spoiled.

Thiɔt The pouring or rushing out of smoke.

Thiɔɔt The rushing out of smoke from the sources.

Thiɔtthiɔt State of smoke rushing out frequently.

Thip To give or let out very little quantity usually liquids (water, milk etc).

Thi̱pthi̱p State of pouring or producing little quantity of milk,water,rain drops every time.

Thirbäc A domestic tree brought to Nuer lands during colonial period.

Thirbäcni Plural of Thirbäc being a kind of tree as explained above.

Thir A long log or pole which is used for supporting a large cattle hut roof.

Thi̱r Having much to do with Thiir plant.eg. Wia ræy thìr : Get into this plant.

Thiir 1. Plural of Thir being a log or pole which support a cow hut as explained above. 2. Slang for poor food which support the stomach or the belly when it collapses due to hunger. 3. A plant which is used for building or making art utensils.

Thi̱rthi̱r To walk or run one way direction or straight line when being whipped, beaten or punished.

Thi̱rthi̱i̱r Being an aimless walk or leisure time walking.

Thit To hit or beat something continuously such as when pounding grains or whatever.

Thiit Having much to do with Thiet plant eg. Cɛ wä thiit: He/she has gone to look for this type of plants for making ropes.

Thitthit 1. That can be hit or beaten several times in pounding or grinding. 2. Spongy item or cotton which gives this characteristic above.

Thitpiny To seat a baby roughly. Is a resting by placing one buttock down on something.

Thiw The flow or leakage of liquids such as blood, milk, water etc.

Thi̱w To be straight forward. State of being on one direction.

Thi̱wthi̱w Flow of liquids, water,butter, blood etc.

Thoa Having anything to do with Thow tree Acacia Nilotica or the second name of the origin. eg. Biel Thoa Thow Biel.

Thow Lual Lual Thoa

Thoac Being what to do with high ground made by accumulation of rubbish. see Thoc.

Thoak Plural of Thok being useful nonsense which passes the time as explained below.

Thoal 1. Having what to do when one misses inflicting big wound or kill with one hitting or spearing. 2. To stay in morning sun in order to get warm. To warn before fire, or boil once more. 3. A type or style of making ropes. 4. Having much to do with Thɔl snake eg. Dɛy thoal.

Thoam Having much to do with Thom being the canoe seat.

Thoan Being what to do with Thon the ox or being the second name of the origin eg. Gatbɛɛl Thoan -Thon.

Thoaŋ 1. A distance direction eg. Wer kɛ thoa̱ŋ ɛmi: Go to the other Way or distance. 2. Plural of Thoŋ being the ground dug hole for pounding grains as explained below.

Thoar 1. Floating on water or any liquid. 2. Plural of Thow being a kind of tree Acacia Nilotica as explained above.

Thoat 1. Half dried material such as stalk or grass for calves. 2. A situation when one pretends to be sleeping or dead.

Thoc 1. A cow or any animal horn made device for fishing purposes where it is used for fitting Rɔɔc or Köör being fishing devices. 2. A rubbish heap or mound.

Thoc 3. Full or compact as with cotton or cushion mattress or pillow.

Thocthoc Being the high ground such as Thöcthöc as explained below.

Thok 1. Mouth, language, information, piece of news. 2. Any opening for pouring in or out, entering or putting in or through eg. -Thok dueel.-Thok waath.-Thok Diar. 3. The hard shell of a coco nut.

Thok kiir A kind of trees that grows along the river banks.

Thokthok A Nuer generation group which followed Litjaŋ. They are also known as Mathok.

Thol 1. Plural of Thöl being the bending or curving part as explained below. 2. To push fire wood burning into the inner fire so as to increase burning while cooking,warming or boiling. 3. To hit with spear slightly but not deep to disable. 4. The morning warm sun in cold weather of winter.

Thom 1. A Nuer musical instrument. 2. A faction or a group of animals or human being walking or moving together. 3. To cut something at once with axe or spear etc. 4. Slang for having taken a sharp decision. 5. An iron ring device which is worn on finger as defensive tool. 6. To jump up or over something be it water, mud, thorn, bush etc. 7. The seating place of the canoe at the front or the back.

Thomni Plural of Thom being both iron rings or musical instrument as explained above.

Thomthom 1. Being in pieces when cut. 2. Style of running or jumping here and there such as people, animals or fishes.

Thon 1. An uncasterated bull (ox). See Tut. 2. A feeling or behaviour when very angry to move. 3. State of having anything to do with Thoän as explained above or when it is a second name eg Biel Thon.

Thonon A state of being, behaving, sitting in such a way or style.

Thoonä Having much to do with Thoän eg. Tuac thoonä: Fur of this type of games.

Thony Difficult to be overcome such as disease eg. Top mi ci thonyæ Ral, Thiet etc.

Thonythony Common cold, flu or running nose.

Tho̱ŋ Plural of Thöŋ being murdering case as explained below.

Thoŋdiit A certain creeping plant that has orange or brown colour fruits when it gets ripened.

Thop 1. To hand over someone or something. 2. Being full to the brim with liquids. 3. Is a yeast like preparation from grains. 4. To have grey hairs started on the head.

Thopthop Having much to do with being full to the brim.eg Ci yier thiaŋ tä Pi kæ thopthop ni wic juaacni:The river is full where the water is on the top of grass.

Thor 1. To break something into small pieces as that with bone, wood etc. 2. To throw or beat something very fast with out giving a chance for retaliation or hit back.

Thoor An iron made part of the pipe that is used for smoking.

Thoori Plural of Thoor being an iron made device as explained above.

Thorthor 1. A game where the young boys are expected to be quick, fast in running or handing over whatever is being chased. 2. State of having something been brokern or cut into smaller pieces, or parts.

Thot 1. To pull something to a different directions. 2. A noise of gas released through anus. See Thöt.

Thoot State of pulling something such as a rope in competition or game.

Tho̱ttho̱t State of having something which is not hard or rigid and that can be manipulated easily.

Thow A kind of tree which grows in rainy savanna region or Acacia Nilotica.

Thowthow The few drops of rain water or light rain.

Thoy A wooden device container made for catching fish in water.

Thooy Having much to do with Thoy being such a device eg. Tut Thooy, Luak Thooy.see Thooy Deang.

Thoyni Plural of Thoy being a wooden container as explained above.

Thoyoy State of being in a very high seat or bed which does not need to be shown to people.

Thɔl 1. Snake of all types. 2. A grass made rope which is used for making grass stands. see Thac.

Thɔɔl 1. Plural of Thɔl being a snake of all types as explained above. 2. Having much to do with the period of morning sun of winter. eg. Ci piny thɔɔl.

Thɔlthɔl State of being not series in doing something.

Thɔnɛthɔn A type of smell which is released by he-goat or ox.

Thɔŋ 1. A pit hole dug purposely for pounding grains. 2. State of having much to do with a distance from the speaker eg. Wer thɔŋ ɛmi. Go there.

Thɔr 1. To appear on top of water surface as crocodile or grass. 2. State of having a light wound but not deep into flesh.

Thɔhr Premature birth. A state of birth which takes place before nine months.

Thɔɔr A premature born person, animal etc.

Thɔri Plural of Thoor being a premature born baby as explained above.

Thɔrɔl Camel.

Thɔrɔali Plural of Thɔrɔl being a camel as explained above.

Thɔt 1. A half dried grass, sugar cane or Sorghum stalk. 2. To pretend to be sleeping while you are not.

Thu 1. A suffix which indicates sort of relationship when joined in marriage With in-laws.eg Guan thu. Man thu ino : Father in-law,Mother in –law etc. 2. A sound that is heard when spitting.

Thuak To chew something half way such as meat, sugar cane, stalk etc. among children.

Thuakthuak Having been half chewed where it becomes tasteless due to this action.

Thuany A kind of crocodile which has become wild and attacksPeople on the sight.

Thuanyni Plural of Thuany being a wild crocodile as explained above.

Thuanythuany The appearance of an ugly wound or any bad appearance.

Thuaar 1. Flowers of maize, sorghum bundles when about to yield seeds. 2. A distorted word from Arabic Language for night watchmen on horses. In Nuer context it is a group of young men in drum dance style.

Thuat 1. Liquids leakage or dropping one by one. 2. To distil or filter ashes to produce salt like substance.

Thuc 1. To push someone or something forward to allow space a head.eg Thuc dow. 2. A bundle of growing or grown plants, sugar canes, sorghum, stalk etc.

Thuk 1. Plural of Thok being news, reports as explained above 2. Stage when a cow stops producing milk. 3. A state when sorghum turns black due to infections.

Thuuk Having been completed, finalized or finished.eg Kak æ puur yænæ Ci kuic mi diit thuuk: The field you have been weeding the bigger part is completed.

Thul Dusty storm which is caused by Mansoon Winds from Indian Ocean.

Thuul A person who keeps on checking or trying to find out things every time.

Thum To kill, to put the end of so many lives or to annihilate.

Thumbaŋ Unwarranted murdering of people in a lawlessness cattle camp.

Thumthum A sort or a series jumping in unorganized ways like locusts or children.

Thuny 1. That secretion the nose releases when in flu. 2. Plural of Thuny being what the nose releases with stress under (u) as explained above. 3. To elbow, hit or push someone or something intentionally or unintentionally.

Thuunyni Plural of Thuny being the way to elbow or hit as explained above.

Thunythuny State of being very short or a piece.

Thuŋ 1. A pit hole made on soil for pounding grains. See

Thɔŋ another pronounciation. 2. Just eg Ci thuŋ ben: You have just come.

Thup 1. A sound that is made when one throws a stone, brick, soil etc. into water, river, lake or water pond. 2. A sound of spitting saliva out.

Thupthup The sound of the hands when swimming.

Thur 1. To demolish or break the building or walls. 2. A dirt that appears on the eyes in early morning before one washes the face.

Thurbiil A borrowed word from Arabic language meaning Automobile-car.

Thurthur State of being rather fat or healthy young man.

Thut 1. One of the early generations of Nuer lineage system. 2. A sound of gas released through anus. 3. Slang for an insult meaning you release gas.eg Aa thut :When you are in conflict with someone you tell him/her such a word.

Thuwthuw Scattered rain water drops or slight rain or showers.

Thuypiny To have something completely ended, finalized, demolished or destroyed.

Thuoc Plural of Thuc being a bundle of grass as explained above.

Thuony To blow one nose as when having common cold or running nose.

Thuonythuony 1. The flu or the common cold. 2. A state of being very short.

Thuor 1. To urge or make someone to do something as quick as possible. 2. To break or destroy something into pieces.

Thuorthuor State of having something become in pieces or particles.

Thuɔk Having something finished or completed.

Thuɔ̱k Facts, right news or reports about something.

Thuɔ̱ɔ̱k 1. Plural of Thuɔ̱k being fact or right as explained above. 2. The blackening disease which affects sorghum bundle.

Thuɔl 1. Plural of Thul being a dust storm that causes Monsoon rains as explained above. 2. To collect or put property or things ready before the journey.

Thuɔɔl Plural of Thuul being he/she who puts things together as explained above.

Thuɔny A short piece of wood, metal, bone etc.

Thuɔr 1. State of being very fast or swift as in a race, or a game. 2. A broken piece of wood,iron, bone etc.

Thuɔɔr 1. Plural of Thuɔr being broken pieces of wood, iron, bone etc as explained above. 2. A state of a wall as when broken down in so many places.

Thuɔrthuɔr A game which is played by children where the participants are expected to be very fast or act quickly.

Thuɔ̱tni Plural of Thut being the Nuer lineage system as explained above.

Thäc 1. The state of bull horn gets rounded in a circle. 2. The dews which drop from the leaves in the morning in Autumn.

Thääc Plural of Thac being a grass made device as explained above..

Thäcni Plural of Tha̱c being the waste of a chewed stalk or cane as explained above. See Nyuɛy – Nyuɛyni.

Thäk 1. A castrated bull, goat or ram. 2. A slang for a person who does not produce or impotent.

Thääk Plural of Thäk being a casterated bull as explained above.

Thämthäm A person who is either dull or insane.

Thänythäny State of being huge and clumsy or heavy like clouds, forests or mountains.

Thäŋthäŋ A person who does not hear well or rather deaf.

Thär Plural of Thar being the bottom,under or buttock as explained above.

Thät The art of cooking, the preparation of food or cooking process.

Thäät A person who carries out the actual process of cooking.

Thäy To ignore or to take something lightly, simple or not true.

Thäythäy A person who does not take anything seriesly.

Thëp Plural of Thep a kind of trees as explained above.

Thiäk State of being near, little distance, not far.

Thiäkthiäk State of being quite near or not very far.

Thiäkthiääk Plural of Thiäkthiäk being quite near or in a short distance as explained above.

Thiäŋ 1. To fill a container or something with any thing needed. 2. A small game or Tiang. See Thieeŋ.

Thiäp That can get disintergrated easily.

Thiäpthiäp Being breakable bundle of soil, tobacco etc.

Thiäw It is the way when one smokes less powerfull tobacco. See Thia̠t.

Thiäy To open cowdung fire, disintergrate, demoblize and decompose.

Thiäythiäy 1. State of moving with burning fire. 2. The movements of the body while walking.

Thiööl Plural of Thiɔl being a fat of all as explained above.

Thiöölwan A fox fats being those whitish clouds in the sky which look like fat meat. Any adult Nuer man or woman near you can tell the story.

Thiör To curse away evil deeds which about to fall on the family or people.

Thiöör The name of a large section of Eastern Nuer Jikany which included Walhok, Ŋon and Lony or in two sections Buup and Lony.

Thoäc Having something to do with the horn made device added to fishing tool Rɔɔc or Kɔ̈ɔ̈r.

Thoäcni Plural of Thoc being the cow horn fishing device as explained above.

Thoän A yellowish brown spotted small animal of cat family which looks like a Tiger.

Thoär 1. Plural of Thow being Acacia Nilotica tree as explained above. 2. Having much to do with premature birth.see Thoor.

Thöc To support a person morally or physically in difficult situation.

Thööc A wooden tool for sitting just like a form or a bench.

Thööcni Plural of Thööc a wooden made seat as explained above.

Thöcthöc State of being quite high such as chair, seat, tool or form.

Thök 1. To stimulate the goat to produce milk. 2. Plural of Thok being the language, news etc as explained above. 3. Heart muscles.

Thöök Plural of Thök being the heart muscles as explained above.

Thöl 1. Bending or curve of a straight stalk or stem. 2. To warm or boil water, food etc.

Thölbök A borrowed word from Arabic Language for taxes. See Wadɛ.

Thön A distinguish cattle rich person.

Thöny A circumcised person being both natural or man made.

Thööny Plural of Thöny being a circumcised person as explained above.

Thönythöny State of being so hard to bend down such as bed or seat.

Thöŋ 1. Murderous case. 2. To have speared or hit someone or animal to death.

Thör 1. Drum or a device made for giving sounds when beaten Systematically in traditional festivals 2. To spear in a distance from the target.

Thöör 1. The eighth month of the year August. 2. The heavy rains which cause things to float.

Thöt 1. A noise which is a sudden release of gas through the anus.. See kuok, kuik thɛt etc. 2. A wooden tool which is used for spreading skin to dry in sun rays.

Thötni Plural of Thöt being the wooden tool as explained above.

Thötkany State of being very difficult or hard to tackle in any way.

Thötthöt A slang for difficulty or problem.

Thöw An expression which defys, undermines one achievemnet, work, task made or done. It is always preceded by (a) eg. A thöw.

Thöyöy An expression meaning it is quite difficult to handle.

Thuäŋthuäŋ That have a clumsy shape, appearance or ugly looking sight.

Thuäy The final chances of filtering local beer – White staff.

W

Wa 1. The twenty sixth letter of Thok Nath. 2. A word for surprise when one sees a person or whatever suddenly. 3. An angry word for defying someone statement.

Waa 1. An expression for reported speech which comes after (I) e.g. I̲ waa ber: You are to come. 2. An expression for confirmation of what was said e.g. Waa, Luot i̲ ni jɛ : Ah you are meaning it.

Wac 1. To irrigate or wet whatever with liquids such as water, blood, beer etc. 2. Fluor paste after grinding.eg Wac æmœ baa thàlä : That grinded paste is To be cooked for me. 3. To soak something in liquid or water.eg. Wac mun dueel: Soak the hut soil. water hut wall soil. 4. The lower part of a fish below genitol organ. Eg. Càl baa gim wac dæ:The Nile perch be cut as from below genital organ. 5. Sour taste as that of soaked fluor or fruits.

Waac 1. Having whatever to do with paternal aunt Way as a right in marriage settlement. 2. A meat share for the very aunt.

Wacwac State of sour or bitter taste.

Wacwaac Plural of Wacwac being sour taste of food items as explained above.

Wak 1. To make sudden loud cry, usually in singing or weeping. 2. A type of bushy trees or shrubs. 3. A sound of a falling wooden materials or tool. 4. To suck away the fleshy part of a shell or pull away or out the bark of a stem, e.g. Ɛŋa ci thoa̲r wak ɔ? Who cleared the Acacia Nilotica fruits? Wäh wak kɛ köm: Iam going to collect barks. 5. To open the loading cabin of a gun. 6. To peel the maize.

Wa̲k To smooth the wooden material e.g stick, tool etc. by rubbing the hard or rough parts with hard matter.

Wakni Plural of Wak being the type of bushy trees or shrub as explained above.

Wakak State of having not well covered such as teeth or bones.

Wakwak A sound which comes when wooden materials or tools are disturbed.

Wakar A sort of feeling when one is feverish.

Wal 1. Plural of Wäl being the drug, herbs or grass as explained below e.g. Duel wal: Hospital. 2. Long time ago and it is referred to as Ni wal : long time ago. 3. The movements of a tougue continuously or all the time. 4. Slang for eating after a long time without food e.g. Wal thokdu.

Walɛ Today, this day or later on e.g. Bikɛ ben ɛn walɛ kiɛ Bia ben ɛn walɛ kiɛ bɛ ben ni walɛ.: They will come today or you willcome today or he/she will come today.

Waalɛ This year or later on this year e.g. Bä lät ni waalɛ: *I will do it later this day.*

Walwal A noise of movement inside the water or in a container.

Walou A name of a person which is best pronounced as Wanɛ lou.: Let us go Lou.

Wan 1. Fox. It is the lucky animal which is accepted by the whole worldnations to be the most clever animal. 2. Let us go, for the first person speaker. 3. To keep or delay eatable thing for later time, date or season. 4. Plural of Wan being what is delayed for later date as explained above with stress on (á) but exclude foxes see Wääni.

Wa̱a̱n Plural of Wään being a theaf as explained below.

Wany 1. To move after a long staying in one place. 2. To clean by wiping with something, tongue or hands, e.g. Wany thokdu kiɛ wany nhiamdɛ: Clean your mouth or clean your face.

Wanywany 1. An adjective, a person who speaks very fast. 2. State of being unstable or not comfortable.

Waŋ 1. Eye.2. Water stream.3. Ditch. 4. Wildfire or a wound caused by burning.

Waŋni Plural of Waŋ being a wound caused by burning or wild fire.

Waŋmac A type of plants which causes severe itching when touched.

Waŋmacni Plural of Waŋmac being the type of plants that causes itching.

Waŋwaŋ An expression for scaring young ones from fire or from coming near to it.

War 1. A shoe. 2. To search by feeling with hands in darkness. 3. To collect or remove gravels, and stone particles from ashes or powder.

Waar 1. A type of plant which is used in twin rituals performance. It is used for identifying water base when digging well.

Wààr 2. The goats and sheep droppings which is always in plural.1. A cow dung. 2. Night.

Wa̱a̱ri Plural of War that is a shoe as explained above.

Wa̱ri Plural of Wäär being a certain type of plants as explained below.

Wargak A distorted Arabic word for a paper.

Wat 1. A relative, friend, inlaw etc. 2. A person who has connection with **you** in one way or the other. 3. To cut a fish into long pieces in order to dry. 4. State of having gone very far or got lost from the sight.eg Cæ wee

Wat kuæær : He has had got lost on the way.

Wát With stress on (á) is the plural of Wat being a relative, a friend or an inlaw as explained above

Waat Plural of Wat being a dried fish when cut into long pieces as explained above.

Watwat State of being long, thin or slim.

Wath 1. The shores where boats, canoes and steamers, ships stop, near the town, village etc. The ports or landing side. 2. The female genital organ, through which the baby comes out and some liquids. 3. A rough way of eating where pieces of food, water etc are scattered. 4. Plural of Wäth being a kind of plants as explained below.

Wa̱th To become wild or to change to animal or cannibal.

Wathwath The noise of water when washing clothes or hands.

Waw 1. Clean appearance of colours or decoration networks. 2. The remaining grass in a dead cow or animal cud. 3. The noise or sound which the baby makes when learning how to talk.

Wawwaw 1. The state of being clear or straight forward things or colours. 2. A statement which is said by fishermen when fishing on canoes.

Wawwaaw A type of bird which makes a lot of noise around water ponds.

Wawwaawni Plural of Wawwaaw a bird which makes a lot of noise as explained above.

Way 1. Aunt paternal side or father sister. 2. A group of birds -Vultures hovering above an area to indicate either fishes or dead animal. 3. To clean or clear water path by removing marine plants or debris.

Waywaa An expression for surprise or chorusing warship songs.

Wayni Plural of Way being the paternal aunt or a group of birds hovering as explained above.

Wä 1. The sound of the letter W. 2. An expression for surprise or exclamation. 3. Going or to go by the speaker e.g. Bä wä: I will go – Bi wä: You will go – Banɛ wä: We will go – Bɛ wä: He/she will go – Bia wä: You will go – Bikɛ (n) wä: They will go.

Wäc To wet or soak something e.g. Wäc kɔaaŋni kuæn: The wetting or soaking of marriage white stuff drinks.

Wäcär State of having something suddenly went wrong or spoiled.

Wäcäw A noise of water when people are either bathing or washing see, Cäwcäw.

Wäk Plural of Wak being the cry or weeping when deeply sad as explained above.

Wäl It has several meanings 1. Wäl to make a move or say something to alert people of your presence 2. Wäl single drug, grass, kujurs. 3. Wäl, the movement of boiling water in a container.

Wälwäl State of being restless or suffering from lack of sleep or severe pains.

Wäläŋ A water pond or depression where rainwater flow to.

Wälääŋ Plural of Wäläŋ being water pond as explained above..

Wän 1. To steal or to rob see Diöp. 2. To leave the place without the notice of people.

Wään Thief or robber, see Di̱o̱p.

Wänwän State of being good or dishonest in changing whatever you have had said early.

Wänwään Dishonesty or very bad behavior when one keeps on changing statements.

Wäny 1. To change or replace bad thing with good one. 2. An old rope or so for tying cows or goats on a peg.

Wäŋ Plural of Waŋ being both eyes and water streams, as explained above see Nyin.

Wäŋwäŋ 1. Feeling of burning pains, fire heat or fever. 2. State of severe pain due to fever, see Bo̱o̱r.

Wär Plural of Wa̱a̱r being cow or grass eating animal dung as explained below.

Wäär 1. Night. 2. A type of plant which roots are chewed by young boys along the river banks.

Wääri Plural of Wäär being the night as explained above.

Wärdär The mid night.

Wärwär 1. Bright colours such as black and white. 2. The blink and **wink** sight of the lightning.

Wät 1. To dig ground or soil with horns, hooves, paws, hands etc. 2. A shallow water well or pond in a dry depression, river bed or valley.

Wätni Plural of Wät being a shallow pond in dry depression as explained above.

Wäth 1. A type of tall plants which looks like sorghum stalk in the early stages. 2..Plural of both Female.Genital.Organ as explained above. 3..A port or landing side, the river bank, lake, or sea. 4. Plural of Wääth being brave man or woman as explained below.

Wääth It has two meaning. 1. A brave man or woman who dose not run from the enemy. 2. A pole of wood which is dug and fixed at the hut entrance to hold the door on with a rope.

Wääthni Plural of Wääth being the wooden pole which control hut door as explained above..

Wäthwäth The sound of water when playing or crossing pool or bathing.

Wäw State of having good looking face or appearance.

Wäwwäw The noise or sound of moving water in stream or valley.

Wäy A conditional way of walking in sandy soil or clay.

Wääy 1. State of having something got rotten, decayed or decomposed. 2. Expression for paralystic sad news.

Wäywäy 1. The conditional way of movements in sandy soil. 2. Being not hard but in breakable soil. We An expression for surprise when something has gone wrong or spoiled.

Wea 1. You go-for more then two persons., see Wia. 2. A colour where black and white spots dominate. 3. To sing songs of praising a person or a bull, see Wey.

Wee Weeping, crying, wailing, lamenting, see Röt, Röl.

Wec Village, town city, land, country.

Wéc The Nuer standard male adull way of answering a call (Yes) see Wiew.

Wekwek A style of walking when carrying something heavy on the head.

Wel To turn or go around when inspecting parts of something.

Weel To exchange money or goods with another currencies or goods.

Welɛ An expression for surprise when someone wants to involve someone in doing wrong.

Welwel State of being not stable, unconfortable or restless in bed.

Wen Before and it is preceded by Ni as Ni wen: Before.

Weny To clear what prevents the rays or brightness of something.

Weeny State of becoming quite opened or clear in regard to the sight eg Cɛ wañ path weeny: The moon has become clear.

Weŋ A bad style of sitting or not proper way of sitting.

Wer A command for a single person to go. You go.

Weri Plural of Weer being an untrained long horns as explained below.

Weer A bull with long untrained horns.

Werwer Wer : means go but when it is repeated it expression angerness which amount to someone being dismissed or not wanted any more.

Wet 1. To alert a person by touching him/her to pay attention to you. 2. Slang for invitation to have a meal, talk or fight.

Wew To enlarge the hole or the opening.

Wewwew 1. State of being well opened, enlarged or quite hollow. 2. State of having much air passing which causes disturbances in the place.

Wey Plural of Wɛy being praises in songs as explained below..

Wɛc To cause bruises as in accident or when having fallen.

Wɛɛc 1. A ritual which is belief to cure bruises when a symbol of a hut is burned on the bruise side see Mankwɛac. 2. An eye disease which causes the eyelid disappears leaving only reddish skin cover.

Wɛcwɛc State of being not smooth because of erosion or soil particles.

Wɛk A game which is performed or played in water where the participants should know swimming.

Wɛl 1. To turn over something or someone as when wrestling or arranging Things.see Wɛl piny or nhial. 2. Not completely in order set e.g. Wɛllɛc.

Wɛlwɛal A night dance where its music is played by hitting two sticks.

Wɛleny Failure to stick or fit on something.

Wɛr 1. A snake, mouse or insect hole or path. 2. To state, or tell what you do not want to say when under threat. 3. To scatter by covering a large area. see Wɛrpiny.

Wɛrwɛr 1. A type of small birds with bright black and white colours. 2. A colour of white on the background with black spots all over. 3. Not tied together. 4. A person who does not hide things but very frank, truthful etc.

Wɛth 1. A fatal disease which affects babies. 2. To mismanage, misuse something or mishandle it.

Wɛthwɛth 1. A person who does not take care of the scarce resources available, see Talaŋ. 2. Lack of organization where each person has the right to say, do or make what he wants.

Wɛwwɛw Noise of grains which is a slang for a little quantity of grains left.

Wɛy 1. To praise someone or something in songs. 2. A string or thread use for tying up luggage. 3. To specify the intention or to be clear of what you want.

Wɛywɛy State of being clear or straight forward from crooks and bad deeds.

Wi 1. A surprise statement that is said when a thing got spoiled. 2. Going for second person by first person e.g. Wi nikä? Where are you going? 3. A short for Wic which is the head or top e.g. Ɛŋu tä wi dueel ɔ? What is on top of the house?

Wia You go for more than one persons.

Wic 1. Head, top and upper part etc. 2. Having something to do with the village,home,national country

Wec eg. Bia wä wic: You go to the village, town, city, cattle camp Home town or country etc. 3. Havig become notorious as that of a man eating animal. 4. To cause troubles or looks for problems.

W<u>**i**</u>**c** Clear, to be cleaned after the dirts sunk or filtered.

W<u>**ii**</u>**c** Having troubles or problems.

Wiicwiic State of movements up and down without specific reasons or whenlooking for troubles.

Widɛ A short form for a Wicdɛ that is his/ her head. In colloquial Nuer some pronounce it as Wiju, Wija, Wijɛ for your head, my head and his head.

Wi̱ewi̱e Specific case or cause of what appears in a distance or either up or deep down in a well or valley.

Wik A sound of iron or metallic tools,untensils, weapons etc.

Wi̱kwi̱k Having the same sound of metallic friction.

Wil To undermine or go around not to tell the truth.

Wi̱l To go round and round like a fan, bicycle, tyre etc.

Wiil To delay or cause delaying in telling the correct or truth.

Wilwil Stage when a person does not want to tell the truth or to answer directly.

Wi̱lwi̱l The wind mill pump or whatever has much to do with continuous movements around all the time.

Wi̱n To turn round as in a circle.

Wini A question such as where are you going? Also it means There.eg Jin wini ? Where are you going?. Bia wä wini : You go there.

Wi̱nwi̱n 1. The whirlpool which causes water to turn round and round in river. 2. A game which is played by boys under a tree in the centre of the village.

Wi̱ny The sign of luck or will indication which may be coming very soon or next days.

Wi̱iny State of having a metallic tool becomes clean after being used thoroughly or rusted.

Wi̱nywi̱ny Being quite clean such as metallic utensils or glasswares.

Winith A question, meaning where?" or which place?

Wir Being quite clear such as liquids.

Wi̱r Dues, rights,belongings or whatever is one share.

Wiir A rope tied on poles for hanging clothes etc. inside a hut.

Wirwir State of being transparent such as water surface or a glass.

Wi̱rwi̱r Straight forward, being clear or exact to the point.

Wit To pretend as if you do not want, or need the offer.

Wi̱t 1. To sharpen the bull, or ox horns or wooden tools. 2. The sudden fall of whatever one is carrying such as pot, utensil etc.

Witwit A sound of series beating or hitting something very fast.

Wi̱th A short wooden stick with round thick huge top.

Wiith State of being quite active dancer.

Wi̱thwi̱th 1. State of being clear without fishes, dirts, or deposits. 2. State of difficulties one faces in holding something which is quite heavy on one side.

Wiw A sound of gas or winds blowing.

Wi̱w 1. A belief people believe to have powers of luck and evil. 2. State of being bright or whitish all over.

Wi̱wwi̱w The sound of storm or winter winds.

Wiiy Plural of Wɛc being the village, town, city or country as explained above.

Woc 1. To take, remove, dismiss, put away, switch etc. 2. To go or get away from one place to another.

Woɔc Piece of charcoal for local pipe To̱ny.

Woɔɔc Plural of Woɔc being a piece of charcoal as explained above see mim, jaac kiɛ bapraari.

Wooc The sour milk poured out from a container see Gue̱y.

Wok 1. To move a little bit or to walk a short distance after staying for a long time in one place. 2. To make beads out of ostrich eggs.

Wokwok Not stable, weak, shaking or about to fall or falling.

Wol Water pond full of rain water only.

Woli Plural of Wol being water pond as explained above.

Woul To throw down either by cutting, pushing down or forcing down something.

Won Cloud or being evaporated winds full of water.

Woni Plural of Won being cloud as explained above. see Wun.

Wony To bend or tilt to one side.eg Ca wony juol :He/she has been thrown by turning ....???????? please add that word.

Wonywony An unstable or steady way of walking,sitting, placing a thing.

Wop A dislocation due to an accident of falling or car accident.

Wor To make a hole by applying sharp pointed tool.

Woor A kind of creeping plants which grows in the field and being consumed as wild vegetable.

Wour A race, running, jogging, fleeing or escaping.

Worwor 1. Having a hole made with a sharp metallic tool. 2. A slang for series looking at something or someone with interest.

Woth 1. Plural of Wœth being the buttock as explained below. 2. To dig or destroy by eating or breaking up as a case with rats, ants etc. 3. State of being heated or needs mating as a case with animals or cattle.

Wow 1. Cursing by many people for having made mistake. see A wöö. 2. To cut small or cut to small pieces. 3. To make small or tiny teeth or hooks on metallic tool. See Nyuɛny.

Woy A type of tree that grows along the river banks.

Woyni Plural of Woy being a kind of trees as explained above.

Woywoy State of being not solid or hard but in powder form.

Wɔk Plural of Wœɔk being state of being bald headed or lack of hairs as explained below.

Wɔɔk Bald head or lack of hairs on the head.

Wɔ̱ɔ̱k Shoulder where the difference in pronounciation is very slight you can detect in these sentences, e.g. Ci wɔ̱ɔ̱kɛ dhök:His/her shoulders become big. Ci wɔ̱ɔ̱(k)dɛ dhök: His/her shoulders become big.

Wɔlwɔl A very small water pond, see Wäläŋ.

Wɔɔny A situation when each person at the scene refuses to tell what he/she has seen.

Wɔɔŋ Very ignorant person or inexperienced who knows very little.

Wɔp An expression that show the object is fitting exactly.

Wɔri Plural of Woor being a creeping plant which is consumed a vegetable as explained above.

Wɔt 1. To eat or having eaten, being a literal word from Nuer legend. Eg Gœœk Cæ mactapni wœt: A monkey ate maize. 2. The shape of buttock confluence structure which appears when one is Thin or starving.

Wɔth 1. Buttock or the human being cushion for sitting. 2. Being an opening on cloth, gourd, pot etc.

Wu The sound of the letter (U).

Wuc A surprise expression indicating alarm or sorrow.

Wucwuc Surprise expression as explained above.

Wuk To remove a fixed things or poles by force.

Wul To throw down heavy object by pushing or cutting it down.

Wulwul A movement to left or right or vice versa being a lame person ways or style of walking or a bull hump.

Wum 1. Nose or the front end of a canoe, car,plane, pumkin, gourd etc. 2. To prick with sharp tool or device any sensitive part such as ear, nose etc.

Wuum Plural of Wum being the nose as explained above.

Wumwum 1. State of being quite fragile or delicate to be handled with care. 2. A person who tells what is being condoned or kept silence.

Wun Clouds formation or having grown huge as in legend storics.

Wuni Plural of Wut being a man as explained below. But this word is **Informal** because (T) is missing. see Wutni where (T) is silence.

Wuny To turn someone on the opposite side in order to throw him down in wrestling. see Wuny juɔl.

Wunywuny Not stale or slippery but still active and strong.

Wup 1. To clear by pouring out something. 2. A sound of a falling heavy object.

Wuor 1. To clear the internal or inner parts of a gourd or water ditch or stream. 2. Running a race or to catch up things on the move.

Wur Having much to do with running Wuor eg Tä wur kuaknikä : I was running after my luggage.

Wurwur State of having cleared deposites, debris or particles.

Wut Man, adult male of human being or he who accepts to accommodate the six horizontal marks on his forehead.

Wutni Plural of Wut being a man or an adult male as explained above. Ḥere (T) is in silence.

Wutwut A sound or noise of heavy winds, birds etc.

Wuthɔ̱åk A cattle cult person who has got magic power for calling cows behind him while running.

Wutpua̱ny Gentleman or a person of so many considerations involved on his behavior.

Wutnipua̱ny Plural of Wutpua̱ny being gentleman or a person as explained above.

Wuth 1. The part of the cattle below the neck which is thick with fat meat. 2. An opening on a container, piece of cloth or skin.

Wuthwuth That is an opening on something such as a piece of cloth,fur,skin etc.

Wuy Another pronounciation for Wey being expression for surprise.

Wuywuy The same expression of surprise as explained above.

Wöö An expression for surprise.

Wöc To pour out something usually, water, liquids, grains etc.

Wök To move or remove something such as poles,teeth etc. by force.

Wökwök The action of removing a thing or extracting it by force.

Y

Yac To vow that you can not do or repeat certain behaviour or mistake Done again.

Yacɛ A front shelter of a hut door.

Yak 1. Hyena or wolf.eg æñu röt cie yak œ? What makes noise

Like hyena or wolf?. 2. To mistreat someone on a journey or a traveler. Eg Gat æmœ la

Jaal æ yak æ dupni: That fellow used to mistreat travelers on the roads. 3. To sharpen a knife, axe, spear etc, on the sharpening stone. 4. To move a mouth very fast as with lion, wolf etc.when eating.

Yaak Mistreatment of people who either on journey, mere mistreatment or whatever eg Næmæ æ yaak mi baa gaat mac :This is a mistreatment if the children are to be cheated.

Y̲a̲a̲k Plural of Yak being the Hyena or wolf as explained above.

Yakyak State of little quantity, light or not heavy such as grains or milk, water etc.

Y̲a̲a̲ky̲a̲a̲k The way the dancers show up themselves in front of people in a drum dance.

Yakok An informal pronounciation for Jakok being a crow.

Yal 1. To move about in a dancing style between young men and ladies. 2. State of having weather clear after heavy rainfull or rain clouds.

Yaal State of moving, doing or playing freely on luxurious manner in a town or in your own compound.

Ya̲a̲l 1. A rain screening grass roof around hut, which protect walls from rain water. 2. A slang for a lady who has large or huge waist.

Yalyal A person who does not hide secrets and always jolly to everybody.

Yam 1. Humiliation statement in front of people by uttering a bad word without respect. 2. To shoot, spear, feel or shake any suspected area. 3. A sound which indicates movements in the grass, or in darkness.

Yamɛ A metallic tool for cutting grass.

Ya̲a̲m Plural of Yäm being a person or a lady who lost respect as explained below.

Yamyam 1. A person who does not respect him/herself or others and who says anything that annoys others. 2. A situation or behaviour when a person looses respect and talks to any person rudely.

Yaamyaam The sound of movements in the grass in darkness.

Yany 1. Being not well made or built hut or whatever. 2. Having been properly searched and checked where no, place is left.

Yanyyany 1. State of being badly thatched. 2. Searched or looted properly.

Yaŋ 1. Cow. 2. Slang for any thing pay as a dowry in marriage settlement. 3. Slang for the indoor games requirements except hunting.

Ya̲ŋ To run or start running as in a race, jogging etc.

Ya̲a̲ŋ State of being in troubles or in a hurry as when doing a thing e.g. Ɛŋu ci ya̲a̲ŋ_inɛ mɔ? Why are you in a hurry like this?

Ya̲ŋya̲ŋ State of being fast or very quick in doing something.

Yaŋkuoth Butter fly.

Ya̲p 1. To cut something into pieces such as meat or grass etc. 2. To interfere in any talk or discussion. 3. A piece of any thing be it meat, rope, wood etc.

Ya̲a̲p Plural of Ya̲p being a piece of anything as explained above.

Yar 1. A slight rain or flood. 2. To scatter some liquids on people as blessing or by mistake.

Ya̲r To spoil or to make a thing bad or useless.

Ya̲a̲r State of spoilage, miused or mishandling of things.

Yaari The upper set of front teeth which is always in plural.

Yaryar Not heavy rainfall or flood.

Ya̱rya̱r A person who does not keep things even secrets.

Yat 1. The whitish butter before it is boiled. 2. To clean a untensil: or spoon by tongue o licking. 3. To be fast or light in doing something.

Ya̱t 1. A type of grass which is used for temporary thatching huts in cattle camps. 2. A name of child born after many dead children where his/her hairs are not cut untill rituals are performed.

Yaat State of having cleaned or licked something very fast or quickly.

Ya̱a̱t Plural of Yet being leather, skin and currently clothes which cover the female genital organs as explained below.

Ya̱tya̱t State of being very light in weight or in running.

Yatyat State of being veryfast or light in movements when doing something.

Yath State of having the surface not smooth.

Yaath 1. A type of Nile fish with small scales. 2. Slang for signs or symtoms of aging where the skin becomes dry.

Yathyath State of being not smooth due to dirts of sand, soil or particles.

Yaw 1. The cluster hairy part of animal tail. 2. The weather being clear in the early morning or after rainfall.

Ya̱w 1. A type of grass which is weeded from the field or farm. 2. To milk a little and leave the big quantity of milking to a calf.

Yaaw State of becoming quite cleared at dawn, day light or after heavy rainfall.

Ya̱a̱w The little milk that was milked early.

Yawyaw 1. State of becoming quite clear after rainfall or darkness. 2. light blood or colour.

Ya̱wya̱w The rise of foams when washing with a soap or the boiling milk.

Ya̱a̱wya̱a̱w A noise or sound of winds, milking or filtering white stuff beer.

Yay 1. A feast where a bull is slaughtered and a lot of meat is served to all people around. 2. Sacrifices or feastival day offering.

Ya̱y To clean the food container with staw, butter, soap or with köp kænæ Kuàn.

Yayni Plural of Yay being the day of sacrifices or festival as explained above.

Ye An expression for whatever has gone bad or spoiled.

Yec 1. An expression for surprise or exclamation when seeing an exta ordinary or strange thing happening. 2. A grass made device which is used for cleaning the room, compound etc. 3. Confusion which prevails after the death or when something got lost.

Yeec A person who cleans the compound or a room.

Yecyec State of great surprise or exclamation due to a strange sight or view.

Yek The shrine where the family holy sacrifices are performed around it.

Yekyek A gourd made device for lulling or soothing a baby to stop crying.

Yekni Plural of Yek being the shrine as explained above.

Yel 1. Bluish or grayish colour or mixture of brown and white colour. 2. Dry day, or state of having no rains after several wet morning.

Yelkɛw State of being quite large in size such as fish or a container.

Yem To consume very fast as with fire, ġoat or whatever.

Yeem State of having much to do with quick consumption of something very fast.

Yeny 1. To do something roughtly with out much care. 2. The touching of people, things or walls when moving. 3. To have wound developed again when a scar got healed4. To put off the burning fire or to quench it.

Yenyyeny State of being troublesome or to move while touching people or walls.

Yeop Slang for person who interferes in what he/she does not know.

Yet 1. The removal of snak or whatever with a stick. 2. A grain bundle. 3. A game which is played with mud made devices as requirements of such game.

Yey Plural of Yiɛɛ being the soul as explained below.

Yeöp 1. To sip tea, soup etc.while it is warm. 2. That can be sipped only but not drinkable.

Yɛ A pronoun for the second persons – you or for more than one.eg Bi kæ ben kä yæ:They will come to you.

Yɛc 1. To clean using Yec being a device as explained above. 2. State of being awakening completely, without any sign of sleep.

Yɛɛc Plural of Yeec being the cleaner as explained above.

Yɛk 1. A local made mat for sheltering or shading baby in a cot in journey. 2. To make sounds or noise by moving gourd container Yekyek with some stones in it to lull or sooth a baby to sleep.

Yɛl To drive away cattle or goats to grazing lands.

Yɛn Pronoun for you plural.eg Yæn bia wä may: You will go fishing.

Yɛnɛ You and third person – here two pronouns make a word in Nuer language, e.g. Kɔn, Yɛnɛ etc.: We, You with he/she/it. It is quite unique.

Yɛt 1. Plural of Yiat being a finger as explained below. 2. The state of removing a dead or living snake, etc. with a stick.

Yian 1. A colour which is a mixture of white with brown or orange. 2. A person or animal being taken care of by a person who is the father relative,friend or the owner. 3. Having been tied down eg Ca yian piny: He/she has been tied down.

Yiaan Plural of Yian being a person or cattle in care of a person as explained above.

Yiat Finger or thumb.

Yic 1. Confusion or in confused manner. 2. A type of grass for making soft local brooms.

Yiic State of confusion usually after the death of important person.

Yicyic A person who does not know to answer or act quickly or faster.

Yiicyiic State of being in a confused manner.

Yiec Confusion due to the death of an important person.

Yieh An expression which gives tune to the name of the person being called. e.g. Pal Yieh?Gatluak yieh?

Yieɛ A sound of insect or reptiles when passing by.

Yiel A water lily or plant which seeds are eaten by young boys when they get ripened.

Yien To prison, keep in custody, not to allow anything to move freely etc.

Yieen 1. What is used for tying up things, such as rope, string etc. 2. A bundle of tied things such as fish to be carried for a distance. 3. A name of child born when the family members tied up themselves as a ritual when they lost an important person.

Yieny 1. To cause an old wound to swell or become worse due itching. 2. To touch intentionally or suddenly while passing by. 3. To clean by using a piece of cloth or any material.

Yieeny Anything that is used for cleaning utensils or equipments.

Yiep Whatever that cuts at once such as sharp blade of knife, axe, spear etc.

Yiepyiep State of having such action of sharp blade cutting.

Yier 1. A sound of movement in the dry grass. 2. To smear the body or whatever with oil or butter. 3. A sound of liquid when being drunk. 4. The sound of wind when is blowing. 5. The river, the lake or water ways

Yieryier 1. The frequent hearing of such sound or noise which indicates that there is something moving. 2. A granary made of grass.

Yiet 1. To separate the butter from sour milk before boiling. 2. Some fluid that comes from Female Genital Organ when heated and about to mate.

Yietyiet State of being very light in weight.

Yieth 1. To spear someone or something in playing games. 2. Slang for choosing an area as a compound, homestead, village, farm or garden. 3. To open blood vien to drain some blood out. 4. A bad smell. 5. Slang for checking the legality of an issue of court ruling or decision taken.

Yieeth 1. Luck where one gets a lot of what one is looking for, e.g. fishing. 2. Iron, metal, coins etc. 3. Slang for ornaments such as beads, precious metals, ivory tools etc.

Yiethni Plural of Yieth To spear, or bad smell as explained above.

Yiew Type of plants which disturbs farmers in weeding.

Yieew Plural of Yiɛw being a type of fish that looks like Helicopter as explained below.

Yiey A sharp noise of musical tune or instrument.

Yieyyiey State of such sharp noise of metal or musical instrument.

Yiɛɛ Soul, breathing etc.

Yiɛl 1. A sort of feeling which people enjoy when in action. 2. To get rid of a device as when speared.3. A part of a gourd utensil.

Yiɛn 1. To tie up something or animal.2. A slang for keeping one waiting in a place for quite a long time. 3. To live with someone for long period or sometimes.

Yiɛny Having old wound goes bad or worse again after the signs of healing.

Yiɛŋ Having awful smell as that of urine.

Yiɛŋyiɛŋ That has the same smell or state of such smell.

Yiɛt Plural of Yiat being the finger or the thumb as explained above.

Yiɛw 1. A type of fish which makes noise when caught or speared at. see Yiew. 2. Having much to do with this type of grass, Yiew weed.

Y̱ik A new style of fashion clothes or ornamental materials.

Yik 1. To put up with some one. 2. To rest on something. 3. To pour water down as rainfall. 4. To start a style or fashion for the first time.

Y̱ii̱k The shrine for the family belief, which is always in the middle of the compound.

Y̱ii̱kni Plural of Y̱ii̱k being the shrine as explained above.

Y̱iky̱ik State of being very fast in adopting or imitating a fashion or a way of doing things.

Y̱il 1. To tell or disclose whatever you are not supposed to tell. 2. A sign of something that has just passed the eyes.

Y̱ily̱il 1. A person who tells or discloses secrets. 2. Signs of something passing frequently.

Y̱in Being very tiny, narrow or little.

Y̱iny̱in Very little, tiny or small in size.

Yir The severe pains of recent injury or wound.

Y̱ithy̱ith 1. A game which is cycled or turned round. 2. A bad smell.

Yiiw The heavy sound of engine, plane or birds.

Yiwyiw The sound or engine noise from a distance.

Yoo Latter or after some few minutes etc.

Yoa An ornamental device made of cow tails and some strings for dancing purposes.

Yoac To pull or drag the net or hooks in water while fishing.

Yoa̱c Having pulled away someone into wilderness to die during starvation or famine.

Yoa̱k A cow's tail made device which is put on top of stick of spear.

Yoal A sharp sudden cry when very angery or unhappy.

Yoaal Plural for Yoal being such sudden cry as explained above.

Yoany 1. Type of plants that has sticky thorn. 2. A slang for a problem

Yoanyaŋ A type of marine plants or aquatic plants which is found in swamps and pools.

Yoa̱ŋ Plural of Yo̱ŋ the mad, crazy or drunken person as explained below.

Yoat Whatever is pulled out from the main body as bark of a tree.see Yöt.

Yoc 1. To pull, drail or drag. 2. To take the biggest part of food meant for a group. 3. To show up or to care of one out look.

Yoɔc The hooks chain for catching fish in a shallow river water or pool.

Yocyoc A person who can not do anything very quick or faster.

Yok To shake quickly a tree, pole etc.in order to get the fruits.

Yool A kind of tall grass.

Yohl A kind of taste which causes bitterness in the throat.

Yolyol State of being fat or huge on the upper part of the body.

Yom Being very dry and grey after bath before smearing with oil or cream.

Yon To close or press one mouth.

Yonyon Having been properly tied up.

Yoŋ 1. Mad, crazy or drunken person. 2. To mock or stir jokes to someone suffering.

Yoŋyoŋ An insect which flies in front of a person walking in day light.

Yop To take care of oneself, property etc.

Yoop State of having great care of oneself or property.

Yooy The noise of burning oil, fat or butter.

Yoyyoy The continuous noise of frying whatever with oil, fat or butter.

Yor 1. Expression which shows how a person is angery e.g. Ku yor: You just go. 2. The flow of beads from string when it gets cut.

Yot To pull out, the outer cover or bark of stem or stalk.

Yohtyoht State of being not thick but very light.

Yotyot 1. A food made out of fermented flour. 2. Slang for remarkable and fast movement in fear or flight.

Yothyoth State of being huge in the middle.

Yow Descendant of Kiir lineage clan e.g. Nyayow or Nyakiir.

Yoyyoy 1. The noise or sound of burning fats, butter or oil. 2. The sound or noise of urine. 3. Being of little quantity such as tobacco.

Yɔat To beat, hit or whip with a stick or whatevr.

Yɔk To start or begin running about in drum adance.

Yɔɔk A kind of rats or mice which looks quite big or huge.

Yɔl To curse the evil that is about to happen.

Yɔɔl A game which is played by young boys to train themselves how to spear.

Yɔm A colour mostly whitish with some few grayish hairs.

Yɔɔŋ State of being crazy, insane and drunkeness.

Yɔhr 1. To charge someone with bad word for having asked you something. 2. A sound or noise which indicates movements in sorghum stalks by night. 3. The outer stalk of maize that looks like a paper which is used for rolling tobacco to be smoked as cigar, cigarette etc.

Yɔhryɔhr State of such noise or sound of some movements in darkness or at night.

Yɔt The beating or hitting with a stick or whip.

Yɔɔht Whatever is used for beating, lashing, hitting, whipping etc..

Yɔɔhtni Plural of Yœœht being whatever is used for hitting,beating,lashing as explained above.

Yɔth 1. Zeal, jolly or readiness to join in dance. 2. It is also pronounced as Joth being a part of the hearth where charcoal pieces are kept.

Yɔɔth Attraction to dance according to drum or musical sounds.

Yuadh A line of beads in a string.

Yuadhni Plural of Yuadh being a line of beads as explained above.

Yuak Heavy or bushy beard.

Yuakni Plural of Yuak being the beard as explained above.

Yual To do something very fast or very quick.

Yua̱l The thickness of hairs particularly when one fails to have it cut.

Yua̱a̱l 1. State of being very fast or quick as when escaping. 2. The clustering of hairs when a person failed to have it cut or shaved

Yualyual A state of having something with long parts dangling down.

Yuan 1. A branch. 2. Slang for a problem extended to innocent person.

Yuaan 1. Plural of Yuan being a branch or a slang for a problem as explained above. 2. State of being in panic or in terrible flight or fear.

Yuanyuan A situation where one is in a hurry collecting his/her property.

Yuanyuaan A state, where one is in a hurry when he/she is caught up by time.

Yuaŋ State of throwing things very easily or simply.

Yuaŋyuaŋ Inability to throw a spear or a stick to the target.

Yuaryuar State of being in dangling or hanging position. See Yuɛryuɛr.

Yuat 1. Failure to gain something after many attempts. 2. Slang for having undermined someone doing something.

Yua̱ta̱t 1. State of having uncombed or unshaved hairs. 2. Unweeded field Farm or compound full of grass.

Yuatyuat Being quite tall, long or slim in body.

Yua̱tyua̱t State of having a place is full with flies which need to be scared away.

Yuathyuath State of being quite tall such as human being or tree.

Yuay To touch or to put one hand on a thing. see Yuey.

Yuɛkyuɛk State of movements up and down in order to achieve something.

Yuɛlyuɛl 1. That is not physically strong. 2. Not many or much in quantity. 3. Different heights or length.

Yuɛr Having some of its parts are dangling or hanging.

Yuɛrɛr Being in a separate manner as in uncombed hairs, leaves, branches etc.

Yuɛryuɛr State of having some parts of whatever are hanging down.

Yuɛt State of being not well distributed such as extracted or removed teeth.

Yuɛtɛt State of being very few such as teeth on the gum or whatever on opened space or ground.

Yuɛtyuɛt Being not well tied together due to having some parts are hanging up unremoved.

Yuɛth To take by little till it remains very little to serve the purpose.

Yuɛthyuɛth Very little quantities that remain on the sight.

Yuɛthyuɛath Plural of Yuɛthyuɛth being very little quantities as explained above.

Yuɛy 1. Sharp short live pain such as bee or insect sting. 2. Having the feeling of such pain as explained above. 3. State of having touched something.

Yuie A sound of whipping or lashing with tiny whip.

Yuiy The same sound of whipping or lashing as explained above.

Yuok 1. State of being short in body with long legs. 2. A container for carrying grains, tobacco etc.

Yuokni Plural of Yuok being the container as explained above.

Yuokyuok

Yuokok State of being physically short in body with long legs as explained above. Being physically congested in body while the legs are long.

Yuol Having connection with a certain type plants such as Yuol.

Yuool 1. A type of plant or grass. 2. Having much to do with Yuool plant.

Yuolyuol 1. Being huge at the upper part while thin or slim at the lower part. 2. A style of walking.

Yuom 1. A sound of dried leaves of Tobacco, vegetables etc as when collected. 2. Quantity of dried leaves of tobacco for local pipe.

Yuomyuom State of being dried quantities of tobacco for local pipe.

Yuon To close or tie up something or whatever have been tied up or closed.

Yuonyuon Well tied up, closed or tight.

Yuoŋ 1. Literal name for vulture. See Nyiŋgol. 2. Having very bad smell as that of Diesel oil. 3. State of falling down quickly when in wrestling.

Yuop 1. A piece of something cut from the main body. 2. To cut a piece from a big quantity.

Your 1. To throw something or to spear. 2. To jump up or over something. 3. A style of beating the drum to make the wanted musical sound.

Yuoth 1. To pull very fast or having been pulled towards the speaker. 2. A quick or very fast running in racing.

Yuothyuoth State of being thick or huge at the upper part of the body.

Yuoy To take by breaking pieces of less solid object.

Yuoyyuoy That has characteristic of breaking into small pieces or parts.

Yuɔɔr Plural of Your being a style of jumping in a dance as explained above.

Yuɔt 1. A small portion of hairs, left at centre of the head after shaving. 2. To act before the opponent get prepared in wrestling or fighting.

Yuɔɔt 1. Plural of Yuɔt being the portion of hairs left as explained above. 2. Yuɔt being a surprising action in wrestling or fighting as explained above.

Yuɔtɔt State of being very small in size or the appearance.

Yuɔtyuɔt State of being very little or small portion of hairs, grass etc. left on the head or on the farm.

Yuɔɔth Plural of Yuoth being pulling or sudden starting of running as explained above.

Yuk State of having short and huge body.

Yukyuk The characteristic of being short and huge.

Yul 1. A kind of insects that attack dried fish or meat. 2. A slang for calling a person born after several dead children where his/her hairs, are not shaved as a belief.

Yulyul A series or quick falling of trees, sorghum stalks, grass when being mowed down,with sharp axe, sickle etc.

Yum True, correct, right or exact. It is an old word, which is not any longer in practice.

Yuŋ A kind of smell such as diesel oil smell, or dirty pieces of cloth.

Yuŋyuŋ State of bad smell such as dirty pieces of cloth, diesel oil or whatever.

Yup To cut a part off something such as meat, hairs, grass,trees, fence etc.

Yupyup A small piece cut from a big one.

Yur 1. Plural of Your to jump up as in dance or over something as explained above. 2. A word which is used when one scores meaning goal in hockey like game Diɛɛr. 3. A noise or sound that is heard when throwing heavy thing from above or high place.

Yuryur 1. A sound or noise of moving animals or people in darkness in sorghum farm. 2. Slang for a person who moves up and down taking messages.

Yut 1. To pull out or uproot. 2. Slang for overthrowing someone in contest.

Yutyut State of being not decent or normal due to changes made on something or someone.

Yuth 1. To pull towards oneself or vice-versa in rope pulling game 2. Racing contest or the starting of a race.

Yuy Very quick or short live message, song etc.

Yuuy A metallic device or tool which is used for sharpening or smoothing metallic tool rough surface.

Yä Th sound of the letter (Y) being the twinty seventh letter of Thok Nath.

Yäc Half ripened sorghum bundles.

Yäk To dispose or throw away the waste.

Yäl The falling of grass, stalk,,trees etc. when being cut down.

Yälyäl 1. State of such falling of grass, stalk, trees etc. when being cut down. 2. A land of tall grass which cover the surrounding space or area.

Yähl 3. A person who acts very fast or quickly. To go into grass covered land looking for something.

Yäm A lady or a person who lost respect to others even to himself/ herself.

Yän To act quickly or a quick action when time is limited.

Yään State of being very fast or acting very quick e.g. Ɛŋu ci yään inɛmɛ? why are you quick like this?

Yäny 1. A name for a child whose hairs were not cut due to rituals. 2. Not well prepared hut, makeshift or whatever.

Yänyän 1. State of being very quick or fast. 2. Slang for being light in movements.

Yänyyäny 1. Having been roughly thatched such as hut roof. 2. Slang for a person who does not perform or do good thing.

Yäp 1. To breath heavily after series racing, running, jogging etc. 2. A slang for the native bell, penis and unfinished stick.

Yäpyäp A person who involves him/herself without invitation in any talk, meeting etc.

Yäpyääp A state of being not consistent in doing one thing at ago.

Yär A person who becomes crazy or insane.

Yäär Mismanagement or spoilage of someone property or belonging.

Yät To act quickly or very fast which alert the games as in hunting, fishing, enemies etc.

Yäät State of action that forces animals,enemies or whatever to leave before being attacked.

Yäth State of being in position to exhibit bad habit, behavior or manners.

Yäy Falling on buttocks or the throwing down in wrestling.

Yäyyäy State of being weak to wrestle. State of having hairy or grass like disorder condition.

Yöö Another word for yes from a distance.

Yöc A word of expression of surprise or exclamations

Yöcyöc Expression for great surprise where both hands are used for emphasis.

Yök 1. To take as quick as possible the greater or bigger part of food. 2. To try to tackle what you can not do.

Yökyök State of movement up and down looking for troubles or problems.

Yöm A metallic or iron made container or utensil.

Yööm Plural of Yöm being the metallic made container as explained above.

Yöör Expression remarks from angry person e.g. Kuɛ yöör: Just bring it.

Yöryör State of being very light which can evaporate quickly such as fat, alcohol etc.

Yöw 1. Having subsided a little bit, not paining as before, etc. 2. Money, weapons ornamental tools etc. 3. A lamenting noise when one is so tied, sad or in danger.

Yuädh To exchange the grain pounding tools to make flour. See Læk

Yuäk Over grown with trees, grass, or hairs etc.

Yuääk State of being fully grown up with grass,trees etc.,

Yuäkäk State of being covered with hairs, clothes or grass.

Yuäl To force someone to act or do something very fast or in short time.

Yuääl State of being full grown with hairs, grass or trees.

Yuälyuäl State of being very quick or fast in doing things.

Yuätät State of having been overcome by a lot of hairs or grass.

Yuät State of having been covered with grass or hairs.

Yuätyuät State of being full of hairs. 2. The movements of flies, birds etc.

Yuääth 1. A group way of practicing some dancing styles. 2. To play with a baby by making it jumps up and down.

Ä

Äh The sound of the twinty eighth letter of Thok Nath.
Ääh A word which expresses yes or yeah.
Ähää A surprising word when one sees strange thing or action.

Thok Nath English Dictionary of Eastern Jikany Nuer Dialect

Nuer Word List
Trial Edition
2006
Juba

www.ingramcontent.com/pod-product-compliance
Lightning Source LLC
Chambersburg PA
CBHW050151120726
47903CB00002B/575
* 9 7 8 0 6 4 8 6 5 4 1 0 0 *